DEAR
PRUDENCE

Published by Turtle Point Press

www.turtlepointpress.com

Copyright © 2011 by David Trinidad

All rights reserved

ISBN 978-1-933527-47-5

LCCN 2010935787

Design and composition by Quemadura

Cover art: Billy Sullivan, *David*, 1998.

Oil on canvas, 30 × 20 inches.

Courtesy of the artist

Printed on acid-free, recycled paper

in the United States of America

FOR HELEN ROSENSTOCK

BLACK TELEPHONE

NEW POEMS

DEAR PRUDENCE

SELECTED POEMS

BLACK
TELEPHONE

NEW POEMS

Without a story there is no poem. Not even a writer.

TED HUGHES

SHEENA IS A
PUNK ROCKER

So I'm in the frozen food aisle
at Jewel, trying to find the right
veggie burger, and I realize
"Blitzkrieg Bop" is playing on
the store's P.A. Thirty years later:
the Ramones as Muzak? Hard to believe.
My hair, reflected in the freezer door
and highlighted by fluorescents,
is turning from salt-and-pepper
to gray (or "silver," as Lisa Fishman
says). Joey, Johnny, and Dee Dee
are all dead. Hard to believe it's been
over three decades since Christopher
(my roommate) and I went to see them
at a small club in San Francisco, their
first-album tour. Twenty-three,
with black, straight, shoulder-length hair
and tight T-shirt and jeans, I looked
like I could be a Ramone. The bartender
thought so; before the show, he kept
serving me free drinks. That's about all
I remember, except that the music was
so loud, my ears rang for days afterward.
I was afraid they'd never return to normal.
On the way home from the market, the right
veggie burgers in one of my plastic bags,

the sky above Chicago was clear blue;
a plane quietly moved through it. How
did I, shy Valley boy, end up at a punk concert?
Jenny. Friend of my friend David, who
before he introduced us, enthralled me
with tales about her: "kooky" overweight
art student who lived in a guesthouse in
Granada Hills with cats and movie posters
and a mannequin dressed in thrift-store finery;
who, when she threw parties, greeted her
guests in the driveway, wearing a flowery
muumuu and feather boa, and blowing bubbles
as she sped towards them on roller skates.
She had gay friends, and frequented Astaire
& Rogers marathons at revival theatres.
Still in high school, such a creature seemed
to me a free spirit worth venerating, a kind
of San Fernando Valley Sally Bowles. After
I graduated in '71, David finally got us
together; we became fast friends. I loved
spending time with her in her guesthouse,
surrounded by objects: her collection of
vintage ladies' hats, her childhood dolls;
Art Nouveau pictures taped to the walls,
jars filled with peacock feathers and pinwheels.
She introduced me to Debussy and Fauré,
Anaïs Nin, Joni Mitchell and Dory Previn.
Every week, she'd read *TV Guide*, circling all
the Garbo and Katharine Hepburn and
Hitchcock films she wanted to watch. She'd
sit at her loom, weaving colorful and textured

wall hangings, while I wrote poems and
short stories about her. Our blissful asexual
relationship lasted several years, until
Jenny completed her master's degree at
CalArts. Though she was beginning to
make a name for herself as an artist, her
life took a sharp, overnight turn in early
'76: she discovered Patti Smith. *You've got
to see her!* I resisted as Jenny dragged me
to the Roxy, but found myself spellbound
when, before the band came out, Patti, in her
Rimbaud-esque *Horses* getup (rumpled white
shirt, tie, black jacket), read poems and spit
on the stage. For the rest of the seventies,
Patti would be God. Encouraged by the
pictures she'd taken of her, Jenny decided
to become a rock-'n'-roll photographer.
While I, inspired by Smith's credo of
fearlessness, quit school (six credits
shy of my B.A.) and moved from L.A.
to San Francisco, "to live the poet's life."
Which translated as very few poems, but
lots of sex and alcohol. Christopher
and I met and hit it off; he moved
into my appropriately seedy apartment
on O'Farrell. We'd hang out with Toni
(a.k.a. Tonette), his friend from high
school, who made decent money as a
dominatrix-for-hire. Jokingly, we called
her "brazen hussy." The three of us
drank and smoked and listened to music,

Tonette's neighbor pounding on the wall.
They introduced me to Sparks and Eno,
Rocky Horror, and Leila and the Snakes,
a campy local act whose lead singer,
Jane Dornacker, had co-written the
Tubes' song "Don't Touch Me There."
With her "snakes" (Pamela Wood and
Pearl Gates), Leila sang tunes like "Rock
and Roll Weirdos," "Pyramid Power,"
"Cathy's Clone," and her spoof of Paul
Anka's recent hit "(You're) Having My
Baby": "(I'm) Getting Rid of Your Baby."
Bona-fide groupies, we showed up
wherever they played. Toni and I had
a handbill photo (the band in Retro Chic:
'40s feathers, fishnets, and floppy hats)
transferred onto two T-shirts. When we
wore them to their next performance, Jane,
who went by the name "Leila T. Snake,"
called us onstage to display our "Leila T. Shirts."
Christopher had to prod me: *Get up there!*
Late in the year, Jenny phoned, peeved
that one of the Ramones had told *Creem*
that they'd been followed around L.A.
by "a three-hundred-pound cherub named
Jenny," and announced that even though
she and everyone else on the punk scene
thought Patti's new album, *Radio Ethiopia*,
a complete disappointment, she was flying
up to Frisco to photograph her. We agreed
to meet at the auditorium. I remember it

darkly: a mystified Smith, less charismatic
on a big stage, asking "Where are my maniacs?"
oblivious that the fans who did rush the stage
were being pummeled by musclebound
security guards; Christopher and Toni to
my left, looking unhappy; Jenny to my right,
flailing to the music. When I'd had enough,
I shouted, "Jenny, please stop pushing me!"
She turned, screamed a Ramones lyric ("I
don't wanna walk around with you"), and
stormed away, but not before Toni brazenly
called her a Jewess. After the concert, we
sat in Union Square, dejected, while a stoned
Patti Smith groupie, who'd attached herself
to us, kept moaning, "I'm so fucked up."
Burned out on promiscuous sex, I moved
back to Los Angeles to finish college and
concentrate on my writing. By then, Jenny
was living in an apartment off the Sunset
Strip, close to the clubs. She dragged
me to see Blondie at the Whisky a Go Go:
Debbie Harry, in dark sunglasses and
hot pants, coyly enacting "X-Offender."
One morning the phone woke me at 3 a.m.
It was Jenny, proclaiming with triumph that
she'd just been "butt-fucked" by Iggy Pop.
As the years passed, I avoided her more
and more. The last time I saw her, she
was house-sitting in the Hollywood Hills.
Freaked out by the Wonderland murders,
she kept checking the window, talking

incessantly. Shortly after that, we had
a blowout over the phone. I told her
I never wanted to speak to her again.
"OK," she said, and hung up. Years
(hard to believe how many) later, after
I'd relocated to Chicago (after fourteen
years in New York), Jenny tracked me
down via the Internet. *Well, look how far
you've gotten.* We spoke a couple of times,
reminisced about her guesthouse. She
revealed that it was one of my stories,
depicting her as a lonely shut-in, that
prompted her to branch out, and led to
her involvement with punk rock. But
we quickly were at odds all over again.
I wished her well; she sent a final, insulting
email. To spit out the bitter taste, I did a
search for Leila and the Snakes. (I always
thought if I ever wrote a novel about those
days, I'd call them Vera and the Vipers.)
And was dismayed to learn the fate of Jane
Dornacker. After her rock group disbanded,
she developed a successful career as a stand-
up comic on the San Francisco circuit, and
also worked as an actress and traffic reporter,
first in California and later in New York.
In 1986, she was killed when the news
helicopter she was reporting from crashed
into the Hudson River. The raspy-voiced
Dornacker, who referred to herself as a
"trafficologist" and "Jane-in-a-plane,"

was in the middle of a live report when
the chopper stalled, nose-dived, struck
the top of a chain-link fence at a pier, then
plunged into the river. Thirty-nine years
old, she died on her way to Saint Vincent's.
Her last words, imploring the pilot to avoid
a collision with the pier below them, were
"Hit the water! Hit the water! Hit the water!"

BLACK TELEPHONE

It sits like an anvil
on end tables

in old movies
and rings—

a startling alarm—
only to advance the plot.

Or is auctioned on eBay
to aficionados of the past

who pay a fortune
to ship this relic,

this tar pit appliance
the distance it once

miraculously bridged.
Its frayed cord

a web of
dead roots.

Its dial a circle
of interminable clicks.

Its receiver a lead weight
pressing cold

dead silence
against the eavesdropping ear.

FROM TED HUGHES'
LIST OF SUGGESTED
WRITING EXERCISES
FOR SYLVIA PLATH

Mushrooms, that they think they are going to take over the world.

Person walking through enormous dark house.

Weeping in the garden.

Mould in graves.

The laughing merchant—attempts to kill him only make him laugh louder.

Fish tossed ashore for a moment, then recovered by the next wave.

Warning to the rose-bud, frost is here.

Houses you have lived in, personified as people.

The pleasant and titillating relationship to be had with things seen from a train.

The face that has just turned away.

To find yourself imprisoned in a certain day of your past.

Watching fat bald men eat.

Somebody whistling in the night, perhaps it's a little stone.

To sunbathe and become a sea-beach gradually.

The clock, death of the fox, baying of hounds—tick, tick.

Zoo penguins, while the Poles melt.

The gardener's pipe-smoke.

Single old shoe on moor.

Little jobs as being a process of petrifaction, till you become a stone heroine on a tomb.

The moments of the past which were special, should have memorial
stones—the site commemorated. Why put up stones to show where
people have died, when the precise places where they came most
alive have no more permanence than a thought in the air, or the
resting place of a sunbeam.

Hornets.

Pine-cones.

The pathetic beast, whose tearful mumblings I feed three times a day.

Dancers coming down a street, each one more unbelievably dressed
than the last.

Midnight in a mountain village.

Snakes in a den, midwinter.

The earth, just cooling—first rains, seas collecting.

The orange's ignorance of the apple.

Friar drunk in a cellar.

Woman opening a letter.

Your honest opinion about the ass.

Fat businessman, drinking coffee, mechanical determination.

Nothing more junky than old newspapers, the news of the world.

Things I wish I could kick.

The body remained at the rail but the mind fell overboard.

CHASING THE MOON
(WITH ANNE WALDMAN)

Just a glimpse
just past midnight

Half looming
hugely

about to sink
into black trees

masking
Boulder horizon

Enough time to
catch more of her
we thought

so the chase
was on

Barreling down
side streets

over speed
bumps

barely stopped
at each sign

Where is she?
Where did she go?

Had to settle
for the moon
(and stars)
in a Joe Brainard
matchbook
(not a bad
substitute)

The moon only
half herself

has an expert
vanishing act

The moon has
lady tactics

The moon has
many scarves

JUNE 20, 2010

WITHOUT A TITLE

The photographs
we took of
the five of us—
my mother
(now dead),
my two sisters
(one estranged),
and Ira and me
("divorced")—
on the observation deck
of the South Tower:
locked away with
the rest of my past
in my archive
at NYU.
Weighing heavily
on us that clear
blue spring day in
1990: the stress of
entertaining my relatives,
in town for my
graduation from
Brooklyn College.
Ira, the seasoned
native, me
still green, "schlepping"
(an Ira word) these
even more naive

Californians around
the Big Apple—
from the Statue
to Times Square, from
the city's dark intestine
(my mother bravely
facing her fear
of the subway) to
the Top of the World.
My first time up there
and my first full-blown
attack of vertigo:
legs shaking
uncontrollably and
stomach contracting
as the tower swayed
and creaked
(did it creak?
I remember
it creaking)
and the unreal gray
concrete far below
and the vast
equally unreal
sky (we were in it!)
began to blur
together and
revolve. I
couldn't wait to
get to the elevator.
My family and boyfriend

smiled and posed
for photographs.
While I felt that
unexpected dread
rise up in me and
threaten to tip the
world upside down.
The air too high to
breathe. The whole
continent buckling
towards the west.
Heart pounding out
its quandary.
Everything—
two years of studies,
the huge blue
spring sky, my
mother poised at
the fire escape
window of
our SoHo loft
transfixed by the
noise of Manhattan,
the uncertainties
of work and of
friendships (more
and more lost
the more I changed)
and of my new
future with Ira—
no way to keep

it from revolving
and creaking
and swaying, no
way to make it
slow down.

MY MAN GODFREY

From this cab, the clouds look like rumpled sheets.
The driver's accommodating: shuts off
the radio when I ask him to turn it down.
Still raw after last night—laughter lapsing

so suddenly, so deeply into tears.
Where are my bright particulars?
To be brought a breakfast tray and not be forgotten!
Black-and-white seems a sublime frame of mind.

PEYTON PLACE

A HAIKU SOAP OPERA

Episodes 1–31, released on DVD May 19, 2009

1

Dolorous premiere.
Worth it for tidal wave of
Dorothy Malone's hair.

2

Ryan O'Neal fresh
from shower. Eyes glued to bare
chest, bulge in towel.

3

Betty has morning
sickness; Rod and Allison,
a date; Norm, wet pits.

4

Every episode
that same couple keeps crossing
the street, hand in hand.

5

Malone mugs with her
jaw, open mouth. O'Neal takes
off his tennis shirt.

6

Small-town slut Betty
ditches buff Bud to chase Rod,
the hunk who dumped her.

7

"Stars, I have seen them
fall . . ." Dreamy Mia Farrow
quotes A.E. Housman.

8

Who's she quoting now?
Something about leaves and snow.
No hits on Google.

9

Close-up of Barbara's
pained face. Pause DVD. Count
every single mole.

10

Contagious coiffure:
a surfer could shoot the curl
in Betty's mom's hair.

11

Betty finally tells
Rod she's preggers, but car crash
should take care of that.

12

Blonde nurse looks like she
was separated at birth
from Julia Stiles.

13

First she can't tell him
that she's knocked up, now she can't
tell him that she's not.

14

If you had to choose:
Connie's art or the owl lamp
at the Anderson's?

15

Despite his bad hair,
Norman's hot. Great playground shot:
his ass in white pants.

16

Can we talk about
Constance MacKenzie's big fat
black false eyelashes?

17

The only title
in paperback rack I can
make out is *The Robe*.

18

Watched this episode
twice and still can't come up with
idea for haiku.

19

At the hospital,
everyone's too worried to
notice the Grant Wood.

20

Odd frame: Norman bent
over water fountain. Is
he giving Dad head?

21

So much depended
upon sponsors: *Peyton Place*
is brought to you by . . .

22

Note the orderly.
No lines, but that look he gives
Malone speaks volumes.

23

Lies, secrets, gossip
and fucked-up families make this
black-and-white world tick.

24

Both brothers shirtless
in Norman's bedroom. Who cares
what's in Mother's will.

25

Did Dorothy dream I'd
gape, forty-five years later,
at her queer blonde hair?

26

For days I haven't
been able to get the theme
song out of my head.

27

After the credits,
autumn leaves litter the path.
Jealous George gets smashed.

28

Full moon, mist, Rossi
filmed through the neck of a lab
flask. Very arty.

29

Morality, truth,
courage, integrity—big
words for the small screen.

30

Will George see a shrink?
Carson be paroled? Connie
have a cavity?

31

Confessions and hard
facts, secret exits. Fake snow,
I have seen it fall.

This is the continuing story of Peyton Place . . .

MOTHERS

When Wanda Hoyt converted her garage to a ceramics studio, rows of chalk-white figurines—clowns, angels, nativity scenes—waited to be painted and glazed in her kiln. The Hoyts had the only color TV on the block; every year we'd watch *The Wizard of Oz* at their house.

Mrs. Boyer claimed our cat leapt off the fence and attacked one of her toddlers. My mother tried to reason with her, but an argument ensued and Mrs. Boyer threatened a lawsuit. "Hysterical" is the word I heard my mother use when she described the incident to my father. She and Mrs. Boyer stopped talking, each tensely aware of the other's comings and goings. Later they made up, right before the Boyers moved.

The day Marilyn Monroe died (I was nine) I saw the newspaper, with her picture on the front page, on Jean Silvernail's coffee table. Jean was a mysterious housewife, revealed, as I got older, the details of her unhappy past. Because she knew I wanted to be a writer, she bought me a copy of Daphne du Maurier's *Rebecca*. "This is *my* story," she said. In high school, when I'd go next door to complain about my father, Jean let me smoke her Virginia Slims. I'd leave as soon as her husband, a contractor, pulled his truck into their driveway. After she divorced him, she changed her name to Deveraux.

Shirley Goode, my mother's best friend, let me borrow her *World Book Encyclopedia* (a volume at a time) for school reports. Her own sons, she'd wistfully say, seldom touched them. One summer evening, the Goodes (who'd immigrated to Los Angeles from Canada) taught me how to play Michigan Rummy, using pennies instead of poker chips. I'd never had so much fun. Shirley chain-smoked Marlboro Reds and drank Cutty Sark, and had a tiny TV on her kitchen counter, which she watched as she prepared meals. Later in life her gambling got out of control—but she won big, I was told, finally won big. The last time I saw her, at my mother's funeral, she was suffering from a fungal brain disease.

Straight-laced and formal, Lauren's mother, a teacher, was one of the few single parents in the neighborhood. Instead of a lawn, she put a cactus and rock garden in their front yard. When my wagon ran off the sidewalk and crushed some of the plants, Lauren's white-haired grandmother, whom they called Boo, ran out of the house and screamed at me.

Once when I went over to Hal's, his mother was dancing to "Walk Right In" in front of a mirror in their living room. The Weilands owned an aluminum Christmas tree—the first I saw—which they decorated with all red balls and lit with a rotating color wheel. Mrs. Weiland opened Hal's bedroom door without knocking, discovered us with our hands in each other's underwear. I was afraid she would tell my mother. Suddenly Hal didn't want to hang around with me anymore.

Mary DeMario (my friend Nancy's mother) took diet pills and did her weekly grocery shopping in the middle of the night, at a 24-hour market. Known as a "kook," she'd eventually have breakdowns. Two strong memories of her both involve water. The first: Stuck inside on a rainy day, Nancy and I sit at their kitchen table, coloring. Mary reacts, excitedly, to news on the radio: a local boy drowned when water suddenly flooded the drain tunnel where he was playing. The thought fills me with panic and dread—a sick, breathless feeling at the bottom of my throat. The second: Because it was cheaper than carpeting, the DeMarios had had their floors laid with linoleum. One day, to avoid sweeping and mopping, Mary drags furniture into the backyard, then sprays down the living room with the garden hose.

Vera Holmes lived next door to the DeMarios. She and the woman next door to her, Mrs. Scott, joined Weight Watchers (new at the time) and everyone commented on the pounds that they lost. Vera's husband was a policeman. After I was raped, my mother showed him the credit card receipts we'd found hidden in my guesthouse. He looked into it, disclosed that the card had been stolen from a woman in upstate New York. She too had been assaulted by Nick, but chose not to report it. He said I was in a "tricky" (meaning humiliating) position, and advised us not to pursue criminal charges.

Kathe Lindsay (a year and a half older than me) battled cancer from the time we were in junior high until she died in the early '80s. Newly sober, I accompanied my mother to her memorial service. Kathe had worked in the library at Cal State Northridge; I'd say hi to her when I went there to listen to recordings of Anne Sexton and Sylvia Plath. A few years after her death, shortly before I moved to New York, I published a poem in *The Jacaranda Review*. The journal was put out by UCLA's English Department, where Kathleen, Kathe's mother, worked. Kathleen called my mother and said, "I've just read one of David's poems."

Priscilla Moran bought her daughter every Barbie outfit, and watched over them like a hawk. The day Linda opened a black wardrobe case and displayed the doll (blonde ponytail) and all her clothes, she gave me one of the booklets (she had dozens of them) that came with every costume: colorful drawings of Barbie's ensembles and accessories. That night I studied each picture, read each description. The next morning, Priscilla knocked on our side door and spoke to my mother, asked for the booklet back. But I'd already committed those images to memory: the pink negligee, the yellow bathrobe, the glamorous black nightclub dress. . . .

Odessa Miller, who was older than other mothers, had a dry sense of humor (and cackle to go with it) and little patience for her rotund husband's religion, Mormonism. I was friends with her daughter Marsha in high school. Marsha had dated my brother, but broke up with him because, like my father, he had a bad temper. Once, stoned on marijuana, I crawled laughing through Marsha's bedroom window. Soon after graduation, she moved to Utah and married a Mormon. To earn spending money when I was in college, I worked part-time as a PBX operator at the answering service Odessa managed.

Scott Small's mother was never home. His older sister was taking hula lessons: I can still hear the lyrics of "My Little Grass Shack," which she played over and over on her portable phonograph. I persuaded Scott to sneak her Barbie Queen of the Prom game out of his house and bring it to mine; we set it up on my bedroom floor. The board had the same graphics as the booklet: Barbie in a blue party dress, in a flowing pink evening gown. We'd just started to play when my mother came in the room. She saw which game it was and made us stop, made Scott take it home.

Melanie Brown complained that her mother would give money to any solicitor who rang their doorbell. Mrs. Brown complained that their houseguest, a friend of Melanie's, used up all the hot water taking long showers. She was separated from Melanie's father, who was black, a serviceman stationed in Victorville, California. Melanie and I were friendly for a while in high school, but she hurt my feelings when she said that I was a racist because I didn't know enough black people.

Mrs. Messerschmidt could have become an opera singer (she had had talent). Instead, she'd ended up in the suburbs, with two teenage daughters, a husband in construction, and a job as a secretary at one of the factories below Plummer. Her brunette hair always in a perfect bubble (she had it done once a week), she'd sit at the kitchen counter inhaling menthol cigarettes while her nails dried. Everything in their living room—furniture, carpet, curtains—was white. No one spent time in it. Janice wanted to be a fashion model; her younger sister Vicky, a roller derby star. I felt closer to Vicky, who seemed to understand (and believe in) my dream of becoming a writer. I related to her, in vivid detail, the entire plot of *Valley of the Dolls*. One Saturday night, I went with the Messerschmidts to the Winnetka Drive-In, to see *Who's Afraid of Virginia Woolf?* (I'd lied to my mother about which movie.) Though the swearing and flare-ups were riveting, the dialogue went over my head. I introduced Vicky and Janice to Mark, my friend in the housing tract on the other side of the wash. Mark's father was a security guard at location shoots; he'd taken Mark and me to see an episode of *Adam-12* being filmed. His mother also smoked menthols: Alpine— the strongest cigarette I ever tasted. I loved the way she made scrambled eggs (with lots of milk and cheese); when I told my mother this, she acted miffed. Mark's mother worked as a cashier at K-Mart. The summer after we graduated from junior high, Mark and I would take her car from the parking lot (he had a secret set of keys) and drive it around the neighborhood. I was always anxious that we'd get caught. Once high school started, Vicky, Janice, Mark, and I began playing hooky. We'd go to the girls' house, watch soap operas and smoke. Home from such a day, I found my mother at the screen door, furious (the school had phoned about my absences). Helpless, I confessed. *What else have you been up to?* I told her about Mark's and my joy rides. She meted out my punishment (grounded for weeks), then said she intended to call my friends' parents; I pleaded with her not to. The three of them got in trouble, and stopped talking to me. Despite Mark's in-fraction, his parents bought him a car, a green station wagon. For the remainder of high school, whenever they passed me walking home, they'd lower the car windows and tauntingly call out my name. Some-times Mark would honk the horn. I waited ten, fifteen, twenty minutes before leaving school, tried taking different routes, to avoid them; in-variably, they'd drive by and yell. Their new friends, kids I didn't know, happily joined in. I'd focus on Vicky, sitting stiffly in the middle of the back seat, staring straight ahead as the others shouted, as the station wagon sped down the street.

DELETED SCENE

Drunk, I go with Danny
to midnight movie in Sherman Oaks.
Rocky Horror. Appropriate:

that early eighties waste
between the accident and sobriety.

He hands me a pill; I swallow it.
Is that me yelling at the screen?

Employees find me on floor
of bathroom stall.
Movie over. Danny gone.

They try to rouse me,
fish John's phone number out of wallet.

Luckily call him, rather than police.

In lobby, waiting for John
to drive from Hollywood,
usher sits with me.

Focus on his face.

"You're cute," I say, and
tears flowing, ask for a date.

9773 COMANCHE AVE.

In color photographs, my childhood house looks
fresh as an uncut sheet cake—
pale yellow buttercream, ribbons of white trim

squeezed from the grooved tip of a pastry tube.
Whose dream was this confection?
This suburb of identical, pillow-mint homes?

The sky, too, is pastel. Children roller skate
down the new sidewalk. Fathers stake young trees.
Mothers plan baby showers and Tupperware parties.
The Avon Lady treks door to door.

Six or seven years old, I stand on the front porch,
hand on the decorative cast-iron trellis that frames it,
squinting in California sunlight,
striped short-sleeved shirt buttoned at the neck.

I sit in the backyard (this picture's black-and-white),
my Flintstones playset spread out on the grass.
I arrange each plastic character, each dinosaur,
each palm tree and round "granite" house.

Half a century later, I barely recognize it
when I search the address on Google Maps
and, via "Street view," find myself face to face—

foliage overgrown, facade remodeled and painted
a drab brown. I click to zoom: light hits
one of the windows. I can almost see what's inside.

THE SYLVIA PLATH CAKE COOKBOOK

FOR CATHERINE BOWMAN

Today I made a Devil's Food Cake for the first time.

Monday I baked a cake, vanilla, with lemon icing.

I had not made enough frosting to spread over the side of the cake to conceal the messy uneven edges, so I cut three pieces of the worst-looking part for our lunch.

Mrs. Watkins had taken my cakes carefully off the plate, washed and dried the plate, and handed it back to me.

There was a great frosted layer cake.

And a cabin boy who could decorate cakes in six-colored frosting.

I am a pig and have three hunks of cake.

With one finger I nudged a cake crumb into a drop of wet, brown tea.

I was thinking of the few times in my life I have felt I was all alive, tensed, using everything in me: mind and body, instead of giving away little crumbs, lest the audience be glutted with too much plum-cake.

"Who made all the cakes?"

Mrs. Mayo was pouring sliced peaches and juice over a great plate of little white cakes.

There was a startling number of cakes, all painstakingly decorated, some with cherries and nuts and some with sugar lace.

Millions of needly glass cakes!

* * *

four kinds of fancy cake
a Schrafft's cake for her maiden aunt
a package of pink-frosted cakes
coffee cake
pound cake
apple cake
tomato soup cake
a beautiful little two-layer 8 inch cake, yellow with 3 egg-yolks, and a
    maple syrup frosting with walnuts
a Gargantuan fantastical pink palace of a cake
a chocolate cake with white frosting
a yellow-frosted banana cake with cherries
yellow-browned round cakes
a three-tiered square cake
a lemon layer cake
a chocolate cake with rich dark frosting
inedible cream-filled cakes
delicious carrot cakes
maccaroon cakes that soften and cling to the hungry mouth
a plate of fancy tea cakes, all sugar & frosting
a plate of absolutely indigestible "Black Walnut flavored" cupcakes
    from a Betty Crocker mix
a glorious iced cake wrapped in her beautiful shawl

* * *

Meanwhile Prudence licks some frosting off the cake.
So I made and sugared some one-egg cupcakes.
I saw she had a handsome fruit cake, with one quarter cut out, on
    the table, cleared of tea things.
I had baked a big yellow sponge cake.

They ate cake; ate cake and catted about the Saturday night date.
All because of those revolting little cakes.
The model daughter fancily posed before a traditional wedding cake.
A wedding-cake face in a paper frill.
While making a cake found she'd left out one ingredient.
"Cake mix."
I want to eat my cake abroad and come home and find it securely on
    the doorstep if I still choose to accept it for the rest of my life.
What could frost my cake more?

And then the tale of the twenty-four cakes will come.

MOONLIGHT
IN TEMECULA

Dorland Mountain Arts Colony, located at the foothills of
Palomar Mountain in Southern California, was destroyed
by a wildfire on May 2, 2004. All of the buildings on the
300-acre nature preserve were reduced to ash and rubble.

Four months after the car accident
and two before the end
of the decadent seventies,
I find myself the first official resident
at this rustic artists' colony.
I hobble around on one crutch,
afraid of encountering rattlesnakes
or bobcats on the dirt paths.
At night I drink scotch
in my hillside cabin.
Isolated, inarticulate with grief,
no poems are possible.

Lost without electricity,
I wrestle with the wood-burning stove.
Helpless to light
the kerosene lamp,
I read *Remains of Elmet*
by a candle's flutterings.

Ninety-six-year-old Mrs. Dorland
is still vain about her legs.

(I can understand that now.)
She leaves a note in my mailbox
inviting me to Thanksgiving dinner.
Elisabeth makes apple chutney
with Alice B. Toklas' recipe.
I bring a bottle of white wine.
Tipsy, hobbling back in the dark,
I stop to admire the stars;
my crutch flies out from under me
and I fall flat on my back.

Alone in the cabin, I wake
in the middle of the night
to moonlight so bright
you could read a book by it.
Rachel has been dead almost five months.
I look out at the moonlit hillside,
at a future burnt down to the ground.

PINK BUTTON

FOR LISA FISHMAN

plucked from
Lorine's pilled sweater

and deposited on
her lawn

island not
an island

lake not
a lake

fame not necessary
for the poems

each word
eye candy

for the literary
pilgrim

too devout
to sign the guestbook

but graced with
a plastic button

glinting in
shrinking sunlight

She found a pink
flicker ring

in the grass

EIGHT NURSES MURDERED IN CHICAGO

Normally it was comics or movie magazines;
I don't know why I reached for *True Detective*.
Something eye-catching on the cover?

Stood, in mid-sixties drugstore fluorescence, and read
about the body of a woman found in an alley,
between trash cans, in what appeared, from the photograph,

to be a run down neighborhood. there were tall weeds.
I owned several Agatha Christies, had seen murder mysteries
on TV, but this made me feel queasy and strangely ashamed—

wrong to look at or be interested in, like dirty pictures.
But not wrong, not much later, to look at the *Los Angeles Times*.
The drawing reminded me of my Clue board: a floor plan

with furniture and entryways, and arrows
showing the path the intruder took.
Used a glasscutter to score a hole in the pane of a French door,

reached in and unlocked it from the inside.
That was the detail that scared me the most,
what woke the stepmother at 4:50 a.m.—

a shatter of glass. She first thought
one of the children had knocked
a tumbler of water off a nightstand.

Then she heard what she later described as a "baleful moan."
She got up and followed the sound,
opened a door to discover a man standing over the bed

of the senator's twenty-one-year-old daughter,
flashlight illumining her blood-soaked body—
bludgeoned and stabbed numerous times.

The intruder shone his light in the stepmother's eyes,
momentarily blinding her; she ran
screaming for help. He retraced

his path: down a circular staircase, through
a hallway into the music room, then out
the French door.

If that could happen at a senator's mansion,
what about our house?
I was already sick with fear.

Two months earlier, there'd been the faces
of eight nurses—all yearbook smiles and brunette hair—
on the front page of the paper.

How to explain anything so horrible happening in the world?
I read about the ordeal of the ninth nurse,
how she slid under a bed and hid

while, one by one, he took them from the room.
How she listened to the muffled sounds, then to the silence.
Their bodies, strangled and stabbed, strewn

through the house. How she squirmed free
of the torn sheets binding her wrists and feet, but laid still
the rest of the night, until she was sure he had gone

and the room had turned light.
How she pried open the second-floor window-screen
and crawled out onto the ledge.

How many were woken from sleep by her screams.

ON SYLVIA
PLATH'S BIRTHDAY

Psychic says one journal burned (too personal)
One still hidden in family

Psychic sees (next session) a box
Carvings, a beautiful jewel on it

Red satin ribbon on key
16th or 17th century

Sees Sylvia put key into box
And unlock it

She's starting to touch me with spirit vibration
Around face (like my mother)

The tears I cried when her son died
Turned (says psychic) to crystals

She's holding them in her hand

"THE CHAIR THAT SHE SAT UPON IS UP FOR AUCTION."

She sat atop the back of this chair
two weeks before she died,

her final photo shoot in Brentwood
at her L-shaped, Spanish Colonial home,

the only one she owned by herself:
"I live alone and I hate it."

Fired from Fox, her last
completed film would be *The Misfits*,

unappreciated at the time,
a performance given on the edge

of the abyss, much of it out of focus.

And somehow posthumous,
as when Peter Lawford introduced her

as "the late Marilyn Monroe."
Her white hair made her look like a ghost.

Life photographer Allan Grant
chose this chair and placed it below

the window for the light it offered.
He asked her to select casual clothes.

She wore a black V-neck sweater,
capri slacks, spike heels.

At the end of the session, she reportedly said,
"Please don't make me a joke."

She could still be alive
(if she'd gotten off pills),

the users and Svengalis long behind her.

The Italian-style carved chair
has had three owners since Marilyn's death.

The green velvet upholstery bears a little tear
where her heel poked through.

As Monroe sat on it and posed,
she caused a small crack in the wood.

Winning bid: $28,000.00

UNDERLINED IN SYLVIA PLATH'S COPY OF *TENDER IS THE NIGHT*

cone of sunshine

redder than the very sun

dead white hours
her face caught the room's last light
very blonde hair
miles and miles of rolling night

to feel blue

dark world

lost key to the silver closet
stiff white collar
sharp little gray eyes
an emerald hill above

masses of color

suspension between the blues of two heavens

snowy-white transformations, black dresses
lips of cherry red

hair dashed with white like a piano keyboard
"My God," he gasped, "You're fun to kiss."

her softly shining porcelain cheeks

glowing away, white and fresh and new

blue dawn
a large, proud, rose-colored hotel
purple Alp
magic in her pink palms

hot light

brutal sunshine

raw whiteness
blank iron masks
ghostly moonshine
cold blue eyes

ashen faces

white crackling glow of a stage

kaleidoscopic peonies massed in pink clouds, black and brown
tulips and fragile mauve-stemmed roses, transparent like sugar
flowers in a confectioner's window
scherzo of color

a bowl of spicy pinks

white mirrors of her teeth

fireflies riding on the dark air
a yellow evening bag
single dull star
suspended in the moonshine

erotic darkness

high, black shadow

the white caps of a great sea of graves
the darkness of the night, the darkness of the world
pink majesty
white excitement

It was a windy four-o'clock night, with the leaves on the Champs-
    Élysées singing and failing, thin and wild.

white semi-circles of panic

the waves grew black
Grief presented itself in its terrible, dark unfamiliar color
the mad hand clutching the steering wheel
Soaring and roaring into the blue

black shape of a tree

there was the eternal moonlight in it

bloody haze
violet darkness
blue paradise
roofless cavern of white moonlight

another little prison

a white sky

PEYTON PLACE

A HAIKU SOAP OPERA

Episodes 32–65, released on DVD July 14, 2009

32

Betty's still missing.
Carson comes home from prison.
Snow cloaks Peyton Place.

33

Phone call from Betty
cuts short the women's highly
caloric breakfast.

34

Julie and Connie
side by side—a virtual
tsunami of hair.

35

How much did it cost
Fox to stage a snowball fight
on SoCal back lot?

36

Malone's sweater's so
full, she almost pokes O'Neal
in front of fireplace.

37

Drama is promised
and delivered: Allison's
zipper gets unstuck.

38

I thought Connie's taste
in art sucked. Wait till you see
Sharon's bird painting.

39

Mother-daughter chat
completely upstaged by cool
sixties throw pillows.

40

Roy, Betty's near-date
rapist, fears the whole building
will hear her (dubbed) cries.

41

All this talk about
existentialist despair.
Then there's Norman's jeans.

42

Quite a basket on
guy who ogles Allison.
Big college welcome.

43

At the annual
faculty art exhibit,
more horrors await.

44

They just keep talking.
I guess every episode
is nothing but talk.

45

The cameraman
certainly has a yen for
Norman's tight trousers.

46

Last episode, Rod
gave Betty a nice hard slap.
Now it's back to talk.

47

Crotch watcher says: Rod
shows up for annulment not
wearing underwear.

48

We've seen some strange things,
but nothing as bizarre as
Betty's hand puppet.

49

Harrington brothers
in profile. Were they cast 'cause
they have the same nose?

50

What would a haiku
soap opera be without
an evil head nurse?

51

Am I wrong, or does
Dr. Morton don a dish
towel as a scarf?

52

Too perfect: Micky
Dolenz (future Monkee) slips
Norman a mickey.

53

Bullies tie up Norm
in town square, leave him to freeze.
Your standard hate crime.

54

Those ruffled kitchen
curtains: a Roy Lichtenstein
postcard I once sent.

55

The two hipsters who
strut through the hospital are
so on the wrong set.

56

We should all be paged
by a voice that comatose
at least once in life.

57

Didn't hear a word.
Too busy revising last
episode's haiku.

58

Preview: Shooting at
the Harrington house. I hope
it's not Elliot.

59

Ambulance siren
wails in the night. They milk it,
so why shouldn't I?

60

Ryan and Barbara
finally get star billing.
Elliot fights death.

61

I'm sorry, but they
mean to draw attention to
Norman's endowment.

62

Through the picket fence,
at the end of the brick walk,
lurks the Big Secret.

63

Is Allison's dream
world shattered by the truth or
by Hanley's bad art?

64

As Elliot's wheeled
out of surgery, the tide
(Connie's hair) is high.

65

Much has been revealed.
But not the release date of
the next installment.

This is the continuing story of Peyton Place . . .

THREE BEDROOMS

3 CHALCOT SQUARE

"The bedroom is like a bright arbor of roses,"
you wrote to your mother in America, enclosing
a sample of the wallpaper, which you'd picked
out yourself, and especially liked:
clusters of rose blooms, deep and pale pink
on white. Because of Ted's size,
you ordered an extra-large bed—5 by 6$^1/_2$ feet—
"most of my sheets don't tuck
in at the side as the mattress is thick."
Ted painted the floorboards (you were six
months pregnant, so he did the heavy work)
"a whited grey." After you gave birth,
the wallpaper roses made their way
into "Morning Song," your poem about
your infant daughter. Six months later,
on the verge of moving to Devon, you tore
up the check of the "busybody man" who wanted
the flat, leasing instead to the couple Ted liked—
"a nice young Canadian poet and his
very attractive, intelligent wife."
By such "fate playing" (as Ted would one day write),
Assia came to sleep among
the flat pink roses.

COURT GREEN

"Rugs is the main thing now," you wrote
within a month of arriving in North Tawton.
"We ordered a lovely all-wool Indian carpet
for our bedroom (10′7″ × 9′3″) with off-white, rose
& green border & center medallion, at just under $150."
Ted painted the "acres of as yet bare
boards" (you were pregnant again):
"pale grey lino paint, as in our London flat."
When the floral Indian rug was delivered,
the bedroom felt like "a place of luxury."
Until Ted bought a 2′ × 4′ Chinese goatskin,
with "long black and grey silky hairs":
"guess whose side of the bed it will be on!"
Once you were dead, Assia purged the drawers
of your combs and ribbons and brushes,
your miscellaneous half-discarded things.
"The God's bedroom," she facetiously called it.

23 FITZROY ROAD

On your own, you painted all the floors—
"2 coats!" Feeling empowered, you adorned
your bedroom with "bee colors":
"yellow & white wallpaper, straw mat,
black floor borders & gold lampshade."
It faced the rising sun, which you likened
to a blooming geranium. London was
"very Dickensian," an 18th century engraving.
From your "little balcony" you viewed the full moon

"in sheer joy." You would have liked to have lived
in the flat forever. You planned to "furnish it, poem
by poem, in beautiful taste from second hand shops."
In the meantime, you slept in a single bed, on loan
from the Portuguese friend that supplied you
with gossip about Assia, your "evil shadow"
who, after your suicide, would sleep *there*, too.

THE DEAD

The patter of rain on the roof,
a late-night comfort.

The knife in the back,
removed and blessed,

absorbed by the lake.
The faces in the locket:

thumbnail guardians, cut-to-fit
hearts. "When you make

your transition," a psychic said,
"Byron will be there, waiting.

Don't forget it." May he
be the first to greet me—

a running leap
into my arms. Then

Rachel, Tim, Mom, and Jim.
The dead emerge from

the flicker of black-and-white
footage, grainy Hollywood fog.

Ann, ever patient for
her words to be heard.

Jimmy, prisoner in mind,
in body, yet as poet free.

Generous, self-effacing Joe.
Even Bob, his lungs full

of forgiveness. Even
Sylvia and Ted, reconciled

and working closely with
Nicholas, new to this.

Darragh, too, recently
arrived, all-but-blind

painter, lonely and depressed.
(What mixed feelings his

death stirred up in me.)
And now Lola at eight months,

Aunt Louise in her late nineties.
Behind them, shadowy,

out of focus, the figures of
grandparents and teachers,

acquaintances and friends,
strangers drawn to and

crowding the frame, like extras
aching for more screen time.

Tonight, lulled by gentle rain,
I'll claim as many as I can name.

THE DRESS THAT
JOAN WORE

This is the dress that Joan Crawford wore
towards the end of her career (1964)
in the B-horror flick *Strait-Jacket*,
directed by William Castle, King of the Cheapo Box-Office Gimmicks,
in which she portrays an axe murderess
who chops off the heads of her husband and his mistress
as they lay postcoital in her own bed,
and who twenty years later is released
from a hospital for the criminally insane
and reunited with her now-grown daughter (played by Diane Baker)
and is the prime suspect (of course)
in a fresh rash of killings.

This is the dress that Joan Crawford wore
(gray, black, and white floral-printed silk
with scoop neck, capped sleeves, and self-belt)
as she milked her performance for all it was worth,
guzzling (real?) highballs,
jangling twin charm bracelets,
and putting the moves on
her daughter's handsome young fiancé
(by fumbling drunken fingers at
his horror-struck lips).

This is the dress that Joan Crawford wore
in "a camp classic as compulsively watchable as a train wreck"

(so says the Internet)
that was put up for auction in June 2009
in an Entertainment Memorabilia sale at Bonhams & Butterfields
(that included the Emmy Estelle Getty won for *Golden Girls*
and a Marilyn Monroe blank check
and one of Elizabeth Taylor's *Cleopatra* wigs)
and sold for $5,185.00 to god knows who,
probably an impeccably manicured *Queer Eye* type
who'll display the costume on a dressmaker's dummy
and invite over a few flamboyant friends
to ooh and aah (and maybe try it on)
and view the DVD of *Strait-Jacket*
on his 52″ flat-panel HDTV
while sipping blood-red (pomegranate) martinis
and screaming—not in horror
at each lopped-off head, but with shrill glee
as Joan slurs her words
and "insanely" unravels her knitting
and lights a cigarette
by striking a wooden match
on a record spinning on a phonograph
and in the dress at which they'd gasped
brandishes (spoiler alert: it's really Diane) the gore-splashed axe.

DELETED SCENE

I was on my way to teach
a poetry workshop at Rutgers.

Penn Station, downstairs,
boarding the Trenton Local.

I'd selected a seat and
was about to sit when
a young woman slid
into it from behind
and gave me a dirty look.

There were plenty of other seats
but she'd taken the one I wanted.

It was not a good time
in my life. Ira and I had
broken up; there I was,
single at forty-six, stuck
in a noisy apartment
in the midst of SoHo's orgy
of high-end consumerism.
I wanted to leave New York
but didn't know where to go.

I don't mean to
excuse myself.

A few rows ahead
I stared back at her

and I said it. "Cunt."

Then sat down with
all my rage and shame.

FOR NICHOLAS HUGHES

At last we know who
you were, beyond the baby
your mother woke and wrote to,
the baby crying while her body
lay, still warm, in the kitchen one
floor below; beyond the youth
sequestered among the moors,
silently fishing alongside his
famous father. We now know
your "varied pursuits": stream ecology,
pottery, woodworking, boating,
bicycling, gardening, and cooking
"the perfect pecan pie." How like
both of them you were! We now
know you would have nothing to
do with her, whose absence left
you hollow, and yet you found refuge
in the Golden Heart of Alaska, in
her country, an ice fortress blazing
with Aurora's lights. We know
that in the nine years since the death
of the Poet Laureate, that man of brick,
your foundation crumbled; know
that two years ago, you gave up
your professorship to concentrate
on ceramics. *Is there no way out of
the mind?* One by one, the passage
doors shut, and locked behind you.

Still, in your depression you were able
to climb Scafell Pike, the tallest peak
in England. We can see pictures
of you on the Internet now, Nicholas:
movie-star handsome, your stare refusing
us access, guarded against the acolytes
who would tear the very flesh from
your bones in order to possess her.
And now your death, we know that.
What is it, finally, but an image, the
feet of a condemned man that fell from
a poem—first one of hers, then one of his.
As if their poems could ever console
you, or explain away the pain. Death
was—and is—your legacy, we know
that now. At last, Nicholas, we know

MARCH 27, 2009

AIDS SERIES

1

I met Larry Stanton at a party on the Lower East Side, Indian summer, 1982. My maiden trip to New York. Nervous and unsure of myself, pinned against the wall in a room full of poets, cocktail chatter, cigarette smoke. I'd just lit a Marlboro Light when Larry, part of the small group I was trying to converse with, leaned forward and kissed me on the lips. That's all I remember. He might have invited me to visit his studio; Tim might have taken me there. He might have come to my reading at St. Mark's. I only remember that mysterious kiss. And his looks: a boyish blond who had morphed into an unkempt mid-thirties handsomeness. I open the book of his paintings to a self-portrait he did in 1984, the year he died. He stares back, sad and cute. It aches to look into his face.

2

Lee Hickman and I became friends in the early eighties, after he published me in *Bachy*. Peter Cashorali (another young Los Angeles poet Lee had published) and I would hang out with him, ask him burning questions about poetry. Lee was dismayed that he couldn't give away a perfectly good copy of Pound's *Cantos*—nobody wanted it, Peter and myself included. I accompanied him to San Francisco (where he gave a reading); on the way back he got a speeding ticket outside of Santa Barbara. For his birthday I gave him a pair of elegant champagne flutes. He showed me a letter Anne Sexton had sent him, praising his poem "Lee Sr Falls to the Floor." It was confusing when Lee rejected all the local poets he had supported and took up with the Language poets:

he seemed angry for some unknown reason, acted like he wanted to punish us. One day when I was at Astro's with Bob and Sheree, Lee came in and sat at the counter. My book *Monday, Monday* had just come out; I had one with me and debated whether I should give it to Lee. Bob and Sheree encouraged me. I walked over and offered it to him: "I hope you enjoy it." Several weeks later, he showed up at a reading and asked me to sign the book I'd given him, on the last page of my poem "Meet The Supremes." I wrote: "Lee, where did our love go?"

3

I went to Astro's with Glen after one of my first A.A. meetings, fall of 1983. Chain-smoked and drank countless cups of coffee. Glen was loud and funny and overweight. I could do little but listen. I've never forgotten something he said that night: "Even a bowel movement can be spiritual." I didn't—and still don't—know what he meant. He gave me my *Big Book*, wrote in it: "David T., May you have many sober years, Glen." His gesture and message made a difference: I've been sober nearly three decades. Early on, Glen celebrated a "birthday" at the Hollywood Squares meeting on New Hampshire. All of the celebrants stood in line to blow out candles (one for each year of sobriety) on a cake and address the crowd. The man in front of Glen carried his toy poodle with him. When it was his turn, Glen walked up to the podium and said, "I always knew if I got sober, I'd follow a dog act."

4

I was a year and a half sober when I saw Steve at an A.A. meeting. He had three or four months. I couldn't understand why I found his profile so captivating; that had never happened before. A psychic confirmed that it signified a past life connection. A sense of stoic intensity, like T.E. Lawrence. Late twenties. Thinning blond hair. Wore a black-and-white kaffiyeh wrapped around his neck. Estranged (because he was gay) from his family in Albany, New York. In his living room in Pasadena, we slow danced to Carly Simon's "The Right Thing To Do" then laid on his couch and kissed. When he ran his index finger up and down my wrist, I thought of the Ted Hughes line "Under the silk of the wrist a sea." When we moved to Simple Minds at an A.A. dance, he smiled and mouthed, "Don't You Forget About Me." When things became emotionally fraught, my A.A. sponsor insisted I break it off: it was too soon for Steve to start dating. "Maybe when he has more time. . . ." When I told Steve we needed to wait, tears literally flew out of his eyes. After he left, I sat on the floor under my Isermann clock and cried. Before he moved home to Albany (where he would die), we talked on the telephone. He told me how angry he was at me. For once, I didn't get defensive, just let him have his feelings. I'm happy that I was able to respond tenderly. What bothers me is that I can't remember Steve's last name.

5

Ron Cahill was a friend my last year in Los Angeles. We met through Sally, an overbearing woman we both knew from the program. In our early conversations, we tried to make sense of Sally's personality. There was a sadness about Ron—pushing forty, positive, no relationship, fed up with the West Hollywood scene. I've sometimes thought that, under different circumstances, we might have been boyfriends. I still have the copy of Capote's *Answered Prayers* he gave me for Christmas 1987, inscribed with red ink: "Love, Ron." After I moved to New York, we kept in contact: there are twelve letters and eighteen postcards from him in my papers at NYU. I regret that I was standoffish when he suggested a visit; I was swamped with graduate work. He was hurt. His postcards mentioned that he was on a regimen of Chinese herbs, and was considering moving to Texas to be close to his family. Then an abrupt message from Sally on my answering machine: Ron was dead. No details, no number to reach her. Years later, when she found me through the Internet, I told her how her message left me stranded with the news of Ron's death, how difficult that had been for me. Her reply was curt: "You poor thing."

6

A few weeks after I arrived in New York, Raymond Foye took me to lunch with Cookie Mueller, Vittorio Scarpati, and John Wieners. An Indian restaurant in the East Village. I was seated across from Wieners, who was certain he'd encountered me in Canada years before. Every time I'd try to converse with him, he'd first say something coherent, then lapse into incomprehensible utterances. I don't remember talking with Cookie at all. When the waiter brought out our food, he dropped the huge silver tray just as he reached our table. We waited while the meal was prepared a second time.

7

I liked Karl Tierney and I liked his poems, but all I can remember is that in the restaurant in San Francisco where we ate, our booth had a curtain.

8

Amy said that when she visited Tim Dlugos at Roosevelt Hospital in 1989, he was reading *Our Mutual Friend*, Dickens' last novel, a book he'd been reading, off and on, since at least 1981. I think she said there were yellow flowers in the room. Eileen said that when she visited him a year later, during his final hospitalization, Tim was trying to eat pink yogurt, but his lips were too swollen. The radio was on a local station playing "Ruby" songs: "Ruby Baby," "Ruby Tuesday," "Ruby, Don't Take Your Love To Town." Jane said that at the end Tim was on so much morphine it seemed he was in a coma. She held his hand or sometimes, exhausted, laid forward with her head and arms in the bed. Even slept. "It was very peaceful to be with him." For years I lamented the fact that I wasn't able, as he was dying, to talk with him about what was happening. It would have felt intrusive for me to bring it up. Eileen said she just held Tim's hand and told him she loved him. That was helpful to hear. The next time I visited him on G-9, I did the same. Tim said, "I love you, too." It was late afternoon, and we sat, mostly in silence, as the light faded. I remember everything as gray.

9

Joe Brainard was so sweet and polite, so self-effacing, it's hard to summon many specifics. I do remember that when he came to a dinner Ira and I gave, he drew the face of a troll doll in our guest book. And that he flipped over *A Class Apart*: Montague Glover's photographs of soldier boys and rough trade, their large penises showing through trousers and bathing suits. And that he was once sitting in Aggie's, a restaurant that used to be on the corner of West Houston and MacDougal, when I walked by. I didn't see him, but he saw me. "I saw you!" he said, the next time we were together. He mentioned it two or three times after that: "I saw you!" It seemed so significant to him. "I saw you!"

MINIATURE

FOR SUZANNE BUFFAM

Every dollhouse
should have a mirror
so its inhabitant
(in this case you)
can see herself
or at least one eye
peering like Alice
into the tiny keyhole
every book should have
a poem small enough
to slip through
on the flood of her tears

ANNE SEXTON VISITS COURT GREEN

(JULY 1967)

After reading more than her allotted time
(infuriating W.H. Auden, on stage behind her)
then blowing kisses to the audience
at the Poetry International Festival,
Anne accepts Ted's invitation
to visit him in Devon.
Lois at the wheel (still unused to
driving on the "wrong" side
of the street), the two women leave London
and head west toward Herefordshire
(where they will meet a young poet,
D.M. Thomas, with whom Sexton has exchanged letters).
Anne, chain-smoking in the left-hand
passenger seat, is no help with the map.
It sits, a crumpled accordion, in her lap.

Having gotten lost on narrow country roads,
the women arrive three hours late.
Thomas, an "exuberant, curly-haired bear
of a man," is ready with gin. As a fan
he'd written to Sexton: "There is no poet in the world,
not Graves, not Auden, not Lowell,
whose future work I look forward to
with as much excitement as I do yours."

A few stiff shots and they settle in
for a pleasant evening. Anne reads
some of her poems, Thomas admiring
her courage to use material from her own life—
so free of English conventions of decorum.
(In the eighties, his novel *The White Hotel*
will bring him fame and notoriety.)
He drives them to the nearby village of Weobley.
As promised, he'd booked the room at an inn, the Unicorn,
where Rilke slept the year before Sexton was born.

Anne asks him up, then asks him
to turn away while she strips
and slides into her white negligee—
bought, she says, with her Pulitzer Prize.
When Thomas is allowed to look,
he breathes in her splendidness.
Anne counts out her colorful pills.
"Please stay until I fall asleep."
He sits on the edge of the bed,
caressing her hand as she drifts off.
Her husband, he thinks, *must perform this nightly duty.*
I feel like I'm tucking in Sleeping Beauty.

The next day, Thomas shows them
the border country. At a castle
in Shropshire, Sexton feels too lame
to climb the stone stairs. (She is recovering from
a broken hip.) She says to Thomas,
"Better than stones and castles are my bones."
Then: "I'll give that to you." She tears out

a sheet of paper and writes down the line.
(Later he'll use it to start an elegy to her.)
As night comes on, they stop at a pub.
Anne plays the fruit machines
and whoops it up when she wins
a "magic jackpot." In the same breath
she talks about poetry, about death.

When Thomas drops them off at the inn,
he and Anne exchange a passionate kiss.
He thinks: *Wow! I've kissed Sexton!*
The following morning, on their own again,
the women proceed to Devon.
They reach North Tawton in the early afternoon,
easily locate Court Green.
(Ted had told them to look for the adjacent church.)
Lois inches the rental up the crumbling lane,
between hedges and brick cottages,
and parks in front of the imposing manor house.
Painted white, with black trim, its most conspicuous feature
is a primeval peaked thatch.
As both women stare up, they hear the gate unlatch.

Ted and Assia emerge and welcome them.
Less radiant than they were
in London (Ted, one of the organizers
of the festival, seems especially worn out),
the couple usher them into the cobbled courtyard.
Ted requests that they not talk about Sylvia
in the presence of the children, then leads
them around the property—two acres

teeming with vegetation. There is a sense
of ancient wildness about the place.
Trees that Ted points out—
three huge elms, a golden laburnum—
prompt Anne and Lois to share knowing glances:
they recognize them from Sylvia's poems.
There the apple orchard, the remote white hive.
Here the old tennis court, the vegetable garden.
There the "row of headstones" (*It really is true!*),
St. Peter's Church, the graveyard, the Gothic yew.

Assia takes them inside to freshen up,
and to give them a tour of the house.
This is the playroom, with its black-and-white tiled floor,
like a Vermeer, and the children's toys and books,
and the furniture Sylvia painted white and
enameled with primitive hearts and flowers.
Across the hall, the "red room," where Sylvia listened
to French and German lessons on the wireless.
They come to the stairs. These
Anne does not hesitate to climb.
To see where Sylvia wrote *Ariel*
she'll put up with a little pain in her hip.
Still, each step is a production.
"Go on ahead, go on . . . I'll catch up."
But of course Lois insists
on assisting her. "*This* was her study,"
says Assia, gesturing towards one of the bedrooms.
In awe, Anne and Lois follow.
By the window: Sylvia's elm plank writing table.
("Ted refuses to move it.")

Sylvia's typewriter and journals and stacks of pink worksheets
are neatly arranged along its length.
Assia hands Anne the copy of *All My Pretty Ones*
that Anne had sent Sylvia when it came out,
and in which Sylvia had written her name.
"You should take it," Assia says.
Anne considers it for a moment,
then sets it down on the desk, runs her slender fingers
along some ink stains in the wood.
They leave Lois with the journals,
scribbling notes for the Plath biography
that she will never complete.
"You must hate me. She was your friend."
Assia says this to Anne as soon as they're alone.
When it comes to adultery, Sexton doesn't throw stones.

Plus she can't help but admire her dark beauty
and her sexual heat. Assia prepares tea
and they sit under the laburnum.
"All parts of the tree are poisonous," she remarks
as she pours. Anne praises the banana bread.
"It was *her* recipe," says Assia distractedly, staring towards Ted
on the lawn in the sun, with the children.
Shura, her toddler, plays slightly apart.
Assia expresses unease about Aurelia's impending visit.
(In August, fears put to rest, she'll write to Anne
that she finds Sylvia's mother "a remarkable woman—
a kind of near-genius knot herself" whose
generous spirit "makes me feel humbler than I have ever been.")
Anne tries to reassure with some banter
about her mother-in-law, though both understand

the singularity of Assia's situation.
Ted joins them and, when Anne shifts uncomfortably
in her deckchair, recommends bone meal
for her ailing hip. "It has to be taken
regularly, but if you take too much
you'll grow bone all over like a crab, so take it easy."
They smile. Then commiserate about reviews.
"Both kinds are bad," says Ted, "but the favorable
are worst. They tend to confirm one in one's own conceit.
Also, they separate you from your devil, which hates
being observed, and only works happily incognito."
He spies on his wrist, sharpening her needle, a bloodthirsty mosquito.

Late sunlight floods the laburnum,
igniting its "blond colonnades."
In less than two years, Assia and her daughter
will be dead; in a little more
than seven, Anne. Ted will live
for three decades; Nicholas, four.
Only Frieda, age seven, who knows more
than she knows, will survive. Shyly suspicious,
she glances over at the adults
now and again. Ted swats his wrist.
Assia slices Shura a small piece of banana bread.
Anne lights a Salem, exhales upward, and watches a bee
bask in the brilliance of the poisonous tree.

MEDUSA REDUX

You were of two minds about everything—
country or city, teaching or retirement, lesbian
or straight sex. When you judged
that poetry contest and couldn't choose
between two finalists (male or female)

and we used my Magic 8 Ball to pick
the winner (male), you made me promise
never to tell. Just as, years earlier, when I was
your student and you showed me a poem
you wrote about screwing my classmate (male)

you whispered *secret, secret.* Your skirt
bunched up around your hips was one of its
images. Your pull always had a push,
your sweetness a sting. "Disingenuous
former mentor," is what I dubbed you

in a poem. Why, knowing that, did I
let you back in my life? Bring you to my
city, champion you to my own students,
expose them to your threadbare workshop style:
spurious nurturing, ingratiating praise.

When I called you the day my dog died,
you said, "I don't know what you expect
me to say." Your obdurate rebuff put
me off. Then, at Starbucks, as I reiterated
how much pain I was in, you sat mute,

stone-faced. Furious at my grief for
keeping me from you. Who would fix
your computer glitches? Or placate your
complaints about your editor, your book
designer, the director of your low-residency?

Or help unstick you from your latest
mess (an affair with a married man)?
So you ran to my colleagues, my students,
my friends—to anyone who would
listen—with your self-deflecting, under-

mining chant: *What's wrong with David?*
Thus, during the hardest loss of my life,
your resentment twisted, hissed behind
my back. At that reading, the last time
I *had* to see you, I waited till I was ready to

leave, till the crowd thinned a path. I walked
up, looked in your eyes—those hopeless
windows—and said, "Goodbye." I knew
from your stricken expression that you knew:
I was through with you. After I left the room,

your tears (it was later conveyed) coerced
bystanders to comfort you. At our closest,
we joked that we'd been soul mates in a past
life: husband and wife reciting poems
to each other in a cabin in the woods.

Now, in my mind's eye, I see a woman
wrapped in a peasant shawl, hands red

with the blood of her dead children,
moaning *What did I do? What did I do?*
She disappears into the Black Forest.

I see you (one of our last encounters), caught
for a heartbeat like an animal on a dark road,
eyes flashing from martyr-pain to self-
righteous rage, then bolting, to avoid me,
towards an exit I knew was locked.

BURNT OFFERINGS

(C O U R T   G R E E N ,   1 9 6 2)

The place was like a person,
its walls pink-washed

flesh that responded
to the slightest touch.

Though she thought
differently—

stained glass lit up
in the church next door

so pretty through
silhouettes of trees

the house was only happy
when black words

oozed their muck
out of the telephone

and she recoiled from
the dark, airless room

off the kitchen
as if it were a tomb

or closet of ghosts
hooked like hung coats.

Her own personal Hill House,
her private horrors made real.

At night he read
Heart of Darkness to her

while she worked with her hands
(they were never still)

in front of the fireplace,
red carpet and drapes

flickering a furious pulse.
Together they'd furnished

the house with her rage.
It need wait but a short while

longer to speak what for too
long had been mute, through her.

MOON STREET

A poem or story deserves that name. —SYLVIA PLATH

There is the moon in the high window.
The eyes lift after it and find the moon.

It resembles the moon, or a sheet of blank paper
Plague-pitted as the moon: each bud

A full moon, river lapsing
The moon to a rind of little light.

Such queer moons we live with
Under the eyes of the stars and the moon's rictus

While from the moon, my lover's eye
Floats calm as a moon or a cloud.

The moon has nothing to be sad about,
The sour lemon moon.

That night the moon
And I knew it was not the streetlight, but the moon.

A moon loomed, as if set off like a balloon a moment before.
If the moon smiled, she would resemble you.

The moon is my mother.
The moon, also, is merciless: she would drag me

In my moon suit and funeral veil,
Agawp at the impeccable moon.

The moon sees nothing of this.
There is only the moon, embalmed in phosphorus.

O moon-glow, o sick one,
The moon is no door.

The moon's concern is more personal:
Rattles its pod, the moon

As the moon, for its ivory powders, scours the sea.
The night lights are flat red moons.

The moon, too, abases her subjects,
Unloosing their moons, month after month, to no purpose.

But their bones showed, and the moon smiled.
And sung me moon-struck, kissed me quite insane.

There was no moon.
The moon went out in a cloud.

Then blackness again, and land lying flat under the clear moon.
The moon, my

Lady, who are these others in the moon's vat—
Intercepting the blue bolts of a cold moon?

The moon lays a hand on my forehead,
Then she turns to those liars, the candles or the moon.

My head a moon
Round as the moon, to stare up.

To the moon.

THE PATTY DUKE SHOW

THE COMPLETE FIRST SEASON

Released on DVD September 29, 2009

Patty gets a crush on her new French teacher.

Patty cheats on a computerized intelligence test and is pronounced a genius.

Mr. Lane mistakenly thinks Patty and Richard are planning to elope.

Eccentric Aunt Pauline comes to stay with the Lanes.

Patty and Cathy try to prepare Ross for his first date.

Ross blackmails Patty and Cathy by tape recording their conversation at a slumber party.

Patty starts a babysitting service so she can earn money for a new dress.

Stretch, the high school basketball star, causes havoc as the Lanes' houseguest.

Patty and Cathy run against each other for President of the Girls League.

Cathy has a reaction to a flu shot, so Patty pretends to be both of them at a dance contest.

Patty is cast as Cleopatra in the school play, but gets stage fright on opening night.

Cathy wants to be more popular (Frankie Avalon guest stars).

Patty panics when Richard enters a poem she plagiarized in a TV songwriting contest.

Cathy becomes engaged to Kalmere, the crown prince of Buchanistan.

On Christmas Eve, Mr. Lane impersonates his twin brother
Kenneth, Cathy's absent father, then confusion ensues when
the real Kenneth shows up.

To save Kenneth's job as foreign correspondent, Patty and Cathy
decide he should write a best-selling autobiography.

Patty finds she has a knack for fortune-telling—for a small fee, of
course.

Patty and Cathy go into the dressmaking business.

Patty writes a novel entitled *I Was a Teenage Teenager*.

When Mr. Lane is transferred to the Paris office, the family begins
packing to move overseas.

Chaos in the kitchen as Patty and Cathy try to recreate the cake Mrs.
Lane baked for the church bazaar (which they ate).

Richard asks Patty to wear his ring, but Patty's parents think she's
too young to go steady.

Because she feels taken for granted by the family, Mrs. Lane concocts
a plan to call attention to herself.

Patty and Cathy attempt to resell the expensive vacuum cleaner they
bought from a fast-talking door-to-door salesman.

After Patty flunks "teenage" in a magazine quiz, she enrolls in
modeling school to bolster her confidence.

Patty becomes editor-in-chief of the *Brooklyn Heights High Bugle* and
turns it into a scandal sheet.

Hoping to win a TV for their parents' 20th wedding anniversary,
Ross enters Patty in the "Beautiful Teens" contest.

Before Patty can take back a dress she can't afford, Cathy wears it to a
piano concert and accidentally spills punch on it.

Patty's secret pen pal turns out to be her boyfriend Richard.

Patty becomes allergic to Cathy.

Patty inadvertently adopts a Korean boy named Kim.

In order to keep Richard from dropping out of school, Patty pretends to
   quit too, but her tactic backfires.
Patty poses as Cathy to convince a British rock star to perform at the
   prom.
Cathy is appointed student principal and has to discipline Patty in class.
Patty gets a job at the Shake Shop.
Via flashbacks (clips from the unaired pilot), Patty and Cathy reminisce
   about Cathy's arrival at the Lane household.

SHARON TATE AND FRIENDS THE MOMENT BEFORE

LUIGINO VALENTIN,
ACRYLIC ON CANVAS, 2000

Frozen, the seven of them, in front of the fireplace.
Mid-protest, Sebring reaches towards Watson.
His mod black-and-white striped pants clash with the zebra rug.

Lamp-glow highlights the blade in Watson's right hand.
Highlights the white ceiling beams, Sharon's blonde hair

bra and panties. Her arms hold her bare pregnant stomach.
Frozen in fear, Frykowski, on couch, leans away from
the Longhorn revolver in Watson's left hand. Folger steps
unsteadily, Krenwinkel's outstretched buck knife at her back.

Atkins, clad in creepy-crawl black, stands tense behind Sebring.

Frozen, the ladder to the loft. Frozen, the American flag
(the reddest thing in the room) draped over
the couch. Frozen, the sheet music
beneath the upraised piano lid. Frozen, Sebring's foot
on the edge of the zebra rug. Frozen, in the windows,
the midnight glitter of Hollywood's ignorant lights.

The painting unpauses: the chaos and panic, the shooting
and stabbing, the bleeding and screaming and pleading, begin.

NOIR & BLANC

Not scary at all, and hardly

Glimpsed, the blood and the body
In the trunk of the convertible

My fear, that drained it of color
These many years, bootlegged

A bad print in public domain

POEM WRITTEN WITH MY NEMESIS LOOKING OVER MY SHOULDER

You who would judge everything I
say, and how I say it, this is what
I see right now: Earl Grey tea (too hot
to sip) in pink Fiestaware cup to my left;
pile of unfolded laundry (mostly towels
and socks) to my right; arctic Chicago light
casting, through glass bricks, prismatic
shadows—like water inside a swimming
pool—on the wall of my coach house.
You would love to harness that
light for your black magic, filter it
through your pitiless gaze, as through a
magnifying glass, and set fire to this page.
The little plastic magnifying glass I once got
as a Cracker Jack prize! You hate the details
of my life, present and past. The Silly Putty I used
to lift color off of comic strips. The fly I trapped
forever, at summer camp, in clear resin, in
an ice cube tray. The books I read by flashlight, hid
under my mattress. (What I loved most
I had to hide.) You cast your life in a harsh
spotlight, on a bare stage. There's no
redemption there, and nothing is right-sized.
Your mother looms, a giant ghost, a great

inflictor of pain; you cower before her, so small
and yet willing, in her absence, to take on
both roles: victim and tormenter fixed in
their addiction, as in a translucent cube.
The light has moved up the wall, reached
the ceiling. For a moment I'm submerged
in one of the blue swimming pools of my youth.
Then: the red jam on this muffin, the brown
sugar and cinnamon sprinkled on this oatmeal.

ODE TO DICK FISK

Dick Fisk,
one of the first
gay porn stars,
handsome,
short,
muscular,
hung like a horse,
did you ever dream
that someday
you'd be the subject
of a poem,
let alone an ode?
Did I ever dream,
jacking off to
pictures of you
in the 1970s,
snorting Rush
as close
as possible
to orgasm,
the bed in my room
in my parents' house
creaking late
at night,
that I'd be the one
to write it?
Yet here we are,
thirty years later,

sharing the most
intimate of moments
as I enclose
your name
in quotations
and click
"I'm Feeling Lucky"
on google.com.
And what do I get?
Ten color photos
on Al's Gay Porn Stars:
you, nude,
with your straight
brown hair
and mustache,
your washboard stomach,
and your astounding
endowment,
posing in bed
and in a white armchair
with a defiant,
come-hither look,
and lost in action
with a mustached blond
in a red-and-black
plaid shirt,
your mouth
stretched wide
to accommodate
his cock.
And a brief

but informative
bio: "Dick Fisk was a
little guy from Georgia
with a big dick,
and he knew how
to use it too."
Your real name
was Frank Rick Fitts
and you were born
on May 13, 1955.
I again search
the Internet
and sure enough:
the thirteenth fell on
a Friday that month.
Friday the 13th! Dick!
On howstuffworks.com,
Jill M. Phillips tells us
Taurus men possess
a great deal of what
used to be called
"animal magnetism."
Those born May 13th
are rare individuals
with unique and
special talents.
There is a dark side
to these people, yet
they are rarely moved to
reveal this aspect
of themselves.

You were a math
major in college,
Dick, before dropping
out and breaking
into the adult
male film industry.
Your acting credits
include such Falcon
and Bijou Studio classics
as *Axe Master,*
Champs 2, Cruisin'
the Castro, Help Wanted,
Spokes, The Other
Side of Aspen, and
Try to Take It.
At the time of
your death, you
were between films
working at a bar in
Midtown Atlanta.
You and your lover
were killed in an
automobile accident
between Atlanta
and Marietta
on the evening of
Halloween 1983.
I've only been
to Atlanta once,
for a writers
conference

in 2007.
My dog Byron
had just died
and I spent
a lot of time in my
hotel room, crying.
It's not much
of a coincidence,
Dick, but during
that trip I
visited my sister
and her family
in Marietta,
where you
presumably lived.
We ate a pleasant
meal and played
a game of Hearts.
You perished
at twenty-eight.
That October 31st,
I was in a single apart-
ment in Hollywood,
thirty, and sober
exactly one week.
I didn't know it,
but my real life
had just begun.
Gone, all the drugs
and alcohol and
torment of my twenties,

exacerbated by
a 1979 car accident
in which my best
friend Rachel
was killed, and which
I barely survived.
A psychic recently
told me that when
I was in ICU,
I was connected
by a very thin
cord, but I
chose to come
back (I didn't
have to), and
the dream I had
just before I woke,
of a scarecrow
falling down a mountain,
bouncing from rock
to rock, was my soul
returning to my body.
Gone also, the blasé
anthem of those years,
Blondie's reggae-infused
"Die Young Stay Pretty."
Oh Dick, it's true,
for Rachel, for you.
Forever you'll get
to keep your
good looks,

ample evidence
of which
is easily
obtained online.
I drag your image—
cute as Jackson Browne,
only mustached—
onto my desktop.
Unabashedly,
I walk into the
back room
at Specialty Video
and select my
favorite of all
your films,
Steam Heat.
I bring it
home and
slip it into
my Mac.
No dialogue,
just that
monotonous
'70s porn
soundtrack
(depriving
us of what was
surely a sexy
Southern accent).
Running track,
you twist

your ankle.
The hunky coach
leads you into
the locker room
and begins rubbing
your foot. His
hand wanders up
your leg and thigh
and into your
jock strap.
He rims and
fucks you,
cums all over
your lightly haired chest.
And you, versatile
actor that you were,
return—lithely
at first, then like
a jackhammer—
the satisfying favor.

SYLVIA'S HAIR

1

"OUR BONES, OUR HAIR"

June, 2009. I'm at the Lilly Library in Bloomington, Indiana, doing re-
search on Sylvia Plath. Every time I enter and leave the reading room,
I pass one of the library's many display cases. Often, I stop to look. I
am fascinated by the items in this particular exhibit. In the center,
against a background of deep green felt: a lock of Sylvia's reddish-
brown hair. This must be the tress that was snipped in the fall of 1949,
when Plath was a teenager. A whole ponytail, really, tied near the top
with a white string. I study it through the glass. In the same display
are two objects that I find equally fascinating: John Ford's Oscar for di-
recting *How Green Was My Valley* and Rita Hayworth's makeup case
(brown with gold engraved nameplate), in which she kept Orson
Welles' love letters. Some of the letters are spread out among Hay-
worth's monogrammed jars of powder and cosmetic cream, a Midol
tin, a comb, hairpins. Ford's Oscar is tarnished, the contents of Rita's
case battered with age. Both pale beside Sylvia's still lustrous and
healthy hair.

2

"A PIECE OF MY HAIR OR MY CLOTHES"

Looking through Sylvia's Baby Book (ca. 1932–1933), I am astonished
when I come across a mass of fine, golden-brown hair. Aurelia Plath
dutifully cut a lock from her infant daughter's head and taped it in the

book. Over the years the tape dried out and the hair became free; most of it has ended up in the crease between the pages. I consider taking some. It would be so easy to slide, with my pencil eraser, a strand or two into my notebook. But the clerks watch you like hawks; there might be cameras. And if everyone helped themselves, I ponder, eventually there'd be no baby hair left. Plus I'm not sure I'm prepared to pay the price, as Sylvia herself says, the *very large charge* for possessing even this tiny piece.

3

"I RISE WITH MY RED HAIR"

Idea for screenplay. Sci-Fi/Horror. Along the lines of *The Boys from Brazil* (insane plot to resurrect Adolf Hitler). Scientists clone a bevy of Sylvias from a strand of her hair at the Lilly Library. But the experiment is doomed. Though they are raised in different parts of the country, under varying circumstances, each Sylvia, shortly after she reaches the age of thirty, commits suicide. Title of movie: *Lady Lazarus*.

From online discussion about Britney Spears' hair:

You can't clone from hair because there is no DNA in hair
You need the roots.

Don't you watch CSI?

HEAVENLY THINGS

(AFTER SEI SHŌNAGON)

A cab speeds up deserted Fifth Avenue at dawn, deposits Audrey Hepburn in front of Tiffany & Co., where—to the wistful strains of Henry Mancini's "Moon River"—she sips coffee and munches a croissant as she gazes into the store, comforted by "the quietness and the proud look of it."

Endora pops into Samantha's kitchen in her diaphanous purple and green witch outfit (with "vampire" collar).

Cathy's pageboy and Patty's flip.

"After dinner, Natalie Wood checked her makeup in the mirror-bright blade of a butter knife."

The voice of Dusty Springfield.

The wig scene in *Valley of the Dolls*.

Katherine Ross in *The Graduate*.

Blue and green eye shadow. White lipstick.

Empire dresses. Textured stockings. Low-heeled patent leather sling-backs with bows or buckles on the vamp. "And the new square toe was everywhere."

Pinkest of albums: *The Supremes A' Go-Go*. Diana, Mary, and Flo in Mod getups and poses—snapping their fingers, swinging their hair.

Herb Alpert's *Whipped Cream & Other Delights*. Not only did it include two themes from *The Dating Game* ("Whipped Cream," which was used when the bachelorette was introduced, and "Lollipops and Roses," which played when she learned about the bachelor she'd picked), but on the green record jacket was a woman covered with whipped cream. Naked except for a pink rose in her hand and all that white cream. A woman covered with whipped cream!

JACQUELINE SUSANN AND HER HUSBAND IRVING MANSFIELD, LOS ANGELES, CAL., 1969

"It was seen all over the world," Mansfield claimed. "We thought it was
 undignified."
Diane Arbus had been commissioned by *Harper's* to photograph the
 author.
Susann was promoting her novel *The Love Machine*, which was high on
 the best-seller list.
Between interviews (six a day) she was ensconced in a Beverly Hills
 hotel suite.

Arbus had been commissioned by *Harper's* to photograph the author.
She flew to California from Chicago, where she'd photographed and
 interviewed Tokyo Rose for *Esquire*.
Between interviews (six a day) Susann was ensconced in a Beverly Hills
 hotel suite
overlooking banks of geraniums and a smoggy sky.

Arbus flew to California from Chicago, where she'd photographed and
 interviewed Tokyo Rose for *Esquire*.
When she arrived, Susann began patting her jet-black hair fall and
 adjusting her bubble glasses,
overlooking banks of geraniums and a smoggy sky.
Diane asked her to take them off.

When Arbus arrived, Susann began patting her jet-black hair fall and
    adjusting her bubble glasses
and straightening her geometric turquoise, purple, and black Pucci
    blouse and slacks.
Diane asked her to take them off.
"This Diane Arbus character was bossy," Mansfield remembered.

Jackie's geometric turquoise, purple, and black Pucci blouse and slacks
were out. She wanted them to pose in their bathing suits next to the
    TV set.
"This Diane Arbus character was bossy," Mansfield remembered.
"I didn't get it, so I said no to the idea, but Jackie, who was always
    cooperative with the press, said of course."

Arbus wanted them to pose in their bathing suits next to the TV set.
When they were in their suits, the photographer asked Jackie to plunk
    down in Irving's lap.
Jackie, who was always cooperative with the press, said of course.
"We held the pose for what seemed like hours—until my kneecaps
    went numb."

When they were in their suits, the photographer asked Jackie to plunk
    down in Irving's lap.
"The flashbulbs kept blinding us, she kept assuring us we looked
    terrific.
We held the pose for what seemed like hours—until my kneecaps
    went numb."
The result was a classic portrait of tacky tastelessness.

The flashbulbs kept blinding them, she kept assuring them they
    looked terrific.

Irving wore an ankh on his bare chest; Jackie, wearing a matching
    ankh, stared intently at the camera.
The result was a classic portrait of tacky tastelessness:
a couple *in extremis*, middle-aged, paunchy, oily in bathing suits,
    presented in sweetly prosaic terms.

Irving wore an ankh on his bare chest; Jackie, wearing a matching
    ankh, stared intently at the camera.
She later blamed Irving. He should have known Arbus had a
    reputation for photographing freaks:
couples *in extremis*, middle-aged, paunchy, oily in bathing suits,
    presented in sweetly prosaic terms.
It was the legs that upset Jackie most: she thought Arbus had made
    her thighs look too scrawny.

Jackie later blamed Irving. He should have known Arbus had a
    reputation for photographing freaks.
Arbus did not accept all her subjects with grace; if she couldn't
    respond, her reaction was often severe.
It was the legs that upset Jackie most: she thought Arbus had made
    her thighs look too scrawny.
The picture appeared in the October 1969 issue of *Harper's* and
    Arbus sold it to other publications.

Arbus did not accept all her subjects with grace; if she couldn't
    respond, her reaction was often severe.
Susann was promoting her novel *The Love Machine*, which was high
    on the best-seller list.
The picture appeared in the October 1969 issue of *Harper's* and
    Arbus sold it to other publications.
"It was seen all over the world," Mansfield claimed. "We thought it
    was undignified."

TED HUGHES
SEES A GHOST

The narcissi that populate
The orchard every spring

Are innocuous fairy lights

Outnumbered
Overnight

By daffodils
A mob of frilled yellow mouthpieces

Multiplying like the libbers
Who hold up placards

That say "Murderer"
Or chant "You do not do, you do not do"

Whenever he tries
To make his voice heard

The moon does what she
Has always done

Shines her alien beams
Between apple trees

Spotlights the painted hive

Tonight the man in black breaks
His code of silence

And cries

HER LAST PICTURE

The Swedish Sphinx
in a screwball comedy?

Tongue in her teeth
jewels in her hair

arms raised above her head
("her obvious posturings")

in the center of
the nightclub

her undulations transfix
the well-dressed extras

glint in the eye of her
mustached leading man

bubble in the delicate glasses
downed at the edge of
the dance floor

The critics were merciless

"It is almost as shocking as
seeing your mother drunk."

Time called her "a clown, a buffoon,
a monkey on a stick."

Never again would she
submit herself
to such scrutiny

effectively rejecting them

A star's prerogative:
to silver offscreen

"You made me lose
my poise,"

the best line (not hers)
in the film,

"For that I shall never
forgive you."

THE PAST

(AFTER NERUDA)

Today, on the phone
with my friend Rebecca,
I talked about the past.
My "wild" youth
(the gay '70s: so easy
to get a blowjob,
but little else),
the decade-long mismatch
with Ira in New York,
the last seven years
here in the Midwest.
Dust begins to collect
as soon as you wipe the cloth
across the tabletop;
the glue dries, the spine
cracks, the faded pages
slip out . . . the book is tossed.
I'm surprised how alive
my memories are in me:
from odd, transient details
(the fake sunny-side up egg
placed as practical joke on
a "sizzling" summer sidewalk;
how I'd savor Neccos—
those candy wafers
that came in a roll,

like quarters—
as if receiving Communion,
letting each color
slowly dissolve on
my penitent tongue)
to deeply ingrained
disappointments
(friends turned adversaries
by their inability to change,
lovers by their refusal to open up).
"He's emotionally dead," you say.
"She's hopeless and malignant."
How they resent your light!
Yet try to keep their
hooks in you.
Why do low moments
have more staying power
than happy ones,
some downright refusing,
though the theater is dark,
to vacate the stage?
Again and again,
the day of the breakup
comes to mind,
how we sat and faced
each other on the red couch,
how he lied to me
and to himself, cried
and touched my arm
as he left—as if petting
something precious

for the last time.
Why cling to the sadness
of that single moment
rather than the months of
anticipation and
excitement, of making love
while the mood lamp
on the dresser morphed
from red to violet to blue?
I used to think that time
was linear, a road
that stretched and
disappeared into the
future, and that if I
walked that road
I'd get farther and farther away
from everything that had
ever caused me pain.
The name-calling and bullying on
playgrounds (the chain-link prisons
of suburbia), the awareness
of queerness and the retreat
inward (a different
kind of prison),
the constant terror
of being exposed
(as I was one morning
in junior high, by
two girls who snickered
as I delivered a book report
in front of my English class).

And I thought that if
I got far enough away
from the popularity contest
I refused to play
and yet nonetheless made
me feel nonexistent,
and became someone important,
became a published poet,
I'd put every mindless jock
and stuck-up cheerleader
to shame.
(Of course you never
get to show *them*.
The poems are for you
and others like you,
and for others, if
you're lucky, to argue with
and dismiss.)
Then in the mid-'90s,
when my mother died,
the road lifted up,
like a ribbon or strip
of Scotch tape,
and bent back on
itself, future flat
on top of past.
Never again would death
be out of focus.
There would be no peace
until I accepted
each wound, each loss

as necessary for my growth,
and ultimately right
and good.
And learned that what
I call my life
is the result
of a series of choices:
something *I* create.
Half my life
I was trapped
in unknowing,
a slave to the patterns
of the past.
Today I'm the one who
gets to choose
how I spend my time
and with whom I spend it.
I'm not a prisoner here.
Inside: the ticking of
the battery-operated
starburst clock—
red, yellow, and blue—
the first piece of art,
by Jim Isermann,
I purchased over
twenty-five years ago.
It has kept perfect time
through so many changes.
Outside: clear
September light.
To be fully engaged

in the present moment,
eyes wide open,
free of guilt trips and manipulation,
free of narcissistic friends,
free of familial obligation.
That is happiness.

DEAR
PRUDENCE

SELECTED POEMS

I am always drawn back to places where I have lived . . .

TRUMAN CAPOTE

IN A SUBURB
OF THEBES

My father didn't see me
as I sat on the hood of his car
in the dark driveway that night.
How could I know
when he caught my shadow
in the corner of his eye
that I'd become burglar
then bad beat
and that he would fall flat?
Believe me, I did not mean to scare.
I was only getting some air,
only drinking my coffee
to get through Balzac.
How could I know
he'd have a heart attack?

I was always the odd one.
I was always up in my bedroom
reading books and books
while my brothers played baseball
in the street.
I was the yellow crop
that tainted his green thumb
like a nicotine stain.
If only he had accepted me
as a smoker does his cough.

But I was the queer seed
that sprouted full blossom
out of all his straight sperm.
I was the germ,
the rotted pith,
I crept towards his core
like a rebellious worm in the orchard
of apples he grew.
He retired too soon.
I did it,
I bit short his plans
like a late frost.

I admit I killed him—
this one disease in a healthy life,
this sun that came out bright and different
above suburban clouds,
that invaded his house,
cleared his table,
became one with his wife,
this heart with this red that's blue—
murdered
with one soft stroke
by the blood clot hand
of the only son he never knew.

1975

DELPHI

My parents first heard it
    from the school psychologist.
It stood out in my artwork
    like a cardboard kitchenette, a jump rope,
a doll. It seeped from my mouth

in stammered speech.
    It had to be stopped, so they sent me
to summer camps, to Little League, to Cub Scout
    meetings. But still it plagued me
like a tetanus shot. I cried helpless and they

gave me candy to get me through. Afterwards,
    the stain remained on my tongue, my teeth,
my lips—red like blood. It was not the sort of thing
    they could nip in the bud.
The neighborhood first heard it

from the radio, the television, the news.
    They read it on labels.
It disrupted each marriage like a woman's curse
    and clung to the landscape,
a pestilent cloud threatening

to infect every lung.
    I never chose my own clothes.
There was absolutely nothing I could do.
    Like this birthmark on my ankle,
it has always been there.

I first heard it from the playground.
    It flew fast as a football in the air and followed me
across the asphalt like a dirty word.
    In cul-de-sacs, the nosy bitch parted drapes
to taunt me with prophetic glares:

We shall stare at you, we shall always stare.
    It burned in my ear like gossip or parents quarrelling.
Later, I heard it whispered
    during lunch hours and in locker rooms.
I ran home from school every day, but it kept at me,

clawed at my window-screen like a hungry cat.
    I did not know they'd throw me out
like scandal sheets
    and cast me in bad shows.
I was blacklisted by the stars.

And they've been spreading the rumor ever since.

1 9 7 5

IN PRAISE OF HIM

Let the memory of him never fade

For I praise him even now

I praise him in his guest house which could not be seen from
    the street
I praise him in his van which I kicked and carved a dent in,
    like an angry valentine, after a party when I was jealous
For I did not praise his ex-lovers who crept like passing car
    shadows across the bedroom wall and who gleamed
    unexpectedly like caution signs
For I do not praise my jealousy, that tumor eclipsing my brain
I do not praise my jealousy spoiling whole days like my mother's
    migraines

Let his memory never fade like the three photographs I insisted
    he send so I could continue praising him

For I praise him saying "I love you" even though he said it less
    than I said it to him

I praise his awkward piano hands which manipulated all of my keys
I praise him in the bedroom of his guest house where, on the first
    day, he kissed the back of my neck
For I praise him in his double-knit pants which turned me on and
    I praise his eyes which burst like sparklers whenever he
    smiled and his arms which opened warm like an oven door and his
    mustache which numbed my lips like Novocaine

For I praise him in the back of his van on the way to the airport
    and in a Palm Springs motel and under the piano
    and on the kitchen floor and only once in the shower
    and on one twin bed to *Rhapsody in Blue*

For I praised his memory which hung over me, heavily, like years
    of smog

But let this memory of him be hidden beneath old turtlenecks

For I praised him too much, too long
I praised him and his guest house on the porch of which I
    waited like a package towards the end
For I finally praised his ex-lovers who worked like road
    construction to tear us apart
For I praised him as he turned away like a visitor afraid
    to see my scars
For I praised him who, as I slept in his memory like a solar
    eclipse, found a lover who looks like me

1975

THE PEASANT GIRL

Sometimes it is to one's advantage to do good deeds.
I know this from personal experience. You see,
one afternoon my abrasive stepmother sent me
to the spring well over a mile from our cottage
to fetch water for her daily bath. As usual, I
passed through the village in my tattered dress, daydreaming,
swinging the empty pail, alternating it from hand
to hand. At the spring, I sat on a fresh patch of grass
and rested, leaning over and gazing at my face
on the smooth surface of the water. Coal smeared my cheeks.
Suddenly, a warped form disrupted my reflection
like a thrown pebble or stone. It was a decrepit
woman who had appeared out of nowhere, a real witch
Her long nose protruded from beneath her loose black hood
like a half-nibbled cob of corn, her hands were withered
and spotted like old cabbage leaves, and her voice cracked like
the shells of walnuts when she uttered: "Would you be kind
enough to give a tired workingwoman a cool drink?"
What the heck, I thought, I've nothing better to do.
So I dipped the ladle into the spring and held it up
to her parched lips. But she was no longer
an old woman; that was only a disguise. She was
actually a good fairy: wand, glitter, gauzy wings
and all. And she spoke in a sweet unruffled voice:
"I shall reward you for your deed. Whenever you speak,
beautiful flowers and priceless gems shall flow
into the world with your words." I ran home in a stupor
of excitement, my unwashed hair flying behind me

like steam from a locomotive, and told my stepmother
about the fairy and how I had passed her silly
test, and as I spoke, a dozen rubies splattered
on the wooden floor like drops of blood. "Keep talking,"
said my stepmother. I did, and orchids tumbled from my mouth,
and gold coins, and pearl rings, and then white chrysanthemums,
irises, violets, sapphires, jonquils, carnations,
strings of sweet peas streaming as long as my sentences,
crystal goblets, asters, opals, pieces of topaz,
jade pears. Daisies popped into the air like periods,
and turquoise and gladiolas fell until a large pile
shone in front of us so brightly, it seemed
the sun had set in the middle of our living room.
Gaping, my stepmother bent down to stuff all
of the valuables into her apron pockets. When
she looked up, a sudden admiration, like emeralds,
glistened in her eyes. Now a local girl fetches our water
from the distant spring. I'm served breakfast in bed.
I dress in the latest Paris originals and
visit the hairdresser. And whether I speak kindness,
insult, or untruth, the roses roll off my tongue
and diamonds sparkle as they drip from my gifted lips.

1977

WARM WINTER

Every night of vacation
we knelt by the split eucalyptus
on the unlighted edge of the orchard—
dry Christmas, no rain
or cold wind, and fourteen days
without a word
for what we were doing
on that shabby beach blanket:
explorers on a foxtailed raft.

Our clothes landed
here and there like leaves.
Our mouths tasted salty sweat,
our hands slid down the excited surface
of each other's skin; then falling
back, ignorant
as criminals at our clumsy act,
pressing senselessly,
and the white sap spurting,
oozing over us
like crushed ice plant.

Now, years later,
in another city,
in a small room,
I am listening to whispers
sketched in pencil
on the walls. A candle

shakes its light
on a knobless bureau.
A nameless shape pushes
between my knees.

But when I glue shut
my eyes, it is warm
winter again:
that hidden corner
of the lot, that black
mannish smell of eucalyptus,
and the crescent moon
shaped leaves cracking
underneath the thin blanket.

I reach down—
familiar brown hair
brushing my thighs, my stomach.
In this dark, this heat,
these strange lips
I let use me
are yours.

1977

IRIS

Behind wet brick,
the leaves of the rose bushes shine
like shoes just polished.
Tinted petals absorb strength again.
And you, after the downpour,
like a full orange
on a high branch, bright,
tempting.

But I know you, and what you do:
children that wander
under your arch of color
never come back;
or they return, altered,
unaware of the appearance
of the sun and moon
and the slight changes
that occur
in rows
in the vegetable gardens.

Please, keep back that slow death,
that chiseling away
at the senses;
the indifferent choice of the maid
handling strawberries, peaches;
the indiscriminate reach
of fat men at the inn.

Let me be evasive.
A touch remembered.
The odor of damp alfalfa.
A leaf let go, spinning in the wind.
Like the mist that rises
off the thatched roofs
in villages after rain,
let me flourish for an instant only,
splitting and sifting
without noticeable division.

Extraordinary, like you.

Allowed to simply disappear.

1977

THE BOY

Looking back,
I think that he must have been an angel.
We never spoke,
but one entire summer, every day,
he sat on the curb across the street.
I watched him: thin, his skin white,
his blond hair cut short.
Sometimes, right after swimming,
his bathing suit wet and tight,
he would sit and dry off in the sun.
I couldn't stop staring.

Then late one night,
toward the end of the summer,
he appeared in my room.
Perhaps that's why
I've always considered him
an angel: silent, innocent, pale
even in the dark.
He undressed
and pulled back the sheet,
slid next to me.
His fingers felt for my lips.

But perhaps I am not remembering
correctly.
Perhaps he never came
into my room that night.

Perhaps he never existed
and I invented him.
Or perhaps it was me, not blond
but dark, who sat all summer
on that sunny corner: seventeen
and struggling to outlast
my own restlessness.

1978

NIGHT AND FOG

Once, depressed and drunk on the worst wine, Christopher N. and I sat out on the fire escape. That was before he got weird, before I moved back to L.A.: we shared a second-floor single apartment in the Tenderloin. Christopher N. (an alias): seventeen, innocent-looking, runaway from the complacent suburbs across the bay, smiling defiler of the scriptures of his strict father, a Baptist minister. That night on the fire escape: genesis of intense gestalt friendship. Ritual of confession. We hugged each other and cried. That night I told him someday I'd write about us sitting on the fire escape. Somewhere a phone was ringing. He finished the last glass of Ripple (Pagan Pink) and pitched it at the brick wall of the opposite building. It shattered and we laughed.

Later, back inside: steam heat, *Discreet Music*, stamping on cockroaches on red carpet cigarette scars. The walls cracked like in *Repulsion*. Lavender and green lanterned light bulb of Blanche DuBois. Initiation rite: I gave him my junior high school St. Christopher (with a surfer on the other side).

Things he did I thought delightful: took taxis, wore suspenders, spit on silver cars, drew dark circles around his eyes with shoe polish for poetic effect, cut pictures out of library books and taped them to the apartment walls, insisted upon passion, allowed himself spontaneous spasms of unlimited excess, praised Tim Curry, praised Bryan Ferry, praised the gospel according to Pasolini, named his cat Icarus, created his own art form (shock), hocked records he tired of listening to to buy used books which he read and then hocked to buy our booze, spray-painted *D* in front of *ADA ST*, cried when I told him he was my Holly Golightly, cursed money for its ability to corrupt purity.

But then he got weird. St. Christopher of the Club Baths. St. Christopher of the trench coat and collect calls. His Philip Marlowe hat. St. Christopher of the transfer ticket. Turned eighteen. Moved into a condemned flat below Market. Folsom: factories murmuring all night, leather bars. St. Christopher of the post-fascist lost degeneration. Devout disciple of Peter Berlin. St. Christopher of the punk rock safety pin. Pierced his nipples. Placed explicit *Advocate* ad. St. Christopher of the forbidden fetish. The decidedly strange attraction to rubber. St. Christopher of the cock ring and handcuffs. Spiked dildo. Branded asses. Undressing in the balcony of the Strand during *Maitresse*. Blond boy snorting Rush stroking himself underneath smooth leather sucked off behind bushes in Lafayette Park after dark. St. Christopher with super-clap. St. Christopher of the 120 days of the Baptist apocalypse. Sexual dementor. Collector of dentures and dead rats, bloodletters. St. Christopher of the Castro hard hat and jockstrap. St. Christopher kicking pigeons and poodles in Union Square. St. Christopher picked up on Polk and Pine: twenty-five dollars for shitting on his trick.

My last visit to San Francisco: saw vomit on the sidewalks, saw piss streaming down steep streets. Bandaged panhandler. Black kid lifting the crutches of a fallen drunkard. Transvestite prostitute throwing beer bottles at a passing bus. Old women with shopping bag suitcases picking in trash bins as if testing produce. At the airport terminal, before he turned to go, Christopher N. said: "You're so prissy I can't see how we could ever have been friends." I flew home. *Angels of the complacent suburbs! of discotheques! of hostile police!* Got drunk.

Jeannette MacDonald, there's a dark alley for every perversion in your sickening city (water sports, B & D, fist fucking). No one is ever innocent.

1978

[1 4 0]

FALSE APOCALYPSE

FOR RACHEL SHERWOOD

The afternoon you bought that Gypsy deck
black clouds followed us
back to your apartment.
We thought we were prepared, we had waited.
As the somber cloth stretched
over us, obliterating the entire sky
like India ink, we laughed
as if we were mad

and remembered the omens—
the warped record, the drunken cut,
a drawer of dull knives,
sheets full of fleas,
my beer glass shattered and your keys
lost, the sick phone calls,
that X scratched in the window's dust.
No one else seemed to notice;

they tailgated or passed,
strapped tight to the weeknight routine,
rushing from work to catch
acceptable disasters on television sets.
This was it, so you were
extravagant at the liquor store—
select champagne and black caviar
for egg bread spread with butter!

Three days later your check would bounce.
But money had never mattered.
You smiled and shook your dark hair,
threw the sack in the back seat.
High Priestess, sexy
in a see-through pink slip
and black pumps, you read violent
death on my palm, a broken heart-line.

You saw death also
in the strange arrangement
of my stars, a death
unquestionable as your tattered cards.
Candles were lit for this
midnight ritual. Our finger-tips slid
back and forth across the Ouija board,
spelling the month of my death.

"Are you moving it?" I kept asking.
So we set aside the occult.
Then I admired those ankles as you leapt
to let the cat in—
a genuine omen when he walked straight
to your Keltic layout,
set his adorable head
on the Death card, and slept.

"Death!" we shouted.
"I love death!" "I hate death!"
Your lips touched my unexpected tears.
The soft footsteps

of the rapist stopped
halfway up the stairs.
The wine dried in silence like a bloodstain,
a bruise on the abused carpet.

The sky cleared.
The weird laughter left us
alone, with only a glimpse
of what we thought we had witnessed,
with just a taste
bad as tabasco, hung over
the next morning, of how we had
ranted, and raged at the world.

1 9 7 8

PAVANE

The two silhouettes separate
from the shadows, emerge
as distinct figures
poised some distance apart.
They face one another
at the edge of the lake.
A star briefly skims across it,
unsettling the surface
like a small white stone.
Gently, the breeze bends
the grass into the blue water.
One by one, clouds appear
and demand attention,
a procession of familiar gestures—
memories mounting.
There will be grief
There will be a great loss
the woods whisper.
And because it is cold,
because it is dark,
the figures take the necessary steps.
They cling
to each other
and silently,
in defiance,
dance.

1980

ORDINARY THINGS

On the patio, next
to a large, rather
awkwardly transplanted
bromeliad, sits
the blackened hibachi
that hasn't been used
since last summer
when a number
of us, who knew you
intimately, got to-
gether to commemorate
the first anniversary
of your death,

It wasn't much
of an afternoon.
For the most part
I was quiet, kept
myself preoccupied
while everyone ate
and talked about
ordinary (it seemed
to me) things.
Your name came up
once or twice—
I can't remember
in what context.
No one cried.

After we hugged
and kissed each other
good-bye, I rinsed
the glasses and plates
and placed them
in the dishwasher. I
sat down and listened
to music (your
records—they were
all scratched).
I chain-smoked and
drank until I was
numb enough to fall
asleep without
reexperiencing
that impact—
one set of headlights
abruptly intercepted
by another, the unut-
terable welding of
metal to flesh—
instant blackness.

This year it
is different.
Everyone is off
doing the things
students usually
do after graduating
from college:
marrying, starting

families, making
lots of money at
jobs you would
have thought out
of character for
your friends—
such a *gifted* group.

I light a cigarette,
sip at this scotch.
In it, there is one
small ice cube left.
It is still warm out-
side, although it
is getting late.
It is very quiet and
the light is faint.

1 9 8 1

GREAT-GRANDMOTHER SMITH

In the two photographs I have of her,
taken over ten years apart, she wears
the same plain dress. In the first,
she sits in the sun (under a parasol)
next to her daughter, Marguerite, my
mother's mother, whose smile is warm,
while Great-grandmother's is stiff
beneath spectacles. Her white hair
is pinned tight. Her figure is slight,
almost skeletal. In the second picture,
she stands alone on the front steps
of the house on W. Montecito Street
in Sierra Madre, where we visited her
when I was a child. I remember little
but details of those infrequent trips:
the dense oleanders that fenced her
yard from the neighbors', a wobbly
stepladder my brother and I reached
for ripe apricots and plums from,
the knee-high weeds we romped through
out back. The small garage was off
limits; in it, black widows guarded
the steamer trunks stuffed with her
memories—porcelain dolls with vacant
faces, petite high-button shoes, and
the padded velvet family album filled

with photographs of her own great-
grandparents, who migrated from France
to Canada in the mid 1800's, and of
her parents before and after they met
in Cambridge Square, married, and
moved to Bristol, Connecticut, where
she was born (the first of twelve
children), brought up, and, at the
age of fifteen, handed to a local
watchmaker turned homesteader, who
with his "drunkard of a brother"
raised gamecocks on Chippens Hill,
a farm notoriously popular in the
area for the cockfights often staged
there. Great-grandmother gave birth
to two sons, grew and sold vegetables
door-to-door in town, transplanted
roots to the dirt floor of the cellar
each fall. But the goings-on in the
barn unsettled her and she objected
until, eight months pregnant with
Marguerite, she warned the two men
that, should the drinking, gambling
and fighting not stop, she would one
by one wring their prize roosters'
necks. The ruckus continued and she
did just that. The following day, her
brother-in-law left for more amiable
parts and her husband returned to his
former trade. Years later, after he
came to California and couldn't find

work, he took up gardening. The family
lived in Sierra Madre, on the opulent
estate of Arthur Gerlach, who once
photographed Einstein and the Ford
brothers, and invested wisely in
Detroit Edison's prosperous stock.
By then, Marguerite had blossomed
into a young beauty, was crowned
"Queen of the Wisteria Vines" in
an annual spring festival, fell
in love with Harlan, Mr. Gerlach's
youngest son, to whom she was wed
in an elaborate ceremony that made
the front page of the city's daily
paper. Their marriage, although it
introduced the Smiths to money and
enabled Great-grandfather to retire
in comfort, ended when my mother
was three—Marguerite left Harlan
as soon as she learned he had lost
everything they owned in a Friday
night poker game. Not long after
the divorce, Harlan died of a burst
appendix and Great-grandfather passed
away in his sleep. He was seventy.
Marguerite got her driver's license,
worked for the telephone company
while Great-grandmother watched after
my mother, waking her early every
Saturday so they could take the Red
Car to Los Angeles, where she'd

rummage through the Goodwill ware-
house and thrift shops on Skid Row
for wool skirts and coats, which
she would lug back in brown paper
bags, split at the seams with razor
blades, picking off the threads,
then soak and wash, steam press,
cut into inch-wide strips that she
folded, stitched together, wound
into balls like yarn, and used to
braid huge oval rugs. That was
before the Second World War, about
the time Marguerite felt the first
symptoms of a disease later diagnosed
as leukemia. The long, drawn out illness
tainted my mother's adolescence, as
did the news that George, her cousin
and childhood companion, was killed
when a Japanese suicide pilot crashed
into his LST landing craft as it
hauled gasoline off Guadalcanal. He
was seventeen. Marguerite was in her
early thirties when she whispered
"George is calling me" moments before
she died. My mother sat at her side,
dampening her skin. She was fourteen.
Great-grandmother lived to be ninety-
three, although we saw less of her
after she had to be moved to a con-
valescent facility where, heavily
sedated, she simply sat and stared

out the window at passing traffic.
I remember being frightened by the
lady in the next bed because she
mumbled strange things. I was not
quite five, but I can still recall
the living room of her house, how
in its spaciousness I kept myself
silent on isolated Sunday afternoons
by counting her spools of colored
thread and lifting the lid of the
piano bench to examine stacks of
faded sheet music. I remember there
were photographs of people I didn't
know above the fireplace and that
I stared up at them as I stared
up at Great-grandmother as she sat
for hours working wool into rugs, her
severe expression matched only by
the intensity with which her fingers
steadfastly braided the fabric.

1982

TIM'S STOLEN SWEATER

Sunlight which seeps through a part
in the drapes illuminates the rumpled
contents of your suitcase: sweaters
and slacks, and some of those short-
sleeved alligator shirts, the kind
that "clones" wear, though they'd make
you look good—healthy and athletic—
unlike most of the men at the crowded
bar where we met. Before we spoke,
I wanted to reach across and touch
your cheekbone, the scar just under
the left one (I couldn't bring myself
to ask how you'd gotten it, so I
imagined a gang fight in your youth
or a steak knife in the hand of
a lover insane with jealousy). You
introduced yourself. I extended my
hand. Then, in your room, our chit-
chat continued until, abruptly, you
asked, "Do you want to kiss me?" It
was a perfect way to get to the point
and I was impressed. "Yes." Our move-
ments cast shadows of flesh barely
lit by the glow of the motel's neon
sign as it flashed on and off. Just
a few hours sleep. Now, slightly hung
over, I erase one or two of the creases
our bodies made in sheets a maid will

change later in the day, after we've
showered and dressed, gone our sep-
arate ways. You're going out for a
newspaper and a six-pack. I watch you
rummage through your suitcase, pull
on a pair of boxer shorts, jeans, and
the sweater you wore last night—
light blue with thin white stripes
around the chest—which is what I
noticed first, from across the bar,
and then, as I moved closer, how
handsome you were, despite your scar.

1982

"C'EST PLUS QU'UN CRIME, C'EST UNE FAUTE"

FOR AMY GERSTLER

In the small hours, several rounds
at Le Café, "one of the swankier
spots West L.A.'s nightlife offers":
pink neon and napkins, essence of
scampi and chateaubriand. Seated at
a table against the wall, listen-
ing to the couples on either side
of us chat *en français*, I was
about to comment on the "ambiance"
of the place when, struck by
the looks of a certain redheaded
waiter, you inadvertently spilled
your second strawberry daiquiri.
It seemed everyone turned to
stare at us and you blushed. I'm
afraid I didn't help much, the way
I laughed. I meant to tell you
then, but in the confusion for-
got, how last week, at work, I
found myself attracted to a rather
brawny refrigerator repairman.
He wore a tight white T-shirt,

the tattoo of a chimera half-
visible beneath one of its sleeves.
A chimera is an imaginary monster
made up of incongruous parts. It
is also a frightful or foolish
fancy. I wrote my telephone number
on a small piece of paper and
slipped it in his pocket before
he left. *Why had she acted so
very rashly?* I read this that
night at a drugstore, on the back
cover of a Harlequin Romance, as
I waited in line to buy a pack
of cigarettes. Walking home,
Hollywood Blvd. was abuzz with
tourists and various low-life
types. I reached my street. It
was late, but fireworks were still
being set off from the magicians'
private club at the top of the
hill. I stopped and looked up,
then started to laugh (It had
to be for my benefit!) as half
the night sky briefly flared
into a brilliant shade of red.

1982

POEM

again like never I feel
my fool way dreamed me
and so you know me
heart of that me I leave
foolish always like love

1982

POEM

That vast dance floor was the empty universe
I presumed mine alone when I was merely eighteen
and utterly accessible to almost any one of many
made handsome only amidst those rotating lights.

1983

WINDOW SEAT

How much closer are we to the moon?
Tonight it's a mere crescent in
an altogether black sky somewhere
over Kansas, or so the voice of our
captain assures us. I've already
forgotten how many thousands of feet
he said we're flying at. I've also
forgotten how many cocktails the iden-
tical blonde stewardesses have brought
me. I feel, well, like a crossword
puzzle: 5 down, an alcoholic beverage
served on airplanes in tiny bottles,
begins with S-C-O. Back in New York
City, the boys are undoubtedly flir-
ting with the boys at the Boy Bar.
How I wish I were still there, wide-
eyed and excited, in that flurry of
good-looks. Up here, in the section
where smoking's permitted, I'm fin-
gering an empty matchbook and a few
leftover subway tokens. They're as
useless now as the valium I took
on the bus to the airport. Most of my
fellow passengers, however, have nodded
off. Others rented headsets, muf-
fling the purity of the soundless film
on the small screen, a romantic comedy
I observe with little interest until

sudden turbulence signals a familiar
"plink" and FASTEN SEATBELT lights up
overhead. My eyelids are leaden; I'm
too tired to obey. What time is it
on the coast this flight is speeding
toward, enabling me to regain the
three hours I willfully abandoned
last week? But what would I have done
with them then, except sleep and dream?

1983

MONDAY, MONDAY

Radio's reality when
the hits just keep
happening: "I want
to kiss like lovers
do . . ." Why is it
I've always mistaken
these lyrics for my
true feelings? The
disc jockey says it's
spring and instantly
I'm filled with such
joy! Is it possible
that I'm experiencing
nature for the first
time? In the morning
the sun wakes me
and I am genuinely
moved, almost happy
to be alive. For a
couple of weeks it'd
been getting a little
bit brighter every
day. I wasn't aware
of this change until
the morning I noticed
the angle at which
the light hit your

GQ calendar, fully
accentuating the aus-
tere features of this
month's male model, as
I sat in the kitchen,
in your maroon robe,
and waited for my tea
to cool. I was thinking
about my feelings, about
how much I loved the sun
when I was a child and
how I loved the dark
as well, how thrilling
it was to lie in bed
on windy nights and
listen to the sound of
bushes and branches being
thrashed about outside.

Actually, that's what
I was thinking while
you were making the tea.
I was staring at the
calendar, at the smoke
from the tip of my
cigarette as it drifted
in the sunlight toward
the open window, when
you set the steaming
fifties-style cup in
front of me. Was it

at this point that
my manner changed?
Your gesture reminded
me of innumerable
mornings spent with
my parents in the pink
kitchen of my childhood.
I remembered my mother,
how she always wore her
gaudy floral bathrobe
and shuffled about in
her bedroom slippers as
she dutifully served us
breakfast. My father
sat alone at one end
of the table, his stern
face all but hidden
behind the front page
of the *Los Angeles Times*.
They seldom spoke. I
felt the tension between
them, watched with sleep-
filled eyes as he gave
her the obligatory kiss
on the cheek, then
clicked his briefcase
shut and, without a word,
walked out the door.

As I was getting dressed,
you grabbed me, kissed

me on the lips, said
something romantic.
I left your apartment
feeling confused, got
on the freeway and
inched my way through
the bumper-to-bumper
traffic. I was confused
about sex, about the
unexpected ambivalence
which, the night before,
prompted my hesitancy
and nonchalant attitude:
"It's late," I said,
"Let's just sleep."
The cars ahead of me
wouldn't budge. I
turned on the radio and
started changing stations.
I was afraid I would
always be that anxious,
that self-obsessed, that
I might never be able
to handle a mature
relationship. Stuck on
the freeway like that,
I was tempted to get
into it, the pain and
the drama, but the mood
soon passed. (After
all, it *is* spring.)

At last, traffic picked
up and I enjoyed the
rest of the drive, kept
the radio on all
the way to work and
listened to all those
songs, though I finally
realized those songs
were no longer my feelings.

1984

APRIL INVENTORY

This is typical
autobiographical
stuff: five or
so years ago,
at a bar called
The Doppelganger,
I picked up a guy
who looked a lot
like you. I had
been drinking all
night and was in
a blackout by
the time we got
into bed. I
remember his name
(Harry) and that
the following
morning, before
he left, I handed
him my telephone
number. I was
too intimidated
to ask for his.
He said he'd call
and for a couple
of weeks I waited,
but didn't hear
from him. Of

course the lack
of contact was
proof that I would
never be loved.

Lately, you
are the one I
keep rubbing up
against. I'm such
a sucker for blonds,
especially those
that aren't too
tightly wrapped.
I'm trying not to
resent your openness
   your laughter and
your anger, always
on tap—or your
apparent ease with
possible sex partners.
Last night it almost
worked. I found
a spot close to the
dance floor, stayed
there and looked
for you. The crowd
was mostly Latin,
so you stood out.

I watched how
freely you danced.

You were smiling.
Our eyes met twice.
I wanted to loosen
up, but couldn't
move. I sipped
my mineral water
and smoked cigarette
after cigarette
until I couldn't
stand it anymore.
That old tape
started playing
at full blast,
although this
time I didn't
completely
believe it.

I made a mental
note: "Fear to
be walked through
at a later date,
with somebody
else." Abruptly
I left the bar
and, wondering if
you had noticed,
walked to my car.
I'd parked around
the block, under
a jacaranda.

Its lavender
blossoms blew off
the windshield
as I drove away.

1984

TO SIR WITH LOVE

My dear fellow artist—
what a surprise it was
to discover that you
have feelings just
like the rest of us.
Life is full of such
interesting twists.
But then you have always
been a source of fascinating
personal disclosure.
I expect nothing less
than complexity from
the man of my dreams.
There's violence in
your work, for instance,
and yet you have the
softest touch. You
have the most attractive
physical assets. And
you certainly know how
to flaunt what you've
got, I'll give you that.
But I would rather you
let me give my heart.

1984

DREAMS

At the stroke of midnight, we
sat down on a queen-size bed
to watch a special screening
of *The Lost Weekend* on TV.
A previously censored scene
(in which Ray Milland, drunk
out of his mind on Irish whis-
key, tries on Jane Wyman's
stylish leopard coat in front
of a full-length mirror) had
been restored to the film.
I felt privileged to see it.
The bed tilted a little and
I realized it was resting on
the edge of a steep cliff.
Miles below us, the ocean
glistened. It looked like
sheet metal. The drop made
me so dizzy I was almost sick.
I wanted to warn you of the
great danger we were in, but
you were engrossed in the movie
and I was afraid you might get
mad if you were disturbed.
We were fine until you shifted
your weight. We tipped back-
wards and, on the mattress,
started sliding down the side

of the mountain like those kids
that sailed through the air on
a block of ice in Walt Disney's
In Search of the Castaways.
I panicked and shouted: "My bed!
My comforter!" Then I noticed
the sky: it was a shade of the
most amazing blue. You reached
underneath the pillow and
produced a bottle of amyl
nitrate, which you proceeded
to take off the cap of and
sniff as we kept plummeting.
You passed it to me just when
we were about to hit the water.

I woke up and looked at the
alarm clock. It was 3:30 a.m.
My heart was pounding. I calmed
down, fell asleep again, and
dreamed that I was sitting at
a picnic table somewhere in
Sequoia National Park. One by
one, I ripped all the pages out
of an old magazine, an issue
of *Time.* The cover looked
familiar (I think I remembered
it from when I was a teenager),
although inside there was
no text, only glossy stills
of silent movie stars. I

didn't recognize any of them.
My grandfather, who had been
standing near a barbecue pit
with the rest of the family,
noticed I was sitting alone
and walked over to the table.
My grandfather had always
frightened me. I looked
up at him, then down at the
torn photographs. Gently, he
placed his hand on my shoulder.
"The stars are silent tonight,"
he said. I wanted to ask
him to forgive me. Instead,
I turned away from him, hating
myself as I did, but I was
afraid I wouldn't be able
to give enough in return
for the presence of that kind
and forever unknowable old man.

1 9 8 4

MEET THE SUPREMES

When Petula Clark sang "Downtown," I wished I
could go there with her. I wanted to be free
to have fun and fall in love, but from suburbia
the city appeared more distant and dangerous
than it actually was. I withdrew and stayed
in my room, listened to Jackie DeShannon sing
"What The World Needs Now Is Love." I agreed,
but being somewhat morose considered the song
a hopeless plea. I listened to Skeeter Davis'
"The End Of The World" and decided that was
what it would be when I broke up with my first
boyfriend. My head spun as fast as the singles
I saved pennies to buy: "It's My Party," "Give
Him A Great Big Kiss," "(I Want To Be) Bobby's
Girl," "My Guy"—the list goes on. At the age
of ten, I rushed to the record store to get
"Little" Peggy March's smash hit, "I Will Follow
Him." An extreme example of lovesick devotion,
it held down the top spot on the charts for
several weeks in the spring of 1963. "Chapel
Of Love" came out the following year and was
my favorite song for a long time. The girls
who recorded it, The Dixie Cups, originally
called themselves Little Miss & The Muffets.
They cut three hits in quick succession, then
disappeared. I remember almost the exact moment
I heard "Johnny Angel" for the first time: it
came on the car radio while we were driving

down to Laguna Beach to visit some friends of
the family. In the back seat, I set the book I'd
been reading beside me and listened, completely
mesmerized by Shelley Fabares' dreamy, teenage
desire. Her sentimental lyrics continue to move
me (although not as intensely) to this day.
Throughout adolescence, no other song affected
    me quite like that one.
On my transistor, I listened to the Top Twenty
countdown as, week after week, more girl singers
    and groups
came and went than I could keep track of:

> Darlene Love,
> Brenda Lee,
> Dee Dee Sharp,
> Martha Reeves
> & The Vandellas,
> The Chantels,
> The Shirelles,
> The Marvelettes,
> The Ronettes,
> The Girlfriends,
> The Rag Dolls,
> The Cinderellas,
> Alice Wonderland,
> Annette, The
> Beach-Nuts, Nancy
> Sinatra, Little
> Eva, Veronica,
> The Pandoras,

Bonnie & The
Treasures,
The Murmaids,
Evie Sands,
The Pussycats,
The Patty Cakes,
The Tran-Sisters,
The Pixies Three,
The Toys, The
Juliettes and
The Pirouettes,
The Charmettes,
The Powder Puffs,
Patti Lace &
The Petticoats,
The Rev-Lons,
The Ribbons,
The Fashions,
The Petites,
The Pin-Ups,
Cupcakes,
Chic-Lets,
Jelly Beans,
Cookies, Goodies,
Sherrys, Crystals,
Butterflys,
Bouquets,
Blue-Belles,
Honey Bees,
Dusty Springfield,
The Raindrops,

The Blossoms,
The Petals,
The Angels,
The Halos,
The Hearts,
The Flamettes,
The Goodnight
Kisses, The
Strangeloves,
and The Bitter
Sweets.

I was ecstatic when "He's So Fine" hit the #1 spot.
I couldn't get the lyrics out of my mind and continued
to hum "Doo-lang Doo-lang Doo-lang" long after
puberty ended, a kind of secret anthem. Although
The Chiffons tried to repeat their early success
with numerous singles, none did as well as their
first release. "Sweet Talkin' Guy" came close,
sweeping them back into the Top Ten for a short
time, but after that there were no more hits.
Lulu made her mark in the mid-sixties with "To Sir
    With Love,"
which I would put on in order to daydream about
my junior high algebra instructor. By then I was
a genuine introvert. I'd come home from school,
having been made fun of for carrying my textbooks
like a girl, and listen to song after song from
my ever-expanding record collection. In those
days, no one sounded sadder than The Shangri-Las.
Two pairs of sisters from Queens, they became famous

for their classic "death disc shocker," "Leader Of
	The Pack,"
and for their mod look. They were imitated (but
	never equalled)
by such groups as The Nu-Luvs and The Whyte Boots.
The Shangri-Las stayed on top for a couple of
years, then lost their foothold and split up.
Much later, they appeared in rock 'n' roll revival
shows, an even sadder act since Marge, the fourth
member of the band, had died of an accidental
drug overdose. I started smoking cigarettes around
this time, but wouldn't discover pills, marijuana
or alcohol until my final year of high school.
I loved Lesley Gore because she was always crying
and listened to "As Tears Go By" till the single had
so many scratches I couldn't play it anymore.
I preferred Marianne Faithfull to The Beatles and
The Rolling Stones, was fascinated by the stories
about her heroin addiction and suicide attempt.
She's still around. So is Diana Ross. She made
it to superstardom alone, maintaining the success
she'd previously achieved as the lead singer of
The Supremes, one of the most popular girl groups
of all time. Their debut album was the first LP
I owned. Most of the songs on it were hits—
one would reach the top of the charts as another
hit the bottom. Little did I know, as I listened
to "Nothing But Heartaches" and "Where Did Our Love
Go," that nearly twenty years later I would hit
bottom in an unfurnished Hollywood single, drunk
and stoned and fed up, still spinning those same

old tunes. The friction that already existed
within The Supremes escalated in 1967 as Diana
Ross made plans for her solo career. The impending
split hit Florence the hardest. Rebelliously,
she gained weight and missed several performances,
and was finally told to leave the group. The pain
she experienced in the years that followed was
a far cry from the kind of anguish expressed
in The Supremes' greatest hits. Florence lost
the lawsuit she filed against Motown, failed at
a solo career of her own, went through a bitter
divorce, and ended up on welfare. In this classic
photograph of the group, however, Florence is
smiling. Against a black backdrop, she and Mary
look up at and frame Diana, who stands in profile
and raises her right hand, as if toward the future.
The girls' sequined and tasselled gowns sparkle
as they strike dramatic poses among some Grecian
columns. Thus, The Supremes are captured forever
like this, in an unreal, silvery light. That
moment, they're in heaven. Then, at least for Flo,
begins the long and painful process of letting go.

1984

FOOTNOTE

Nancy's question is
aimed at her mean little heels:
"Are you ready boots?"

1 9 8 4

SONNET

The first thirty to sixty days I was

simply insane, if not most mentally

incapable of the simplest tasks: brush

teeth, wash dishes, face, dress for work, drive on

streets, freeways. I had headaches, radio

static, anxiety attacks. Then I

couldn't speak, not in meetings in utter

terror of others and in the fog of

craziest thoughts. The shakes, the coffee pot,

my cigarettes. "Get numbers." "Sit down, shut

up and listen." "Do not drink or use, *no*

matter what." This I did (not alone) and

fell for the most brilliant though mad of them.

But oh I was such a sick one myself.

1984

GOOD TIDINGS

Tonight, a hand-painted and
haloed cherub is watching
over you as you drift off.
It is the same angel that
inhabits the candle's shadows,
the spirit that dwells
in your glass of warm milk.
It is also the protector
of good art and the speaker
of all romance languages,
as well as the guardian of
your dreams and little wishes,
and the keeper of each dark
secret you swore you would
take to the grave, but which
you have given up this time
around—your second and final
chance. So turn away from
the light. Sleep. Let go
of every unknown answer and
explanation. When you wake,
you will own your life.

1984

LIVING DOLL

FOR SHEREE LEVIN

The night we met, I was wearing one of my most exquisite ensembles: formal, floor-length gown with flowing train (in the elegance of pink satin), pearl necklace and drop earrings, pink dancing pumps with silver glitter, white elbow gloves and fur stole. An enchanted evening! I can still hear those distant harps and violins, can still recall how the laughter and chatter of the other guests magically dissolved as we sipped champagne on the lush, moonlit terrace. "He's such a doll!" I thought. "This must be love at first sight!" Right then, I decided I wanted to spend the rest of my days gazing into that dreamboat's blue eyes.

The following Sunday, Ken picked me up for a drive in the country. I took the high fashion road with my beige sweater and striped pants, a car coat fastened with toggles, a straw hat that ties with a red scarf, and wedgies to match . . . perfect for a lunch-stop in a picturesque village. Before I slid into the passenger seat, I noticed the license plate on Ken's sports car. It said MATTEL. I later learned he was the youngest and fastest-rising executive the company had ever employed.

At that point, I was a little bewildered about the direction of my own future. My modeling career seemed to be going nowhere. The photo sessions, fan mail, and fashion shows that had once brought me fame were tapering off. I simply wasn't up for it anymore. (It isn't easy being a teen-age model at twenty-five!) Besides, I wanted to do something different. Oh, I had tried just about everything. As a ballerina, I danced before kings and queens as the Sugar Plum Fairy, costumed in a shimmering silver tutu. As a stewardess, I took off for sky adventures in a navy blue uniform with flight insignia on cap and jacket. I'd even been a registered nurse and cured patients in my trim white uniform and silk-lined cape. Before I met Ken, I had been toying with the idea of pursuing a singing career. Although I'd started to appear at some of the nightclubs around town, I could tell this endeavor would never really get off the ground. The feelings I found myself developing for Ken gave my life new meaning, a definite direction. He seemed to fix it for me.

The next couple of months, we were practically inseparable. We went sailing and ice-skating. We played tennis at an exclusive country club. On our alpine holiday, I sported a swaggering leather coat, a striped t-shirt with jaunty hood, and knit mittens. Often, after cocktails, I twirled on dance floors in a feminine flower print accented with a fancy sash or a powder blue corduroy jumper with colorful felt appliqués and bouffant petticoat. For a garden party, I cultivated a cotton candy look: rosebuds, ruffles, and dainty pink bow at waist. I blossomed out for a fund-raising banquet in a buttercup yellow sheath frosted with sheer overskirt, smart hat, and a bouquet of spring posies to complete the pretty picture. But did Ken notice? Was it my imagination, or was he growing more and more remote?

I sensed something was amiss the night I debuted my new act at The Pink Lady Lounge. Didn't Ken realize what an important event it was? There were no tasteful floral arrangements, no expensive chocolates or vintage wines. I'd spent hours at the dressing room vanity in a frenzy of false eyelashes, mascara, powder puffs, lipsticks, and bobby pins. And still I didn't look right! I was completely beside myself. I'd misplaced one of my gold hoop earrings. I couldn't get the ribbon tied around my ponytail. I could barely fasten my bead necklace. At the last minute, I managed to slip into my dramatic black glitter-gown, the one with bare shoulders and a rose corsage on its netted flounce. I pulled on my long black gloves just as a stagehand ushered me into the wings . . . and before I knew it, I was standing at the microphone, in the middle of my first number, pink scarf in hand. Beyond the glare of the spotlight, I recognized a couple at one of the front tables. It was Allen and Midge. But where was Ken? I nearly collapsed several times during my performance. Afterwards, I kept the bartender company until last call, then took a taxi home.

What went wrong? Why won't he answer my messages? Whenever I phone his office, the curt receptionist says he's either in a conference or at the gym. Why won't he let me get close to him? Lately, all I do is mope around my apartment in a yellow terrycloth robe (with a big monogrammed "B" on the breast pocket). I oversleep and keep the drapes drawn all day. I'm gaining weight. There are dark circles under my eyes. I should try to pull myself together, but what about the plans we made? What about my Dream House and its complete suite of modern, slim-line furniture? What about my magnificent church wedding dress? It's fit for a princess: formal train, diamond tiara, tiered bridal veil, and billowing layers of flowered nylon tulle. What about my trousseau . . . my embroidered peignoir or my full-length pink negligee with its Grecian bodice and low-cut back? Are my dreams as flimsy? Are they as transparent as that?

1985

NOVEMBER

FOR CHRISTOPHER HARRITY

11/4

Sunlight
(the drapes
only par-
tially drawn)
on orange
carpet. Wall
lamp (pink,
green and
black) by
Isermann.
Stereo (on
floor). Stack
of records:
The Go•Go's,
Laurie An-
derson, Lin-
da Ronstadt.
In black
wire rack:
this month's
Vanity Fair,
VALLEY OF
THE DOLLS,
Barbie: The

Magazine
For Girls,
et cetera.
Faded green
cushions on
black chair.
Black lamp
(thanks to
Christopher)
on small round
table. Pink
futon. Star-
burst clock
(red, yellow,
blue), also
by Isermann.
On an end
table (blond
wood): two
spiritual
books, candle,
ashtray and
(thanks to Joe,
Christopher's
beau) red car-
nations in
a white art
nouveau vase.

11/9

Morning fog.
I can't think
clearly yet.

*

Two cups of tea
(Earl Grey in-
stead of Lipton
for a change)
and lots of
cigarettes later.
Not much better.
Suppose these
last addictions
are beginning
to fail me?
Then what?

Oh, maybe just
one more cup.

*

The doorbell
(waiting for
the water
to boil).
Flowers!

Sign here.
What a de-
lightful
surprise!
From Bob R.
A dozen
red roses
swathed in
baby's breath.
I leave a
"thank you
so much"
message on
his phone
machine.

*

Those amazing
girl groups
strike again:
"Da Doo Ron
Ron." "I
Have A Boy-
friend" is
a wonderful
but obscure
number by
The Chiffons.
A truly upbeat
little ditty.

*

Only one piece
of mail today.
I tear open
the envelope.
Some sort of
announcement of—
Pat's death.
It takes my
breath away.
A heart attack,
the note from
her husband
says. I have
to sit down.
Poor Pat.
Patricia Capps,
Rachel's mother.
I wait, but
no tears come.
Rachel's been
gone how long
now? Over six
years. I call
Kathy. She's
out, so I tell
her daughter
the news. I
light a candle
and another

cigarette, then
turn over
the tape.

*

"Wait!
Oh yes,
wait a minute
Mr. Postman..."

11/19

Christopher knocks
on my window, then
the door. "Come
in." "There was an
awful accident on
the freeway! I was
stuck for over two
hours! I'm *so* mad!"
He goes home to
sleep. I sit down
to write. A little
later, Christopher
calls. He likes
the new message on
my phone machine: me
followed by about
thirty seconds of
"Blame It On The

Bossa Nova." "What
are you up to?" he
asks. "Writing."
"Oh, how's it going?"
"Not well," I tell
him. "All I've
come up with is:
A cold and quiet
November night."

11/21

A cold and quiet
November night.
I sit on the floor
next to the heater.
In front of me:
old Smith-Corona,
green loose-leaf
notebook, cigarettes,
lighter and ash-
tray (the one that
Christopher bought
at a thrift shop
in San Francisco:
shaped like a comma,
yellow with orange
specks), diction-
ary, teacup, pen.
The flowers (bur-
gundy mums) that

Joe brought last
week are beginning
to wilt. New ones
would be nice. No
music, not tonight.
It's quiet. A cold
(although quite
cozy here by the
heater) and quiet
November night.

11/22

Friday evening,
Christopher,
Joe and I lis-
ten to *Televi-
sion's Greatest
Hits* (themes
from "Green
Acres," "The
Addams Family,"
"The Patty
Duke Show,"
and so forth)
as we primp
in front of
the full-length
mirror in
Christopher's
bedroom. Joe

wears a tan-
gerine cardigan
and orange and
turquoise Ban-
Lon pullover.
Christopher
wears his new
over-dyed pur-
ple Perry Ellis
sweater. Except
for a brown and
tan plaid muf-
fler and white
high-tops, I
wear all black.
Jay arrives and
we're off to the
1985 Queen of the
Universe contest
(for female im-
personators) at
"the meteoric
Mayflower Ball-
room." Our table
is in front, right
below the stage.
We order cokes.
The lights go
down. The show
opens with an act
featuring Empress

LeRey as a giant
spider with eight
huge furry arms.
On either side
of her, suspended
in webs, several
half-naked boys
writhe and con-
tort their faces
in fear. After
a few more num-
bers, the stage
is cleared. Then,
one by one, the
contestants ap-
pear and parade
on the runway.
Christopher and
Jay roll their
eyes. Joe whis-
tles and shouts:
"¡Ay Chica!" I
look up, applaud
and laugh. Such
exotic outfits!
Many feathers,
veils, jewelled
hairpieces and
heels. Miss Phil-
ippines, Miss Viet
Nam, Miss Hawaii,

Miss Saudi Arabia.
Miss Egypt is
carried onstage
by four men in
loincloths and
chains. The aged
Miss Iceland is
dressed as an
enormous silver
and white snow-
flake. The judges
confer and Miss
Iceland is an-
nounced the winner
of the costume
competition. As
she rushes out to
accept the trophy,
part of her snow-
flake-shaped head-
dress catches on
a lighting grid
and sparks fly.
"I'd love to see
what she does for
the 4th of July,"
someone says.
The swimsuit
competition is
next, but we get

up to leave during
the fifteen min-
ute intermission.

11/23

Saturday morning,
John and Louise
(my mother's aunt)
and I drive four
hours up the coast
to see my parents,
who've recently re-
tired. The time
passes fast, with-
out much small talk.
Light traffic. We
stop in Santa Bar-
bara: Louise buys
us lunch at a res-
taurant on State
St. and complains
about the slow
service. Back
on the road, she
worries about the
rain ("It's only
sprinkling, Aunt
Louise.") and
that we'll miss

our exit, which is
next to impossible:
there's just one
for the entire city
of Nipomo. West
on Tefft (a coun-
try road) to Rose,
left to Chandra,
right to La Loma
(which Chandra
turns into). My
parents' new home
is beautiful: a
pale yellow and
brick ranch house
on a large (over
an acre) lot. No
lawn yet. They're
at the front door:
Mom and Dad, Lin-
da (my sister, re-
cently separated)
and her two kids,
Kristy and Ryan.
We all smile, kiss,
hug and shake hands.
Rita (the Doberman)
sniffs and follows
us. Skipper (the
rat terrier) yaps
and wags in his

little cage (he'll
pee on the furni-
ture if loose).
We sit in the
family room and
visit. Ryan looks
up at me and asks,
"Who are you?"
"He's very bright
for his age," my
mother says. My
father goes out-
side to get more
firewood. Linda
sets the table.
My mother puts
dinner together.
It starts raining
harder and harder
as it gets dark.

11/24

Last night, after
Kristy performed
her baton routine,
we sat in the liv-
ing room and played
several games of
Old Maid. She lost
each time, but didn't

seem to mind. Then
we played with Lin-
da's ancient Chatty
Cathy. I was amazed
it still worked. We
slid the miniature
records in and out
of the doll's side
and pulled the ring
at the back of her
neck. "I always eat
my vegetables," she
said. "Everybody
likes good girls."
Ryan brought out
and demonstrated
his Glow Turtle:
press his stomach
and his face lights
up! We laughed and
played with toys
until their bedtime.
Still excited, they
couldn't sleep.
John stayed up and
talked with my mother.
I laid down on the
couch and was out
like a light.

*

At the breakfast
table, Aunt Louise
says: "Is David
always this grumpy
in the morning?"
She doesn't real-
ize I can hear her.
"Bitch, bitch, bitch,"
I whisper to my
mother in the kitchen.

*

Linda and the children
put on raincoats and go
to church. My father
watches football on TV.
Aunt Louise works on a
crossword. She's staying
through Thanksgiving.
My mother warms up the
car, takes John and me
on a little tour of the
area. A golf course and
half-completed condomin-
ium tract, some other
houses they had looked
at. "Yours is better,"
I tell her. Beautiful
downtown Nipomo: the
post office and a li-

quor store. Santa Maria.
Pismo Beach. The local
nuclear research plant.

*

We say good-bye in
the rain. I try not
to get Christopher's
suede jacket wet. My
mother pulls me a-
side and says: "I
worry about you.
Look at Rock Hudson
—with all his money.
Be careful." I tell
her not to worry a-
bout me, kiss her
on the cheek. We
wave and drive off.
It rains all the way
back to Los Angeles.

11/27

My caseload
at the Housing
Authority is
always crazy
the day before
a holiday week-

end. I'm glad
when it's time
to go. Traffic's
slow on the Gold-
en State; no ac-
cidents, though.
I call Christopher
the minute I get
home. "Come over,"
he says. I bring
some tea bags
and we tell each
other about our
days. Then we
run out to the
video store and
rent a few movies
for tomorrow:
Little Women,
The Thin Man
and (my idea)
The Parent Trap.
Christopher calls
me a "big Teen
Queen" and we
both crack up.
Home again, I
listen to the
messages on my
phone machine.
Jay says he has

to cancel his
Friday night
get-together
due to "tech-
nical diffi-
culties" with
his visiting
mother. Kathy
says she's al-
ways blamed it
on the Bossa
Nova. "Call
me." Amy says:
"Happy Thanks-
giving (almost)."

11/28

I've only been awake
a little while when
Christopher calls.
"Joe's in the shower,"
he says, "I told him
you and I already made
plans to pick up my
mother. Will you go?"
"Sure." I pull on a
sweater, brush my teeth
and dash next door.
"In here!" he calls,
"I just put the bird

in the oven." I smoke
a cigarette while he
cleans up. "Could you
hand me that vase?"
"Sure." A Bauer. He
puts fresh flowers in it.
"What would you do with-
out a boyfriend who
works for a florist?"
I ask. "I don't know.
There! Let's go."
Joe sticks his wet
head out of the bath-
room. "Good-bye, girls."
"I'm mad about you!"
Christopher yells as
we hurry out the door,
"Don't forget the yams."

*

At the airport, we look
at the magazines and
trinkets in the gift
shop, then sit and talk
until Jody's flight
arrives. We greet her
at Gate 5. Christopher
gives her a big hug.
"Hello, you." Jody
wears a trench coat,

hat and boots. "It
was raining when we
left Oakland," she says.
"We've had some here,"
I tell her, "but it's
clear today." We follow
the arrows to the bag-
gage claim area and
wait for her suitcases
to appear on the con-
veyor. "I'm so glad you
could come," Christopher
says, "We're going to
have a *fabulous* time!"

*

I open all the windows
in the apartment. I
fold the sheets, blan-
kets and futon. I dust
and vacuum, get the
laundry going, wash
the dishes, throw the
dead mums in the trash.
I sit down and drink
a cup of tea, call
Bob and Sheree. "Happy
Thanksgiving!" I say
to their answering
machine. I call Kathy.

"Happy Thanksgiving!"
She says she got a
note from Pat's husband,
thanking us for the
flowers. "Can you
stop by later?" I
tell her I probably
won't be able to.
I call my mother.
"Happy Thanksgiving!"
She says my father is
taking her and Louise
out to dinner tonight.
"Someone wants to say
hello to you." "Hi,
Uncle Dave?" "Hi, Ryan.
Happy Thanksgiving!"

*

Christopher leaves a
message while I'm in
the shower: "Dinner's
almost ready, darling.
Where are you?" I
dress up and go over.
They're all in the
kitchen. "It smells
like Thanksgiving,"
I say. Christopher
hands me a glass of

Perrier in a long-
stemmed wine glass
and a shrimp cocktail
in a tumbler with a
copper holder. He
also hands me his
Polaroid. I take a
few pictures: Jody
lifting a pot off the
stove, Joe grinning in
front of the refriger-
ator, Christopher
carving the turkey.
The food's beautiful-
ly arranged on an
orange and green
'40s drapery panel
spread across a blond
Chinese Moderne desk:
homemade cranberry
sauce in a Roseville
dish, stuffing (with
nuts) in an apricot
Vernonware bowl,
broccoli, wild rice,
warm whole wheat rolls.
Joe puts his yams
(Von's canned) in
a fluted orange bowl.
"They have honey and
brown sugar on them,"

he says. Christopher
sets down a platterful
of light and dark meat.
"Come and get it!"
We serve ourselves
on square Franciscan
plates, sit in the
bedroom and watch
The Thin Man on the
VCR. Christopher:
"Myrna Loy is beau-
tiful." Jody: "Oh,
yes." Joe: "Look at
that dress!" Me:
"Dolly Tree outdid
herself." I eat fast,
get up and fix some
tea, slice a large
piece of pumpkin
pie. The three of
them are crowded to-
gether on the bed.
I sit on the floor.
"What's wrong?" Joe
asks me towards the
end of the movie.
"Nothing." "You're so
quiet. What's wrong?"
"Nothing." When he
asks again, I snap
at him: "Stop it,

please." Everyone
looks at me. I take
my dishes into the
kitchen, set them in
the sink. I wait a
few minutes, then go
back into the bedroom.
"I'm going to take
off. Everything was
delicious. Thank you."
Christopher jumps up,
walks me to the front
door. "Are you alright?"
he asks. "I'm fine,"
I say. "Do you want
to take any food home
with you?" "No, I'm
stuffed. Thank you,
though. Goodnight."

11/29

After a late break-
fast, we drive around
to some bookstores
so Christopher can
deliver samples of
the 1986 She-Male
"Pin-Up" Calendar
("Transsexual super-
stars in the most

intimate settings"),
which he designed for
Kim Christy Productions.
At A Different Light,
I run into Larry.
"What are you doing
tonight?" he asks.
"I don't have any
plans." "Why don't
you stop by my place.
I'm having some people
over." "I'll try to
make it. Thanks."
On the way to West
Hollywood, we stop
and look through Have
A Nice Day, a new shop
on Melrose full of
'60s stuff: lava lamps,
a red beanbag chair,
clear plastic pillows,
daisy pins, Peter Max
ashtrays and scarves,
a troll doll with wild
orange hair, Happy Face
place mats, television
sets that resemble space
helmets. We take turns
sitting in a magenta-
lined egg-shaped iso-
lation chair. More

bookstores: Drake's,
Unicorn, Dorothy's Sur-
render. We end up at
George Sand. Christopher
hands the calendar to
the woman behind the
counter. "Would you
give this to the person
who does your purchasing?"
he asks, "A cover letter's
included." The woman
opens the wrapper and
looks at a few of the
pictures. "I don't
think we'd be interested
in presenting women in
such a sexist fashion,"
she says as she passes
it back to him, "Perhaps
you should try some of
those adult bookstores
in Hollywood." "They're
not women," Christopher
tells her, "They're men."
"Really," the woman says,
"That is even worse."

*

Before Christopher re-
turns the tapes, I put

a new outgoing message
on my phone machine: a
song from *The Parent Trap*,
Hayley Mills (as iden-
tical twins) singing
"Let's Get Together"
("Yeah, yeah, yeah").

*

Christopher takes a nap
on the black-and-white
striped chaise in the
living room. Janet (his
cat) curls up in Jody's
lap and sleeps while
Jody and I watch two ep-
isodes of the *Twilight
Zone* marathon. In the
first, a mute Agnes
Moorehead is terrorized
by two tiny, toylike
spacemen. Grunting and
groaning, she captures
one in a burlap sack
and throws him in the
fireplace, then squashes
the other as he tries
to escape in the little
spaceship. Her ordeal
is over. But there's

a twist: the intruders
were actually astronauts
from earth, whereas Agnes
was a giant on a distant
planet. In the second
episode, Anne Francis (as
a lustful country girl)
sells her soul to a witch
in order to win the heart
of the man she loves.
The spell works: he wants
to marry her. She must,
however, pay the devil
his due: every night at
midnight, she is trans-
formed into a ferocious
leopard. This is not ex-
actly what she had in mind.
At the end, she's cornered
by the townsmen and shot.

*

Driving down Vermont,
I see the first sign
of Christmas: a lit tree
in a second-story win-
dow. By the time I get
to Larry's, the party's
in full swing: at least
thirty men crammed in-

to his small apartment.
I stand in the kitchen,
smoke and drink a couple
of Diet Cokes. I talk
to two guys—John and
Kurt—and am attracted
to both of them. "Nice
talking with you," John
says when he leaves,
"Hope I see you around."
"Same here," I say.
After the party breaks
up, Kurt and I go to
Astro's, "the coffee
shop of the future."
We order hamburgers.
He's twenty-one, from
Sacramento, works at
a record store on Sunset.
Walking out to the park-
ing lot, I ask him if
he wants to spend the
night with me. "I'd like
that," he says. And then:
"I only have safe sex."
"Same here," I say.

11/30

I wake up in the middle of
the night and can't get back

to sleep. Carefully, I lift
Kurt's arm and slide out of
bed. I go to the bathroom,
then sit in the kitchen and
smoke until it begins to get
light outside. I take a
shower, shave, straighten
a few things, put some water
on. When Kurt wakes, I make
him a cup of tea. "I had
trouble sleeping," I tell
him. "I didn't," he says,
"This thing is comfortable."
He pats the futon. I light
a cigarette with one that's
almost out. Kurt says he
just stopped smoking a couple
of weeks ago. I tell him
I quit for over two months
earlier this year and that
I plan to try again soon.
Kurt gets dressed and I
drive him to his car, which
is parked across the street
from Larry's building. We
sit for a moment. "Thank
you for last night." "Sure."
Kurt smiles and hops out
of the car. I reach over
and lock the door. I pull

away, turn right at the
light, and drive up Vermont
towards the post office.

*

It starts to rain again in
the afternoon. I wake up
from a nap, turn on the heat
and sit down at my desk to
type for a while. Through
the wall, I hear Christopher
and his mother laugh and talk.
I call and say: "You sound
like a roomful of people."
"We are!" Christopher ex-
claims. He invites me out
to eat with them. I hesitate.
"I'll loan you an overcoat,"
he says. "Okay." We drive
across town in the rain.
Later, if it lets up, we'll
window-shop in Hollywood or
Beverly Hills. Christopher
pulls into the French Quarter,
but the lot's full. We opt
for Noura, a Greek restau-
rant just east of La Cienega.
We park, make a run for it
and shake ourselves off in-

side the door. We're seated
at a corner table. The wait-
er brings menus and a basket
of pita bread. Christopher
and Jody order the Mediter-
ranean salad. I can't decide,
so I try the Taster's Delight:
eggplant, tabbouleh, stuffed
grapeleaves. After we eat,
I get up to look at the bak-
lava and notice a jar of
madeleines next to the cash
register. "Here's dessert,"
I say as I set a small plate
on the table. "One apiece.
Compliments of Marcel Proust."
"That's right," says Jody,
"Remembrance of Things Past."
I take the first bite. "I
tried to read him in college,"
I say, "but only made it
through half of *Swann's Way.*
It was Rachel's copy. In
fact, I still had it when
she died." I tell them about
the accident: July 5, 1979,
2 a.m., the drunk driver who
passed out and hit us head-on.
"He and Rachel were killed
instantly. She was driving.
Christian, her boyfriend,

was in the front seat. I
was in the back. We were
both injured. I was in the
hospital for a long time."
I push the plate towards
Christopher. He eats the
second madeleine, then tells
us that he inherited a com-
plete set of Proust after
his ex-lover's mysterious
death in 1976. "John read
a lot," he says. "His books
are packed away somewhere.
You know, at Land's End in
San Francisco, there's ac-
tually a sign that says:
'Be careful while climbing
rocks: You may be swept to
your death.' The city must
have put it there." The wait-
er comes by with our check.
Jody picks up the last little
shell-shaped cake and exam-
ines it. "Nance and Mother
and I used to bake these,"
she says. "Oddly enough, I
sent Nance a madeleine tin
for Christmas last year."
She pauses to take a bite.
"When Mother died, I told
our friends the service was

going to be as simple as possible. Instead of sending flowers, I suggested they plant something in their yards. The idea just popped into my head. Nance planted a blue rose in Colorado Springs. There's also a daphne bush in Ferndale, a blossoming cactus in Tucson, and another rose, one with the loveliest cream-colored petals, which a dear friend planted in memory of her in Moraga, California."

1985

MOVIN' WITH NANCY

It is almost time to grow up
I eat my TV dinner and watch
Nancy Sinatra in 1966
All boots and thick blonde hair

I eat my TV dinner and watch
The daughter of Frank Sinatra
All boots and thick blonde hair
She appears on "The Ed Sullivan Show"

The daughter of Frank Sinatra
She sings "These Boots Are Made For Walkin'"
She appears on "The Ed Sullivan Show"
The song becomes a number one hit

She sings "These Boots Are Made For Walkin'"
She sings "Somethin' Stupid" with her father
The song becomes a number one hit
She marries and divorces singer/actor Tommy Sands

She sings "Somethin' Stupid" with her father
She sings "The Last Of The Secret Agents"
She marries and divorces singer/actor Tommy Sands
She sings "How Does That Grab You, Darlin'?"

She sings "The Last Of The Secret Agents"
She sings "Lightning's Girl" and "Friday's Child"
She sings "How Does That Grab You, Darlin'?"
She sings "Love Eyes" and "Sugar Town"

She sings "Lightning's Girl" and "Friday's Child"
She puts herself in the hands of writer/producer Lee Hazelwood
She sings "Love Eyes" and "Sugar Town"
She co-stars with Elvis Presley in *Speedway*

She puts herself in the hands of writer/producer Lee Hazelwood
Three gold records later
She co-stars with Elvis Presley in *Speedway*
She rides on Peter Fonda's motorcycle

Three gold records later
She has developed an identity of her own
She rides on Peter Fonda's motorcycle
The wild angels roar into town

She has developed an identity of her own
Nancy Sinatra in 1966
The wild angels roar into town
It is almost time to grow up

1986

FIVE HAIKU

OCTOBER 20TH

I was so surprised.
I'd never have thought you were
waiting, watching me.

DRIVE

One hand on the wheel
and the other, your right one,
gently clutching mine.

DRY KISSES

The safest kind. "I
could get used to kissing like
this," you said at first.

"OPEN YOUR HEART"

Madonna sang this
on the radio the day
yours suddenly closed.

WHAT LASTS

How we opened up
and were affectionate for
one brief, sweet moment.

1 9 8 6

HAND OVER HEART

I look up at the clock.
It's time to go, so
I cover the typewriter
and calculator, lock my radio
in the file cabinet
and straighten my desk.
On the way out, I unplug
the Christmas tree lights.
I am rarely the last one
to leave the office.

Alone in the elevator,
I listen to a lilting
rendition of "Frosty
The Snowman." The door
slides open. Outside,
it's already dark. I say
good night to the guard
in the parking lot, wait
for my car to warm up.
It does and I drive off.

Halfway home,
I turn on the radio.
Madonna sings
her new hit, "Open
Your Heart." At
the same time, on

another station,
Cyndi Lauper sings
her latest song, "Change
Of Heart." Not that long
ago, it might have
been Brenda Lee
singing "Heart In Hand"
and Connie Francis
belting out any number
of her most popular
tunes: "My Heart
Has A Mind Of Its
Own," "Breakin' In
A Brand New Broken
Heart," "When
The Boy In Your Arms
(Is The Boy In Your
Heart)" or "Don't
Break The Heart
That Loves You."
I don't know why
I think about
such things.

I park the car
in the garage, walk
across the courtyard
and check the mailbox.
A few bills, ads,
Christmas cards
from friends I no

longer feel that
close to. No
messages on my
phone machine.

"I'm sorry,"
you said last
night. You seemed
sincere. Later,
I sat in my car
and cried. *Was it
love? I thought
it was love. I mean
it felt like love.*
It really did.

1986

DOUBLE TROUBLE

Patty:

"Hi, Mom! I'm home!"
I shouted as I burst
through the front door.
"Hello, dear." I dashed
upstairs, threw my books
on the floor, tossed
on a stack of singles
and flopped down on
the bed. Chad & Jeremy
sent me instantly to
Dreamsville. I rolled
over and reached for
my princess phone. "Hi,
Sue Ellen." "HI! Oh,
Patty!" she gushed,
"You're absolutely the
talk of the campus! I
mean you're practically
a celebrity!" We gig-
gled about how I'd
been dragged to the
principal's office
for cutting my geome-
try class and spying
on Richard in the
boys' locker room.

Cathy:

From the beginning, I
was opposed to Patty's
"wild" idea. It just
didn't seem feasible.
Her enthusiasm, how-
ever, was dizzying.
After listening to her
plan, she persuaded
me to exchange clothes
with her. Frantically,
she threw on my white
blouse, plaid skirt,
knee socks and oxfords
while, reluctantly, I
slipped into her sweat
shirt, blue jeans and
scruffy tennis shoes.
Next, she brushed her
flip into a pageboy
and wiped the makeup
off her face, then
spun around, brushed
my pageboy into a flip
and applied her fa-
vorite Yardley shade
(Liverpool Pink) to my

"Have you told your dad yet?" "And miss my date with Richard tonight? Not on your life! I'm meeting him at the Shake Shop at eight." There was a knock on my door. "I gotta run, Sue Ellen. See you tomorrow." We hung up. "Come in!" It was Dad. I'd never seen him look so mad. "I received a call from the principal of your school today," he said. My heart just about stopped. "Gosh, Pop-O . . ." "Don't 'Gosh, Pop-O' me, young lady. *You* are grounded. For the next two weeks, you're to stay home and study every night. You're to be in bed by nine o'clock. No phone privileges." "OH!" I cried. "No music." He switched off the phonograph. "And clean up this mess!" The door

pursed lips. We stood back and looked at each other in the mirror. It was perfectly uncanny: I couldn't even tell us apart. Patty squealed with delight and grabbed my hands. "Now, Cath," she coached, "Try not to act so brainy, or we'll never pull this off!" She picked up a few library books and said "Bye-eee," then glided out the door. I sat down and studied for my geometry mid-term. At one point, Ross stuck his head in the room. "What's up, Sis?" he asked. I took a deep breath, turned around and said "Scram, brat!" in the harshest tone of voice I could mus-ter. He made a nasty face and stomped off. The real test came at nine o'clock, when Uncle Martin stopped

slammed behind him. I
moaned and buried my
head in the pillow. My
whole life was ruined!
What about my date???
How in the world could
I be in two places at
once? Just then, Cathy
came into the room.
"Hello, Patty," she
smiled. I stared at
her. She blinked back.
"Anything wrong?" "Yes!
No! I mean LIKE WOW!"
I yelled as I jumped
up and down. "I have
the *wildest* idea!!!"

by to turn out the
lights. "I hope you
understand this is for
your own good," he said.
"I dig, Pop-O," I uttered
with a weak smile. He
didn't seem the least
bit suspicious, so I
slid into Patty's bed
and blew a goodnight
kiss at him. Then, for
a convincing finishing
touch, I blew another
kiss across the room,
at Patty's heart-shaped
framed photograph
of Frankie Avalon.

1987

RERUNS

SPLASH!

Like a rock, Elly
May's cake sank to the bottom
of the "ceement" pond.

IN OUTER SPACE

Judy Jetson spins
a disc and does the Orbit
to "Comet of Love."

WITH A LITTLE GRIN

Morticia snipped off
the rose and placed the stem in
the tombstone-shaped vase.

PATTY TO CATHY

"While you study as
me, I'll leave as you, then go
as me on my date!"

HOUSEWORK

Samantha looked at
the dirty dishes. "Just this
once," she thought, and twitched.

NEW YEAR'S EVE

The cork popped off the
bottle and, effervescent,
Jeannie overflowed.

HONEY IN THE FLESH

She knew how to use
her high-voltage curves like an
unconcealed weapon.

BATMAN AND ROBIN

hang by threads above
a bubbling vat of acid.
To be continued . . .

MODEL CHILDREN

Kitten told the truth.
Princess set aside her pride.
Bud made right his wrong.

ISLAND GIRLS

Mary Ann dons one
of Ginger's dresses, but it
falls flat on her chest.

GOSSIP

Gidget and Larue
knock heads as they press their ears
to the princess phone.

FRED'S BREAKFAST

With a club, Wilma
cracked open the three-minute
pterodactyl egg.

PUBERTY

Wally pounds on the
bathroom door, "C'mon Beav! You've
been in there for hours!"

FRACTURED FAIRY TALE

This kissing princess
was such a dog that the frog
she smacked simply croaked.

GREEN ACRES

The smoke from Lisa's
burnt pancakes slowly blackens
the fresh country air.

THE MOD SQUAD

Julie, Pete and Linc
bust some thugs, then head back to
their pad to turn on.

LIKE BIRD OR BALLOON

Sister Bertrille fades
to a speck in the blue sky
above San Tanco.

1987

OSCAR NIGHT

When two-time Oscar winner
Olivia de Havilland comes
out in a red dress with see
-through sleeves to present
the award for Best Cinema-
tography, Christopher gasps:
"She's so affected! I just
love her!" Christopher, Joe
and I sit on the couch eating
pizza. "How splendid!" says
Olivia after she announces
the winner. An award or two
later, Janet (the cat) walks
into the room with a dead
bird in her mouth and deposits
it in front of the TV. "Oh
Janet!" Christopher sighs. He
picks up the bird and takes it
outside. "She does this at
least once a week," he says
when he returns, "I'm sure it
satisfies her somewhere deep
in her nature." Joe doesn't
miss a beat: "Just like Miss
de Havilland satisfies *you*?"

1988

THE MUNSTERS

Among cobwebs and
dust, Lily sits in
the parlor reading
this month's issue
of *Better Tombs
and Graveyards.*
In the lab, Grandpa
hangs upside down,
dreaming of fara-
way Transylvania.
Up in his bedroom,
Eddie sleeps off
the effects of last
night's full moon.
When the doorbell
rings (to the tune
of a funeral march),
Spot roars flames.
Herman stomps to
the front door and
opens it. Hair on
end, Marilyn's date
runs screaming down
Mockingbird Lane.

1988

DRIVING BACK
FROM NEW HAVEN

Tim looks at his watch, reaches into his
pocket, takes out a small plastic container
and swallows an AZT pill with a sip of Sprite.
"Poison," he mutters under his breath. I
glance over at him. We haven't talked about
his health the entire trip. "How does it
make you feel?" I ask. "Like I want to live
until they discover a cure," he snaps. We
travel in silence for a while. I stare out
the window at all the green trees on the
Merritt Parkway. Then he says: "I resent
it. I resent that we were not raised with
an acceptance of death. And here it is,
all around us. And I fucking resent it.
I resent that we do not know how to die."

1 9 8 8

POEM

Friday evening:
Jimmy's private
reading at Raymond's.
I've come early to
help out. The guest
of honor's already
there: he sits in
the blue armchair
sipping seltzer.
I'm about to hear
him read! A handful
of equally privileged
friends will arrive
soon. Raymond sends
me to the Korean
market to pick up
some last-minute things:
plastic cups, paper
napkins, one lemon,
sugar cubes, ice.
It's a beautiful
fall night. A slight
breeze. I walk down
9th St. in a shower
of small, yellow
headlight-lit
leaves.

NOVEMBER 6, 1988

THE PORTRAIT OF A LADY

She wished to make her peace with the world—

Far afloat on a sea of wonder and pain

A mixture of the effects of rich experience

Like mere sweet airs of the garden

When one returned from it with a lapful of roses

A sort of passion of tenderness for memories

"You're drifting to some great mistake."

She stood a moment before the mantel-glass

Alone in a wilderness of yellow upholstery

A wandering tress of hair

The impression of her ardent good faith

An end to the pretty tea-parties on the lawn

Signified more than lay on the surface

Kindness, admiration, bonbons, bouquets

And was an open-handed gift of fate

A suggestion of perfume and murmuring boughs

Rustling, quickly-moving, clear-voiced

The place, the occasion, the combination of people

The dark, shining dampness of everything

1988

HOCKNEY:
BLUE POOL

Los Angeles,
California:
a summer afternoon.
One boy sunbathes
on a yellow towel
beside the pool;
another stands
at the end of
the diving board,
gazing downward.
Palm trees sway
in the blue water.
Overhead, a few
clouds float by.
To the right,
sprinklers lightly
spray the green
lawn. The sunbather
slips off his red
and white striped
swimsuit and rolls
over; the other
boy dives into the
pool. The artist
snaps a photograph
of the splash.

1989

SONG

"You Don't Own Me"
was a hit that summer. Up in
my room, I played
it till the single was all scratched

while, below, my
brother's friends caught softballs in the
street. They drove me
nuts as the song, all summer long.

1989

THINGS TO DO IN
VALLEY OF THE DOLLS
(THE MOVIE)

Move to New York.
Lose your virginity.
Become a star.
Send money to your mother.

Call pills "dolls."
Fire the talented newcomer.
Have a nervous breakdown.
Suffer from an incurable degenerative disease.

Sing the theme song.
Do your first nude scene.
Wear gowns designed by Travilla.
Become addicted to booze and dope.

Scream "Who needs you!"
Stagger around in a half-slip and bra.
Come to in a sleazy hotel room.
Say "I am merely traveling incognito."

Get drummed out of Hollywood.
Come crawling back to Broadway.
Pull off Susan Hayward's wig
and try to flush it down the toilet.

End up in a sanitarium.
Hiss "It wasn't a nuthouse!"
Get an abortion.
Go on a binge.

Detect a lump in your breast.
Commit suicide.
Make a comeback.
Overact.

1989

EIGHTEEN TO TWENTY-ONE

I

He said his name was Nick; later I learned
he'd crossed the country on stolen credit
cards—I found the receipts in the guest house
I rented for only three months. Over
a period of two weeks, he threatened
to tell my parents I was gay, blackmailed
me, tied me up, crawled through a window and
waited under my bed, and raped me at
knifepoint without lubricant. A neighbor
heard screams and called my parents, who arrived
with a loaded gun in my mother's purse.
But Nick was gone. I moved back home, began
therapy, and learned that the burning in
my rectum was gonorrhea, not nerves.

II

Our first date, Dick bought me dinner and played
"Moon River" (at my request) on his grand
piano. Soon after that, he moved to
San Diego, but drove up every week-
end to see me. We'd sleep at his "uncle"'s
quaint cottage in Benedict Canyon—part
of Jean Harlow's old estate. One night, Dick
spit out my cum in the bathroom sink; I

didn't ask why. The next morning, over
steak and eggs at Du-par's, Dick asked me to
think about San Diego, said he'd put
me through school. I liked him because he looked
like Sonny Bono, but sipped my coffee
and glanced away. Still, Dick picked up the bill.

III

More than anything, I wanted Charlie
to notice me. I spent one summer in
and around his swimming pool, talking to
his roommates, Rudy and Ned. All three of
them were from New York; I loved their stories
about the bars and baths, Fire Island, docks
after dark. I watched for Charlie, played board
games with Rudy and Ned, crashed on the couch.
Occasionally, Charlie came home with-
out a trick and I slipped into his bed
and slept next to him. Once, he rolled over
and kissed me—bourbon on his breath—and we
had sex at last. I was disappointed,
though: his dick was so small it didn't hurt.

IV

I made a list in my blue notebook: *Nick,
Dick, Charlie, Kevin, Howard, Tom. . . .* Kevin
had been the boyfriend of an overweight
girl I knew in high school. I spotted him
at a birthday bash—on a yacht—for an

eccentric blonde "starlet" who called herself
Countess Kerushka. Kevin and I left
together, ended up thrashing around
on his waterbed while his mother, who'd
just had a breakdown, slept in the next room.
Howard was Kevin's best friend. We went for
a drive one night, ended up parking. His
lips felt like sandpaper, and I couldn't
cum—but I added his name to the list.

V

Tom used spit for lubricant and fucked me
on the floor of his Volkswagen van while
his ex-lover (also named Tom) drove and
watched (I was sure) in the rearview mirror.
Another of his exes, Geraldo,
once cornered me in Tom's bathroom, kissed me
and asked: "What does he see in you?" At a
gay students' potluck, I refilled my wine
glass and watched Tom flirt with several other
men in the room. Outside, I paced, chain-smoked,
kicked a dent in his van and, when he came
looking for me, slugged him as hard as I
could. It was the end of the affair, but
only the beginning of my drinking.

VI

I ordered another wine cooler and
stared at his tight white pants—the outline of

his cock hung halfway down his thigh. After
a few more drinks, I asked him to dance to
"The First Time Ever I Saw Your Face." He
pressed himself against me and wrapped his arms
around my neck. I followed him to his
apartment but, once in bed, lost interest.
I told him I was hung up on someone.
As I got dressed, he said: "If you love him,
you should go to him." Instead, I drove back
to the bar, drank more, and picked up a blond
bodybuilder who, once we were in bed,
whispered "Give me your tongue"—which turned me off.

VII

As one young guy screwed another young guy
on the screen, the man sitting a couple
seats to my right—who'd been staring at me
for the longest time—slid over. He stared
a little longer, then leaned against me
and held a bottle of poppers to my
nose. When it wore off, he was rubbing my
crotch. Slowly, he unzipped my pants, pulled back
my underwear, lowered his head, licked some
pre-cum from the tip of my dick, and then
went down on it. As he sucked, he held the
bottle up. I took it, twisted the cap
off and sniffed, then looked up at the two guys
on the screen, then up at the black ceiling.

1989

YVETTE MIMIEUX
IN *HIT LADY*

All I remember is she drives a red
sports car and wears an ankh around her neck
and is instructed by The Company
to bump off some union bigwig because
he's scheduled to testify against a
Mafioso so she assumes a new
identity and starts dating him and
naturally he falls madly in love
with her not suspecting that this pert blonde
sitting on the other side of the pink
roses at the fancy restaurant is
actually the best assassin in
the business but when the time comes to pull
the trigger she breaks out in a cold sweat
and can't go through with it because all she
really wants is to quit The Company
and marry her struggling artist boyfriend
who's played by Dack Rambo and who of course
has no idea she kills people for a
living so she slips away and puts her
silencer in a storage locker at
the airport and flies to this picturesque
seaside village in Mexico where Dack
paints his unsalable masterpieces
and hoping to make a fresh start she tells

him everything but it turns out that Dack
works for The Company too so he shoots
her in the back on the beach and she dies.

1 9 8 9

LOVE POEM

At 4:30 a.m., I wake up
from a nightmare, bump
through the dark apartment
to pee, then sit and smoke
a cigarette in the living
room. When I get back
in bed, Ira wakes up
and says: "You're a sweet
man, do you know that?"
I tell him I've been having
bad dreams. I'm lying on
my back; he tells me to roll
on my side. As I do, he presses
against me from behind and
wraps his arm around my chest.
"You're safe now," he whispers
into my neck. "Go back to sleep.
You won't have any more bad dreams."

1989

LAST NIGHT

Ira knocked

one of the mums

in the makeshift vase

(a blue glass)

beside the bed

in his sleep

and we woke up

with white petals

in between

the sheets

1989

SUNDAY EVENING

Back from Boston,
Ira and I listen
to a tape of Anne Sexton
reading her poems—
part of my $87.00 binge
at the Grolier Book Shop
in Harvard Square.
Ira likes her "smoky" voice,
which is interrupted
by the kettle's shrill whistle.
I go into the kitchen
and prepare our tea:
Cranberry Cove for Ira,
Mellow Mint for me.
We sip, smoke and listen
to Anne. Toward the end
of the tape, Ira unpacks
the little black bag
of Godiva chocolates
and, one by one, eats
a butterscotch-filled coat
of arms, a light brown starfish
and a gold-foiled cherry cordial.
He chews and smiles.
I regret that I ate all
of mine on the train.
But wait! He offers me

his last one (which he
makes me earn with kisses):
a dark chocolate heart.

1 9 8 9

PEE SHY

I waited till
the boys' room
was empty, then
stood at one
of the urinals.
It always took
me a long
time, even when
I was alone.
Before I could
do it, someone
came in and
stood next to
me. Anxiously, I
glanced over. It
was Steve, the
good-looking son
of an actor
on a popular
detective series. He
was one grade
ahead of me.
Everyone said he
was stuck-up,
but I'd always
had a crush
on him. As
we stood beside

each other, my
legs began to
shake. I tried
to look straight
at the wall
in front of
me. Without realizing
it, however, I
pressed my whole
body against the
urinal. "Don't worry,"
Steve said disdainfully,
"I'm not looking
at you." He
pulled the handle
above his urinal,
zipped up his
pants. Out of
the corner of
my eye, I
watched him wash
his hands and
check his hair
in the mirror.
Then he left.

I can't remember
anything after that.
How long did
I stand there?
Did I rush

to my locker?
Was I late
for a period
I dreaded—woodshop,
drafting, gym? How
did I hide
my shame, convinced
as I was—
as I'm sure
I was—that
everyone would know
my hideous secret
before I even reached
my next class?

1990

ANSWER SONG

FOR TIM DLUGOS

Lesley Gore got her rival good
in the smash answer to "It's My Party,"
"Judy's Turn To Cry," when her
unfaithful boyfriend, Johnny, suddenly
came to his senses in the midst
of yet another apparently unchaperoned shindig.
I picture Judy—hot pink mini-dress
and ratted black hair—being swept away
by a flood of her own teenage tears.
In triumph, Lesley rehangs Johnny's ring
around her neck. She has no idea that
the British are coming, that her popularity
will wane and she'll watch her hits drop
off the charts like so many tinkling
heart-shaped charms, and that there she'll be:
a has-been at seventeen. Naturally
she'll finish high school and marry
Johnny. They'll have a couple of kids
and settle down in a yellow two-story
tract house with white-shuttered windows
and bright red flower beds. At the supermart,
Lesley will fill her cart with frozen dinners,
which she'll serve with a smile as the family
gathers round their first color TV.
Week after week, she'll exchange recipes,
attend PTA meetings and Tupperware parties,

usher Brownie troops past tar pits
and towering dinosaur bones. Whenever
she hears one of her songs on an oldie station,
she'll think about those extinct beasts.
She'll think about them too as, year
after year, she tosses headlines
into the trash: Vietnam, Nixon, Patty Hearst.
Then one afternoon—her children grown
and gone—she'll discover a strange
pair of earrings in the breast pocket
of Johnny's business suit. It's downhill
after that: curlers, migraines, fattening
midnight snacks. Or is it? She did,
after all, sing "You Don't Own Me,"
the first pop song with a feminist twist.
What if Lesley hears about women's lib?
What if she goes into therapy and begins
to question her attraction to emotionally
unavailable men? Suppose, under hypnosis,
she returns to her sixteenth birthday party,
relives all those tears, and learns that
it was Judy—not Johnny—she'd wanted
all along. There's no answer to that
song, of course, but I have
heard rumors.

1990

PLAYING WITH DOLLS

Every weekend morning, I'd sneak downstairs to play
with my sisters' Barbie dolls. They had all
of them: Barbie, Ken, Allan, Midge, Skipper and
Skooter. They even had the little freckled boy,
Ricky ("Skipper's Friend"), and Francie, "Barbie's
'MOD'ern cousin." Quietly, I'd set the dolls

in front of their wardrobe cases, take the dolls'
clothes off miniature plastic hangers, and play
until my father woke up. There were several Barbies—
blonde ponytail, black bubble, brunette flip—all
with the same pointed tits, which (odd for a boy)
didn't interest me as much as the dresses and

accessories. I'd finger each glove and hat and
necklace and high heel, then put them on the dolls.
Then I'd invent elaborate stories. A "creative" boy,
I could entertain myself for hours. I liked to play
secretly like that, though I often got caught. All
my father's tirades ("Boys don't play with Barbies!

It isn't *normal*!") faded as I slipped Barbie's
perfect figure into her stunning ice blue and
sea green satin and tulle formal gown. All
her outfits had names like "Fab Fashion," "Doll's
Dream" and "Golden Evening"; Ken's were called "Play
Ball!," "Tennis Pro," "Campus Hero" and "Fountain Boy,"

which came with two tiny sodas and spoons. Model boy
that he was, Ken hunted, fished, hit home runs. Barbie's
world revolved around garden parties, dances, play
and movie dates. A girl with bracelets and scarves and
sunglasses and fur stoles. . . . "Boys don't play with dolls!"
My parents were arguing in the living room. "All

boys do." As always, my mother defended me. "All
sissies!" snarled my father. "He's a creative boy,"
my mother responded. I stuffed all the dresses and dolls
and shoes back into the black cases that said "Barbie's
Wonderful World" in swirling pink letters and
clasped them shut. My sisters, awake now, wanted to play

with me. "I can't play," I said, "Dad's upset." All
day, he stayed upset. Finally, my mother came upstairs
    and said: "You're a boy,
David. Forget about Barbies. Stop playing with dolls."

1990

IT'S NOT UNUSUAL

My platinum blonde hair

held in place

by a paisley scarf

as I speed down

Route 66

in the pink convertible

I won

behind Door Number 3

1990

THE BOMB SHELTER

The photograph on the front page of the paper showed a supermarket after an attack of mass hysteria: shelves stripped bare as Old Mother Hubbard's. At home, my mother filled our pantry with cans of Campbell's soup and Spam, while my father—who had quit smoking on the very day the Surgeon General announced that cigarettes could be hazardous to health—hired a contractor to install a bomb shelter in our backyard. Our dream of a swimming pool (my brother and sisters and I were always begging our parents to put one in) went up in smoke as, out of nowhere, a crew of potbellied construction workers appeared and started digging in the same spot we'd buried a pet turtle, goldfish, rabbit, and guinea pig. A few months later, my father proudly took us on a tour. We climbed down a ladder and huddled in darkness behind him. Like a strict teacher pointing at a blackboard with a stick, he waved his flashlight at a couple of sleeping bags and boxes of provisions, at a port-a-potty, and at the handle of the air vent we'd all have to take turns rotating in order to breathe. "Will I be able to bring my comic books?" I asked. "No. No toys." In the first place, my family were the last people on earth I wanted to sit with in a tiny subterranean room with a port-a-potty and a five-month supply of Spam and wait however long it took for the radiation to wear off. But without my comic books, I decided it would be better to take my chances above ground. I wondered if they would drop The Bomb while I was at school. In Mrs. Bialosky's class, we'd started having drills. Suddenly, in the middle of a lesson, she'd call out "Drop," and we'd all crouch underneath our desks with our hands cupped over our heads. My parents informed us that we were not to tell any of our friends about the bomb shelter. It was a secret. If there were a war, they explained, our neighbors might show up with guns and try to get in. They might even try to kill us—they might be that desperate. I imagined the Hillsingers and DeMarios and Scotts marching down Comanche Avenue carrying baseball bats and rifles—friends suddenly turned enemies, like in an episode of *The Twilight Zone*. "Your father will have a gun, too," said my mother. "To protect us with."

As time went by, the drop-drills and discreet lectures occurred less and less. One Halloween, I wanted to turn the bomb shelter into a haunted house—with spider webs, skeletons, and flying ghosts—but my father forbid it. For a while, he periodically changed the water and canned goods, and aired it out. Eventually, though, it just sat there in the middle of our backyard, a neglected reminder of my father's fear.

1990

IT

was over
yesterday

but tonight
seems all right:

no tv

warm sheets

his knee in my back

sleep-breathing

lilacs

1991

WHAT IRA SAID
IN HIS SLEEP

1

Lights out

Brassiere too tight

2

What did you do?

What didn't you do?

Taxes

3

Indian Chief

4

Ow! Fatso!

5

Go fuck yourself!

How dare you talk to me that way!

6

Oranges

Innocuous things, mostly

7

Is it sit-down or buffet?

1991

THE TEN BEST EPISODES OF *THE PATTY DUKE SHOW*

1. Patty cheats on a computerized intelligence test and is pronounced a genius.

2. Ross blackmails Patty and Cathy by tape recording their conversation at a slumber party.

3. Patty is cast as Cleopatra in the school play, but gets stage fright on opening night.

4. Patty writes a novel entitled *I Was a Teenage Teenager*.

5. Cathy wears Patty's expensive new dress to a piano concert and accidentally spills punch on it.

6. Patty and Cathy run against each other for class president.

7. Frankie Avalon's car breaks down in front of the Lane house.

8. Patty raffles a date with Richard for the church bazaar, then gets jealous and tries to buy all the tickets back.

9. Patty's tonsils are taken out by a dreamboat doctor (played by Troy Donahue).

10. Patty pretends to be Cathy and flirts with Richard to see if he'll be faithful to her.

1991

THE SHOWER SCENE
IN *PSYCHO*

She closes the bathroom door to secure her privacy, slips off her robe, drapes it over the toilet bowl, steps into the bath, and closes the shower curtain behind her, filling the frame with a flash of white (5.89).

Shortly before midnight on Friday, August 8, 1969, Manson called together Family members Tex Watson, Susan Atkins, Patricia Krenwinkel, and Linda Kasabian to give them their instructions.

From Marion viewed through the translucent shower curtain, Hitchcock cuts to (5.90), framed from within the space bounded by the curtain. At the top center of this frame is the shower head.

Fortified with drugs and armed with a gun, knives, rope, and wire cutters, they were to take one of the Family cars and go to 10050 Cielo Drive in Beverly Hills.

Marion rises into the frame. Water begins to stream from the shower head. She looks up into the stream of water and begins to wash her neck and arms. Her expression is ecstatic as the water brings her body to life (5.91).

In the secluded ranch-style house at the end of the cul-de-sac, Sharon Tate, aged twenty-six, a star of *Valley of the Dolls* and now eight and a half months pregnant, was entertaining three guests: Hollywood hair stylist Jay Sebring, coffee heiress Abigail Folger, and Folger's lover Voytek Frykowski.

At this point, there is a cut to Marion's vision of the shower head, water radiating from it in all directions like a sunburst (5.92).

(I had just turned sixteen, was about to start my junior year at Chatsworth High.)

Hitchcock cuts to the shower head viewed from the side (5.93) at the precise moment Marion turns her naked back to the stream of water.

(Every Saturday, I went to the matinee at the Chatsworth Cinema.)

Marion takes pleasure in the stream of water emanating from the shower head (5.94).

(The theater was next to the Thrifty Drug where, two summers before, I'd bought a copy of *Valley of the Dolls*.)

From the side view of the shower head, Hitchcock cuts back to Marion, still ecstatic (5.95). Then he cuts to a setup that places the camera where the tile wall of the shower "really" is.

(I took it home and hid it under my bed. I knew it was the kind of book my mother wouldn't let me read.)

The shower curtain, to which Marion's back is turned, hangs from a bar at the top of the screen, and forms a frame-within-a-frame that almost completely fills the screen (5.96).

(The summer before that, she'd found the box of newspaper clippings on the top shelf of my closet.)

The camera begins to move forward, until the bar at the top becomes excluded from the screen (5.97).

(For weeks, I'd been cutting out articles about murders.)

Synchronized with this movement of the camera, Marion slides out of the frame, so that the shower curtain completely fills the screen (5.98).

(It started with the eight nurses in Chicago. Right after that was the Texas sniper. Then there was the politician's daughter who was bludgeoned and stabbed to death in her sleep.)

A shadowy figure, barely visible through the shower curtain, enters the door that can just be made out in the background. It steps forward toward the camera, its form doubled by and blending into its shadow cast on the translucent curtain (5.99).

After cutting telephone wires to the house, they gained access to the property by scaling fences, careful not to set off alarms.

The curtain is suddenly wrenched open and a silhouetted knife-wielding figure is revealed (5.100).

As they walked up the drive, a car approached from the house and caught them in its headlights.

The silhouetted figure is symmetrically flanked by the raised knife on the one side and the light bulb on the other (5.101).

At the wheel was eighteen-year-old Steven Parent, who had been visiting the caretaker, William Garretson. In his apartment over the garage, Garretson listened to his stereo with headphones on, unaware of what was happening just yards away.

When the camera reverses field to Marion, turned away (5.102), her figure displaces the silhouette in (5.101).

Parent slowed down and asked who they were, and what they wanted.

It is through the silhouetted figure's eyes that Marion is now viewed, as she turns around clockwise until she looks right into the camera (5.103). What she sees makes her open her mouth to scream.

Watson's response was to place the barrel of a .22 against the youth's head and blast off four rounds.

Jump cut to a closer view of Marion's face (5.104).

(I didn't know why I was so fascinated by murder.)

Second jump cut to an extreme closeup of her wide-open mouth (5.105).

(I told my mother the clippings were "research," that one day I wanted to write about crime. She made me throw them away.)

From Marion's point of view, the silhouetted figure strikes out violently with its knife (5.106).

Watson slit one of the window-screens, crawled into the house, and admitted the others through the front door. Linda Kasabian remained outside as lookout.

The knife slashes down for the first time (5.107).

Frykowski, who was asleep on a sofa in the living room, woke up to find Watson standing over him, gun in hand.

The knife slashes through the corner of the screen. The arm and the knife remain silhouetted (5.108).

Atkins reported to Watson that there were three more people in the house. He ordered her to bring them into the living room, which she did at knife-point.

In a slightly closer variant of (5.107), the knife is again raised, its blade gleaming in the light.

(The first time I saw *Psycho*, I was baby-sitting for a couple who lived at the end of a dark cul-de-sac.)

This shot frames part of Marion's body along with the intruder's arm, still shadowy in the frame (5.109).

(I prayed they'd stay out late. I wouldn't have been allowed to watch it at home.)

Viewed from overhead, the shower-curtain bar cuts across the screen. As Marion tries to fend it off, the knife strikes three times (5.110).

(There was a storm that night: rain and branches beat against the windows. I waited anxiously for "The Late Show" to come on.)

Marion's face fills the screen, expressing bewilderment and pain (5.111).

(They'd cut most of the shower scene for TV.)

Marion holds onto the shadowy arm as it weaves three times in a spiraling movement (5.112).

(I felt cheated.)

Reprise of (5.111).

(I wanted to be scared.)

Reprise of (5.112).

When Sebring was told to lie face down on the floor, he tried to grab Watson's gun, whereupon Watson shot him through the lung.

Another variant of (5.107). The knife again slashes down.

Watson looped one end of a nylon rope around Sebring's neck, threw the free end over a beam and tied it around the necks of Folger and Tate, who had to stand upright to avoid being choked.

Marion turns her face away, her head almost sliding out of the frame (5.113).

Watson ordered Atkins to stab Frykowski, who got to his feet and ran outside. Atkins pursued him onto the lawn, and knifed him in the back.

The slashing knife (5.114).

Watson followed, shot Frykowski twice and, when his gun jammed, continued to beat him over the head with the butt.

A shot of Marion recoiling, still bewildered (5.115).

In the living room, the two women struggled to free themselves from their dual noose.

This shot approximates (5.114), but this time the knife slashes through the center of the frame.

Like Frykowski, Folger got as far as the front lawn. She was chased down by Krenwinkel, who stabbed her repeatedly.

Reprise of (5.115). Marion's bewildered reaction.

Watson also descended upon her, after first knifing Sebring.

The hand and knife come into clear focus. Water bounces off the glinting metal of the blade (5.116).

Then they turned on the heavily pregnant Miss Tate.

Juxtaposition of blade and flesh (5.117).

(In secret, I read *Valley of the Dolls* several times.)

Marion recoils, but still looks dazed, entranced (5.118).

(My mother found my hiding place and made me throw the book away.)

A low-angle view facing the door. The knife slashes through the frame (5.119).

(I bicycled to Thrifty Drug, bought another copy, and snuck it into the house.)

Marion's back and arms. The intruder's arm again enters the frame (5.120).

Watson told Atkins to stab her.

Closeup of Marion's face. She is now clearly in agony (5.121).

When the actress begged to be spared for the sake of her unborn child, Atkins sneered, "Look, bitch, I don't care . . . "

Blood drips down Marion's writhing legs (5.122).

"I have no mercy for you."

Marion turns her face from the camera. The knife enters the frame (5.123).

She hesitated nonetheless, so Watson inflicted the first wound.

Reprise of (5.122), with a greater flow of blood.

Within moments, Atkins and Krenwinkel joined in, stabbing her sixteen times.

The screen flashes white as the camera momentarily frames only the bare tile wall. Marion's hand, viewed from up close and out of focus, enters and then exits the frame (5.124).

Finally, Susan Atkins dipped a towel in Sharon Tate's blood and wrote the word "Pig" on the front door.

The intruder exits (5.125).

It was not until the next day, when they watched TV at the Spahn Movie Ranch in Chatsworth, that any of them knew who they had murdered.

Marion's hand pressed against the white tile (5.126). It slowly slides down the wall.

(The same summer I read *Valley of the Dolls*, the book was being made into a movie.)

Marion's hand drops out of the frame and her body slowly slides down the wall. She turns to face forward as her back slips down, the camera tilting down with her (5.127).

(After Patty Duke, my childhood idol, was cast in one of the lead roles, it was practically all I could think about.)

She looks forward and reaches out, as if to touch someone or something she cannot see (5.128). The camera pulls slowly away. Then her hand changes its path.

(I made a scrapbook of pictures I had clipped from movie magazines:)

In extreme close-up, Marion's hand continues its movement until it grasps the shower curtain in the left foreground of the frame (5.129).

(Patty reaching for a bottle of pills, tears streaming down her face;)

The shower curtain, unable to bear her weight, pulls away from the support-ing bar, as the hooks give way one by one (5.130).

(Barbara Parkins in a white bathrobe, collapsed on the beach;)

Marion's arm falls, followed by her head and torso. Her body spills over from within the shower, and lands on the curtain (5.131).

(Sharon Tate in a low-cut beaded dress, her blonde hair piled up high.)

From (5.131), there follows a cut to the reprise of the sunburst shot of the shower head viewed frontally.

(Later, when the movie premiered at Grauman's Chinese, I begged my mother to take me to see it.)

The camera cuts to Marion's legs, blood mixing with the water (5.132), and begins to move to the left, following this flow of water and blood.

("Wait till it comes to the Chatsworth Cinema," she said.)

At the moment Marion's legs are about to pass out of the frame, the drain comes into view (5.133).

(The Saturday the bodies were discovered, I saw *Mackenna's Gold*, a western starring Omar Sharif and Gregory Peck.)

The camera reframes to center the drain as it tracks in toward it, so that the blackness within appears about to engulf the screen (5.134).

(The "Coming Attraction" was for *Goodbye, Columbus*, a serious adult drama.)

At this point, there is a slow dissolve from the drain to an eye, viewed in extreme closeup (5.135).

(The following week I would ride up to see it, but they wouldn't let me in. It was recommended for mature audiences.)

This eye, which fixes the camera in its gaze, displaces the drain in the frame, and appears to peer out from within it (5.136).

(We lived a few miles from the Spahn Movie Ranch.)

The camera spirals out clockwise as though unscrewing itself, disclosing the eye, Marion's, dead (5.137).

(There was a newspaper machine in front of the Chatsworth Cinema. I always chained my bicycle to it.)

The camera keeps spiraling out until we have a full view of Marion's face (5.138).

(When I left the theater that afternoon, I saw the face of Sharon Tate.)

Death has frozen it in inexpressiveness, although there is a tear welled in the corner of her eye (5.139).

(Then I read the headline as my eyes adjusted to the sun.)

1991

FAMILY PORTRAIT, 1963

My father sits in his dark
armchair, under a store-bought
painting of Paris,
reading *Fortune* magazine.
As a young man
he read Shakespeare and Poe,
dreamed of being an artist
(my mother tells me this).
Now he works somewhere
every day, and at night
barks orders: *Sit up*
straight! Get out
of my sight! Stop
that racket! Goddamnit!
Turn down the TV!

*

My mother sobs
behind her locked bedroom door:
Your father's a tyrant.
Go away. Other nights
she has migraines
and lies in agony
on the living room couch
while my father yells
Get up, you fat slob!
Do some work around here!

I do chores for her, sneak
her cigarettes and chocolate bars
into the house, hide them
in the pots and pans.
When they fight, I lock
myself in the pink bathroom,
play with the soap roses
in the shell-shaped dish,
with her delicate perfume bottles
and her Avon lipsticks—
so many names for red.

*

My brother collects
baseball cards,

         for my father

builds model airplanes
and race cars,

         for my father

watches *Gunsmoke*
and *Combat*,

         for my father

joins Boy Scouts
and Little League,

         for my father

mows the lawn,
pulls the weeds,

rakes the leaves,

for my father

excels in batting
and tackling
and running,

for my father

and brings home
poor grades on
his report card.

And is punished
by my father.

*

One of my sisters stands
at a miniature bassinet
changing the diaper
on her Hush-a-Bye Baby.
(Someday she'll have four
children of her own, bounced
checks, bruises and black eyes,
a husband she'll try, repeatedly,
to leave.) With a makebelieve
iron, she unwrinkles the doll's
frilly pink party frock.
She's my father's favorite:
the quietest one.

*

My other sister learns
to walk early, is always
breaking things. One night,
when my father barks an order
at the dinner table, she puts her
little hands on her hips
and barks back: *You're
not the boss! I am!*
After a tense silence,
my father's face seems to
crack, and he laughs.
Then we all laugh.

*

At school, I spend
most of the lunch hour
in the library.
I belong to
the Bookworm Club:
the more I read,
the higher my name moves up
the bespectacled paper worm
on the bulletin board.
I'm reading the *Little House*
series and the blue biographies
of famous Americans,
but only the women:
Pocahontas, Martha Washington,
Betsy Ross.

In the afternoon,
I do homework
at the kitchen table
while my mother cooks and cleans.
I ask her questions,
but there's a lot she doesn't know.
She hands me a warm Toll House cookie,
tells me to look for the answer
in the book.

Around 4:30, she sprays
lilac-scented Glade
to cover up the smell
of her cigarettes.
When my father's car
pulls in the driveway,
she franticly sets out
napkins, glasses, handfuls
of silverware.
Make yourself scarce.
I gather my books and papers
together, rush down the hall
to my bedroom, hear
the door slam.

1991

AT THE GLASS ONION, 1971

He stood behind me while I played pinball
in a corner of the bar. He rubbed his
hard-on against my jeans. It was the fall
after the rape. Nineteen, I was a wiz

at the game, but as he ran his large hand
along the inside of my thighs and said
how much he wanted to take me home and
fuck me, I glanced up at the flashing red

and white lights and let my last ball slide past
the flippers. Instead of getting more change,
as I'd said, I bypassed the bar and dashed
into the bathroom. No lock, though. "You're strange,"

he said, tugging. I looked down at his head
till someone knocked, stuffed my wet cock, and fled.

1992

ANCIENT HISTORY

1949 Hedy Lamarr snips Victor Mature's hair while he sleeps, but he regains his strength in time to heave the pillars apart. George Sanders, an urbane leader of Philistines, raises his glass with rueful approval as the temple collapses about him.

1955 Condemned to wander the Mediterranean after the fall of Troy, Kirk Douglas is bewitched by Silvana Mangano, while his crew are transformed into swine.

1956 Charlton Heston turns his staff into a snake, refuses Anne Baxter's advances, frees the Jews from Pharaoh Yul Brynner, majestically leads the Exodus and parts the Red Sea, and witnesses a rather jet-propelled inscription of the Ten Commandments.

1959 Gina Lollobrigida smoulders and heaves in a series of plunging gowns, drives a chariot with abandon, dances in a curious balletic orgy, and seduces Solomon (Yul Brynner) for political purposes.

Charlton Heston wins a chariot race and an Academy Award.

1960 Kirk Douglas excels in gladiatorial school, falls in love with Jean Simmons, and rebels after a private games staged for Roman general Laurence Olivier. Olivier makes a casual (but unmissable) come-on to slave-boy Tony Curtis.

1961 Stewart Granger rescues the Hebrews from the city of Sodom, whose depravity consists largely of dancing girls, sprawled bodies sleeping off orgies, and Stanley Baker chasing Lot's daughter (Rossana Podesta) into the tall grass. When fire and brimstone are about to descend on her palace, wicked queen Anouk Aimée is called upon to deliver the memorable line: "It's just a summer storm. Nothing to worry about." The city is then overwhelmed in splendid ruin, Granger and Co. escaping to high ground, all except Pier Angeli, who looks back and is turned into a pillar of salt.

1963   Elizabeth Taylor enters Rome enthroned on an enormous Sphinxmobile hauled by sweating musclemen. After Rex's assassination and Dick's suicide, Liz outwits Roddy McDowall by sticking her hand in a basket of figs.

1964   Christopher Plummer shows tyrannical tendencies which alarm the dead Emperor's protégé, Stephen Boyd (his hair dyed blond and marcelled), who is in love with Plummer's sister, Sophia Loren, whom Plummer marries off to Omar Sharif. Confusion ensues: the talk is endless, and there are ambushes, troop decimations, high-speed chariot crashes, and a ridiculous spear-duel between Boyd and Plummer (in the Forum, of all places), which ends with Plummer dead and Boyd nobly refusing the imperial crown. To Dimitri Tiomkin's pensive cello, Sophia prays to Vesta in a fabulous fur-trimmed cape.

1965   An all-star cast populates the Holy Land: Max von Sydow, Dorothy McGuire, Charlton Heston, David McCallum, Roddy McDowall, Sidney Poitier, Carroll Baker, Pat Boone, Telly Savalas, Angela Lansbury, Martin Landau, José Ferrer, Claude Rains, Donald Pleasance, Van Heflin, Ed Wynn. Sal

Mineo is healed by Christ, as is Shelley Winters, who crieth: "I am cured! I am cured!" John Wayne, the centurion managing the Crucifixion, utters: "I believe this truly was the Son of God."

1966   Clutching his fig leaf, Michael Parks is expelled from Paradise; Richard Harris kills his brother, Franco Nero, in an Irish frenzy; John Huston builds a massive Ark and potters among pairs of elephants, hippos, penguins, polar bears, and kangaroos; Stephen Boyd (wearing heavy eye shadow) climbs an impressive Tower of Babel and has his language confounded; God talks to patriarch George C. Scott.

Raquel Welch, clad in a bikini of wild-beast skins, is carried off by a squawking pterodactyl.

1993

FLUFF

FOR LYNN CROSBIE

O Fluff, no one knows who you are.
You were produced for one brief year
(nineteen seventy-one) after
Mattel discontinued Skooter,
Barbie's little sister Skipper's
best friend. The toy company feared
the first generation of Bar-
bie consumers, baby boomers
nearing their teens, would disappear
once puberty struck. So you were
invented, a fresh face to lure
the next wave of greedy youngsters,
pink pocketbooks full of gener-
ous allowances or hard-earned
baby-sitting money, to stores
with well-stocked doll departments, where
you were displayed, a wide-eyed, cheer-
ful, puffy-cheeked tomboy, blonde hair
in twin ponytails, wearing your
green, yellow and orange striped over-
alls. You came with a skateboard, per-
fect for cruisin' the park after
school with your pal, Growing Up Skipper.
Mattel executives were sure
that you would be a best-seller,
but your short shelf life was over

almost as soon as it had start-
ed. In essence, Fluff, you flopped. More-
over, today, when collectors
are willing to pay ten dollars
for a pair of Barbie shoes, you're
not worth a lot, even NRFB (Never
Removed From Box). I remember
you, though. As a child, I smeared your
cheeks with grease and slid you under
my girlfriend's orange plastic camper.
Barbie dolls were far too mature
for a girl like me to endure.
But not your flat-chested allure!
O tiny mechanic! The cars
I made you tune up and repair!
The engines you put together!
The windshields you washed, the batter-
ies you changed, tires you filled with air!
After work, you'd smoke a cigar-
ette, then skateboard home in the dark.
O smudged kid! O angry loner!
All my friends think that I'm bizarre
'cause Fluff, no one knows who you are.

1994

ESSAY WITH
MOVABLE PARTS

From Broadway to Hollywood, this is the fastest-selling, most whispered-about novel of the year. *And no wonder!* Jacqueline Susann's VALLEY OF THE DOLLS reveals more about the secret, drug-filled, love-starved, sex-satiated nightmare world of show business than any book ever published.

*

These tiny, whimsical characters were manufactured by Mattel from 1966–1971. Their name came from the combination of Little and Kid; thus the name Liddle Kiddles was born.

A wide variety of dolls was marketed, ranging in size from 3/4″ to 4″ tall. The larger of these dolls are marked at the base of their neck "© Mattel Inc." Their bodies are made of a soft vinyl material and have wires in them that enable them to bend.

Kiddles came in just about everything imaginable—jewelry, perfume bottles, lollipops, ice cream cones, soda bottles and tea cups.

*

Show business—a world where sex is a success weapon, where love is a smiling mask for hate and envy, where the past is obscured and the future is oblivion. In this sick world where slipping youth and fading beauty are twin specters, the magic tickets to peace are "dolls"—the insider's word for pills—pep pills, sleeping pills, red pills, blue pills, "up" pills, "down" pills—pills to chase the truth away.

*

One of the most sought-after series by collectors are the Storybook Kiddles. These truly enchanting little dolls were created around storybook characters and nursery rhymes.

A series of seven were made: Liddle Biddle Peep, Liddle Middle Muffet, Liddle Red Riding Hiddle, Sleeping Biddle, Cinderiddle, Alice in Wonderiddle and Peter Paniddle.

*

When Pugsley abandons his pet octopus to befriend a puppy, wear a Boy Scout uniform, and play baseball, Gomez and Morticia fear their child is becoming normal.

*

The Kosmic Kiddles Series, a zany little crew of Martians, had their own spaceship to ride in and a purple plastic rock to park on. There were four Kiddles in this series: Yellow Fello, Greeny Meeny, Purple Glurple and Bluey Blooper.

*

Investigators from the MSO (Mysterious Space Objects) mistake the Addams Family for aliens while the family is enjoying a moonlight picnic and snail hunt.

*

Being an avid Kiddle collector myself, one of my fondest memories as a young girl is of my sister and me sitting on Granny's rug and zooming our Kosmic Kiddles into outer space and back to earth again. As we were tucked into our beds at night, we were reminded of the fun we'd had as our Kiddles glowed back at us in the dark.

*

Visiting dignitaries from an Iron Curtain country assume the Addamses are the typical uncultured American family. After witnessing Morticia's carnivorous plants and Uncle Fester's penchant for electricity, the officials conclude that Americans have vastly progressed in technology.

*

Player turns crank (A) which
rotates gears (B) causing lever
(C) to move and push stop sign
against shoe (D).

*

Morticia prods the family to donate objects of art from the Addams home to a charity auction. These treasured items include Wednesday's headless Mary, Queen of Scots doll, the old flogging table, and a shrunken head. Gomez donates Pugsley's beloved wolfs'-head clock, but decides to bid at the charity auction to retrieve it. Thing's box is accidentally donated as well.

*

Shoe tips bucket holding metal
ball (E).

*

Meet Cathy who's lived most everywhere
From Zanzibar to Barclay Square
But Patty's only seen the sights
A girl can see from Brooklyn Heights
What a crazy pair

*

Ball rolls down rickety stairs (F)
and into rain pipe (G) which

leads it to hit helping hand rod
(H). This causes bowling ball (I)
to fall from top of helping hand
rod through thing-a-ma-jig (J)
and bathtub (K) to land on div-
ing board (L).

*

But they're cousins
Identical cousins all the way
One pair of matching bookends
Different as night and day

*

Weight of bowling ball cata-
pults diver (M) through the air
and right into wash tub (N)
causing cage (O) to fall from top
of post (P) and trap unsuspect-
ing mouse.

*

Where Cathy adores a minuet
The Ballet Russe and crepe suzettes
Our Patty loves to rock 'n' roll
A hot dog makes her lose control
What a wild duet

*

She comes in a lovely dress which has a red "velvet" top and a skirt made of white lace over taffeta. Chatty Cathy's pretty hair is in twin ponytails. You can get her as a blonde, brunette, or new auburn. There's a complete line of Dress-Up Fashions for her, too.

*

Still they're cousins
Identical cousins and you'll find
They laugh alike they walk alike
At times they even talk alike
You can lose your mind
When cousins are two of a kind

*

One record is already in the doll, so to make Chatty Cathy talk to you just pull her Chatty-Ring out gently as far as it will go (about 10 inches). When you release the Chatty-Ring, Chatty Cathy will talk to you!

*

After watching Ginger sing "I Wanna Be Loved By You" to entertain the castaways, Mary Ann, wishing she could be like Ginger Grant, falls and hits her head, causing her to believe she is Ginger. After examining Mary Ann, the Professor suggests the castaways go along with her fantasy until he can come up with a cure, advising Ginger to dress like Mary Ann.

*

When you want to turn the record over, or change the record, put Chatty Cathy on her right side. You'll see the record slot, with the lever, on her left side, like this.

Move the lever to lock position (A). Now turn Chatty Cathy over on her left side, and the record will drop out.

Put Chatty Cathy on her right side (with button still in position A). Drop the record into the slot and gently move the button back to position (B). The side of the record you want to hear should face up toward the lever.

*

Mary Ann, dressed like Ginger, asks Gilligan to practice a scene with her, kissing him passionately, while the other men dress Ginger like Mary Ann, using one of Lovey's wigs. That night Ginger serves the castaways an unappetizing dinner and later finds Mary Ann shortening all her gowns.

*

The records which come with Chatty
Cathy include:

Let's Get Acquainted (2 sides)
Let's Talk Scary
Let's Make Animal Noises
Let's Say Proverbs
Let's Make Up a Poem
    (Listen to Chatty Cathy's line—
    Then make up your own to rhyme!)
Let's Play "If I Were Mother"
Let's Be Ridiculous
Let's Be Good
Let's Pretend We're Famous

*

The next day when Mary Ann sees Ginger hanging up laundry without her wig, she faints. Explaining that Mary Ann is experiencing traumatic shock, the Professor decides to try hypnosis. Gilligan peeks through the window to watch the Professor hypnotize Mary Ann, falling into a trance as the Professor tells her she'll become Mary Ann when she hears the name Mary Ann. The Skipper pulls Gilligan away from the window, and when the Professor wakes Mary Ann and says her name, she remains convinced that she's Ginger.

*

Anita: I had a great collection when I was a kid. Lots of dolls and outfits. My favorite Barbie was a redhead with a bubble do. She had bright red lips. I loved to

dress her in her nightclub gown—it came with long
black gloves and a pink scarf. I'd stand her in front of
the microphone and she'd sing songs like Brenda Lee's
"I'm Sorry."

*

When the Skipper finds Gilligan taking a bath in his hut and mentions
Mary Ann, Gilligan screams, splashes the Skipper, and chases him
from the hut. Gilligan, thinking he's Mary Ann, wraps himself in a
towel and runs to the girls' hut, where he finds Ginger wearing what
he thinks are his clothes. After pulling Gilligan out from under Gin-
ger's bed, the Professor hypnotizes him back to his normal self.

*

Once I got too old to play with them, I packed them
away. I ironed each dress and folded them in pink tis-
sue paper. I wrapped the dolls up, too. I put every-
thing in shoe boxes that I taped shut and stacked in the
back of the hall closet. I was saving them for when I
had a daughter.

*

VALLEY OF THE DOLLS is the
story of three of the most ex-
citing women you'll ever meet;
women who were too tough or
too talented not to reach the top
... and unable to enjoy it once
they were there!

*

My parents divorced when I was little. I lived with my mother. As time went on, she grew really angry with my father and wouldn't let me visit him. I think she thought I saw him anyway. One day, when I came home from school, she said that she'd thrown away all my dolls. I raced outside, but the garbage men had already taken them away. All she said was: "I needed the closet space."

*

ANNE WELLES: the icy New England beauty who melted for the wrong Mr. Right . . . an Adonis famous for his infidelity.

*

Finally, I told my mother that I was seeing my father all along. That's when things *really* went downhill. On the day I turned eighteen, I came home from my after-school job and saw all my belongings on the front lawn. My clothes, my books, even my white canopy bed—right there on the front lawn! She threw me out, even changed the locks.

*

NEELY O'HARA: the lovable kid from vaudeville who became a star and a monster.

*

Rae: My parents bought me all the Kiddles I wanted. Kiddles were my life. Calamity Jiddle and her little plastic rocking horse. Soapy Skiddle and her bathtub and towel. Millie Middle with her sandbox and pail. Telly Viddle with her tiny TV set and box of Mattel pretzels. I had so many, I filled several pink Kiddles Kollector cases. I even had some in my vinyl 3-story Kiddle Klubhouse.

*

JENNIFER NORTH: the blonde goddess who survived every betrayal committed against her magnificent body except the last.

*

I have a younger cousin whose parents aren't as well-off as mine. Growing up, she always wanted what I had—clothes, games, books, dolls. For years she tried to get her hands on my Kiddles. I never let her near them. She played too rough.

*

Each of them was bred in the Babylons of Broadway and Hollywood. Each of them

learned about making love,
making money, and making
believe. Each of them rode the
crest of the wave. And each of
them came finally to the Valley
of the Dolls.

*

My cousin's interest in my Kiddles seemed to grow in
proportion to my collection. The more Kiddles I got,
the more she begged to play with them every time they
visited.

*

The Brady boys are having a hard time adjusting to living with girls in
their house. The difficulties reach a boiling point when the girls want
to move into the boys' backyard clubhouse. Mike agrees that the boys
should have their own space, but eventually he changes his mind, in
the spirit of sharing and family unity.

*

One time my aunt and my cousin came over when I
wasn't home. My mother let my cousin into my room.
When I got back, I found my Kiddle collection—com-
pletely trashed! She'd cut off all their hair, written with
magic markers on their little bodies, ripped off some
of their heads. And she didn't get in trouble for it!
"She's just expressing herself," said my aunt. "She's
artistic."

Years later, she ended up marrying one of my husband's cousins. She'd met him at our wedding.

*

Someone has stolen Kitty Karry-All, Cindy's favorite doll. Cindy suspects Bobby, who had angrily told her that he hoped her doll got lost. Bobby didn't steal the doll, but he has his own problems, too: someone has stolen his kazoo. Even with that, Bobby does try to make amends by buying a new Kitty Karry-All for Cindy—but Cindy refuses to accept the present because it's not the real Kitty. Eventually, both items turn up—in Tiger's doghouse.

*

The first troll doll was carved from wood in the 1950s by a Dane named Thomas Dam, who made it as a birthday gift for his teenage daughter. It was a homely little imp with a spray of woolly white hair, a flaring nose, jug ears, big black eyes, a toothless grin, and spatulate, four-fingered hands—an effigy of the mythical Scandinavian elves visible only to children and childlike grown-ups. If one of these pixies is ever captured, he is supposed to provide his captor with a lifetime of good fortune.

*

Marcia is devastated when she learns she has to wear braces. Even though her family assures her she still looks pretty, she becomes even more upset when Alan, a boy who was going to ask her to the school dance, cancels on her. She assumes it was because of the braces. To make her feel better, Greg, Alice, and her parents try to con three other boys into taking her to the dance. All three show up at the Brady residence at the same time—as does Alan!

*

A Danish toy-store owner encouraged Dam to manufacture more of them. Known as Dammit Dolls, his comical gnomes arrived in the U.S.A. in the early sixties, at a time when cuteness of all sorts was glorified—from the Singing Nun with her lilting ballad "Dominique" and the adorable mop-top Beatles to 1963's number-one television show, *The Beverly Hillbillies*. In the fall of 1963, college coeds began adopting troll dolls for their dorm rooms and carrying around miniature ones in their purses.

*

The children have been moaning to Mike and Carol that the house is too small, so Mike decides to sell. But then the kids realize their attachment is too strong, and so to scare off prospective buyers and change Mike's mind, they make it seem as if the house is haunted. When a house hunter shows up, so do two ghosts—actually Bobby and Cindy in sheets. When Mike sees the extreme measures the kids have been taking, he realizes he can never sell.

*

Suddenly, they were a phenomenon. That same year, the belief that a troll doll provided its owner good luck was attested to by Betty Miller, the daredevil pilot who retraced Amelia Earhart's long-distance flight with only a troll doll as her copilot. Troll dolls soon became the second-biggest-selling doll of the decade, after Barbie.

*

I'm Chi-qui-ta Ba-na-na and I've come to say,
I want to be your friend to-day and ev-ry day
I come from sun-ny trop-ics where the skies are blue
I wear a happy smile just like the sun-shine too

*

Original trolls were naked, but as the fad caught on, they were sold in tunics, diapers, aprons, and sports jackets and with hair in kicky, mod colors. There were baby trolls, Grannynik and Grandpanik trolls (old ones with wrinkles), trolls on motorcycles, troll piggy banks, a complete troll wedding party in formal wear, a superhero troll in a black cape and mask, animal trolls (cows, giraffes, monkeys), and trolls to dangle from rearview mirrors in cars. At the height of the fad, a rumor spread that if you put a troll doll in the freezer overnight, its hair would grow. Montgomery Ward's 1966 Christmas mail-order catalogue offered a troll village complete with cave, rocks, trees, and fourteen prehistoric 1 1/4"-tall troll villagers.

*

Golden yel-low is my col-or
My dis-po-si-tion is so sweet
Just one bite and you'll dis-cov-er
I'm a yum-my treat!

*

PARTRIDGE CARD

MOM just loves to cook for
the little Partridges.

MOVE

AHEAD 2 SPACES

*

So come dance and play and learn my song
We'll all have lots of happy fun to-ge-ther
We'll make some merry merry mu-sic
No mat-ter what the weath-er
Si-si-si-si

*

PARTRIDGE CARD

KEITH has broken a string
on his guitar.

MOVE

BACK 3 SPACES

*

Chiquita ® Banana, the winsome animated cartoon figure, was born in 1944 and became an overnight hit as she sang her calypso tune over the radio and in movie theatres. The song, one of the very first singing commercials, was aired nationwide 376 times daily, making Chiquita Banana a household word and a universal pet. She has been recreated as a doll to hold and love. The recording is for pure musical fun.

*

PARTRIDGE CARD

TRACY is headed for the bus
on her mini bike.

MOVE

AHEAD 4 SPACES

When Darrin tries to surprise Samantha with an antique rocking chair, Endora—because of a call from the antiques shop saleswoman —suspects he's fooling around with another woman. To prove her point, Endora causes Darrin's ears to grow each time he lies. The more he lies to keep Sam from finding out about the rocker, the larger his ears get. Finally Sam is surprised with the chair, which Darrin has been hiding in the Kravitzes' garage. In disgust, Endora returns Darrin's ears to normal.

PARTRIDGE CARD

LAURIE belongs to the
"now generation".

LOSE
I TURN

While baby-sitting for Tabitha, Endora learns that she is expected at a party at the Taj Mahal. She breathes life into Tabitha's toy soldier so that it can take her place as sitter. Later, Larry believes he's missed out on a masquerade party, when Tabitha copies her grandmother's incantation and brings all her toys to life. Larry goes out for a drink with the human toy soldier, thinking it works for another agency that's trying to hire Darrin.

I come from a family of pack rats and I've lived in the same house for thirty years. As my friends will attest, that's a dangerous combination. Though I got rid of many Barbie items through the years, consciously (when they were damaged) and unconsciously (when they were swallowed by the vacuum cleaner), I've also kept a variety of oddities that most women would have pitched years ago. As an adult collector, I'm thrilled. But I can't help wondering what neurotic child hung onto boxes and earrings and other minutiae some twenty years before Barbie was a hot collectible.

When Larry comes over to discuss ideas for a beauty account, Esmeralda accidentally conjures up Julius Caesar while making a Caesar salad, and she can't send him back. It seems that Caesar does not want to return. Sam conjures up Cleopatra to lure him back. When the client, Mrs. Charday, sees the two historic figures, she approves the ad slogan, "The Great Romances of History," for her beauty line.

When I packed away my Barbie in junior high school, many miscellaneous items landed in boxes destined for storage shed and basement. Who knew that those shoes, earrings, and accessories were valuable? Who knew that sixteen years later I'd be tearing my hair out looking for them!

Samantha and Endora take Tabitha to a live taping of the *Ho Ho the Clown* show on TV, which is sponsored by Darrin's client, the Solow Toy Company. Endora is enraged when Tabitha is excluded from the show's contest because she's related to Darrin, so she magically makes sure her granddaughter wins anyway—while on the air. Darrin then feels his career is over when Solow finds out he's Tabitha's father. Ever to the rescue, Sam conjures up a "Tabitha" doll, and claims that her daughter's TV appearance was a publicity stunt for the new toy.

*

During the last two years, I've been on a virtual treasure hunt. Combing every nook and cranny, box, case, and container I can find to see what Barbie items I might have tucked away during my hiatus from collecting. Things have turned up in the unlikeliest of places. Maybe there was some logic in putting Casey's earrings in my jewelry box. But what were a pair of silver glitter open-toe shoes doing in a 45 rpm record case with some amusement park novelties?

*

This is the doll,
JACQUELINE SUSANN,
who wrote

VALLEY
OF THE
DOLLS

which has been Number One on *The New York Times* bestseller list for 28 consecutive weeks—8 weeks longer than *The Group* or *Exodus*—10 weeks more than *Peyton Place* or *Hawaii*—15 weeks longer than *Marjorie Morningstar*! Everything you've heard about it is true!

*

The moral of this story is don't give up the search. If your parents are still in your childhood home, comb the place. You never know what might turn up in a hard-to-vacuum corner of the carpet or that antique candy dish on the top shelf or in the dark caverns of a basement or attic. The key to success is familiarizing yourself with Barbie's accessories. Would you recognize Miss Barbie's planter without its plant? If Casey's earring lost its triangle, could you pick it out of a pin cushion? How many "Floating Gardens" bracelets have been tossed because they look like broken bits of plastic? Here's another hint. Be sure and check behind the drawers in all your cases. They're great hiding places.

*

Big, brilliant, savage, and sensational—Jacqueline Susann's shocking, true story behind the headlines of a glittering generation.

Jacqueline Susann's
VALLEY OF THE DOLLS

Don't miss it. And don't lend it to a friend. You'll never get it back.

1994

BITS 'N PIECES

Barbie's charm bracelet
Skipper's butterfly net

(net and butterfly torn)

Skipper's ice skate
Tammy's fruit plate

(banana missing, plate cracked)

Tammy's telephone directory
Ken's car keys

(ring rusted)

Ken's camera
Barbie's umbrella

(tassel, handle missing)

Barbie's candlesticks
Skipper's cookie mix

(box crushed)

Skipper's yo-yo
Tammy's transistor radio

(antenna chewed)

Tammy's pizza
Barbie's tiara

(tip chipped)

1994

THE GAME OF LIFE

I start with $2,000 and a car.
Click, click, click . . .
spin the Wheel of Fate and

eagerly advance.
At the first fork in the road, I
decide to take

the longer way through college
with a chance
for a larger salary. *Click, click, click.*

Lawyer! (Salary $15,000)
Move ahead four spaces. PAY DAY!
On the first mountain

range, I find a uranium deposit
and collect $100,000.
At the church I stop and get

married: add
spouse, collect presents and go
on honeymoon

(five spaces). *Click, click, click.*
Many surprises
are in store for me on Life's

winding road:
win $50,000 at the race track
and triple it by

betting on the wheel; add a baby
daughter (pink peg)
then twin sons (two blue pegs);

become a sweep-
stakes winner; even take revenge
on my opponent

(sending him back ten spaces).
After I cross
the third mountain range, I

incur some
major expenses: buy a helicopter
($40,000); take

world cruise ($8,000); expand
business ($50,000);
pay $9,000 to get rid of uncle's

skunk farm.
But I keep passing PAY DAY!
and collecting

dividends on my stock. Stop
to fish on
Toll Bridge: lose turn. Cyclone

wrecks home!
(I'm insured.) Pay $5,000 for tou-
pee. The Day of

Reckoning is a breeze—no Poor
Farm for me!
I receive $20,000 for each child

and proceed.
Click, click, click. Buy phony
diamond from

best friend. Pay $10,000. This,
just one space
before Millionaire Acres!

1994

MONSTER MASH

Frankenstein, Godzilla, The Blob, Phantom
of the Opera, The Wolf Man, The Hunchback
of Notre Dame, Children of the Damned, Them,
Queen of Outer Space, Creature from the Black

Lagoon, Curse of the Cat People, The Mum-
my, The Green Slime, The Brain that Wouldn't Die,
Invaders from Mars, It! The Terror from
Beyond Space, Dr. Cyclops, Freaks, The Fly,

Bride of Frankenstein, The Invisible
Man, The Mole People, Dr. Jekyll and
Mr. Hyde, Mothra, The Incredible
Shrinking Man, Dracula, The Crawling Hand,

Attack of the Fifty-Foot Woman, King
Kong, Tarantula, 13 Ghosts, The Thing.

1995

RED PARADE

Depressed because my
book wasn't nominated
for a gay award,

I lie on the couch
watching—not listening to—
the O.J. trial.

Byron, who senses
something's wrong, hides under the
bed until Ira

comes home, carrying
a bouquet of beautifully
wrapped tulips. I press

the mute button. "*This*
is your prize," he says. "Guess what
they're called." A smile in-

voluntarily
overcomes my frown. "What?" "Red
Parade." "That sounds like

the name of an old
Barbie outfit," I say. "That's
exactly what I

told the florist. And
you know what she told me?" "What?"
"When she was a girl,

she turned her Barbie
into Cleopatra: gave
her an Egyptian

haircut and painted
her nipples blue." "How cool." "Yeah,
but now she thinks that

her doll would be worth
eight hundred dollars if she
hadn't messed it up."

Once in water, the
tulips begin to unclench—
ten angry fists. Their

colors are fierce, like
Plath's "great African cat," her
"bowl of red blooms." Poor

Sylvia, who so
desperately wanted awards,
and only won them

after she was dead.
Byron jumps up, Ira sits
down and massages

my feet. "You guys." My
spirits are lifted by their
tulips, kisses, licks.

1995

PLASTICVILLE

The train goes round and round
Our tiny little town

The milkman drives his truck
Up and down the block

The housewife pushes her cart
Through the supermart

The girl holds her doll
The boy catches the ball

The train goes round and round
Our quiet little town

The mailman hoists his sack
And carries it on his back

The gardener tends the lawn
Till all the weeds are gone

The mechanic works on cars
The grocer straightens jars

The train goes round and round
Our simple little town

The engineer waves hello
And lets his whistle blow

The policeman extends his arm
To protect us all from harm

The gentleman tips his hat
The neighbors stop to chat

The train goes round and round
Our perfect little town

The couple strolls through the park
As it begins to grow dark

The streetlights go on one by one
As the businessman hurries home

And the stores close for the day
Here in Plasticville, U.S.A.

1 9 9 5

OF MERE PLASTIC

FOR WAYNE KOESTENBAUM

The Barbie at the end of the mind,
Beyond the last collectible, is dressed
In "Golden Glory" (1965–1966),

A gold floral lamé empire-styled
Evening dress with attached
Green chiffon scarf and

Matching coat with fur-trimmed
Neckline and sequin/bead
Detail at each side. Her accessories:

Short white gloves, clear shoes
With gold glitter, and a hard-to-find
Green silk clutch with gold filigree

Braid around the center of the bag.
It closes with a single golden button.
The boy holds her in his palm

And strokes her blonde hair.
She stares back without feeling,
Forever forbidden, an object

Of eternal mystery and insatiable
Desire. He knows then
That she is the reason

That we are happy or unhappy.
He pulls the string at the back
Of her neck; she says things like

"I have a date tonight!"
And "Let's have a fashion show
Together." Her wardrobe case

Overflows with the fanciest outfits:
"Sophisticated Lady," "Magnificence,"
    "Midnight Blue."
3 hair colors. Bendable legs too!

The doll is propelled through outer space,
A kind of miniature Barbarella.
She sports "Miss Astronaut" (1965),

A metallic silver fabric suit
(The brown plastic straps at the shoulders
And across the bodice feature

Golden buckles) and two-part
White plastic helmet. Her accessories:
Brown plastic mittens,

Zip boots, and sheer nylon
Mattel flag, which she triumphantly sticks
Into another conquered planet.

1 9 9 5

CHATTY CATHY
VILLANELLE

When you grow up, what will you do?
Please come to my tea party.
I'm Chatty Cathy. Who are you?

Let's take a trip to the zoo.
Tee-hee, tee-hee, tee-hee. You're silly!
When you grow up, what will you do?

One plus one equals two.
It's fun to learn your ABC's.
I'm Chatty Cathy. Who are you?

Please help me tie my shoe.
Can you come out and play with me?
When you grow up, what will you do?

The rooster says *cock-a-doodle-doo*.
Please read me a bedtime story.
I'm Chatty Cathy. Who are you?

Our flag is red, white and blue.
Let's makebelieve you're Mommy.
When you grow up, what will you do?
I'm Chatty Cathy. Who are you?

1995

PINK POEMS

FOR ELAINE EQUI

1

EMILY DICKINSON PINK

Frequently the woods are pink –
Of a Despatch of Pink.
Pink – small – and punctual –
A Pink and Pulpy multitude

Is pink Eternally.
The swamps are pink with June.
Shame is the shawl of Pink
To that Pink stranger we call Dust –

2

ANNE SEXTON PINK

I wear bunny pink slippers in the hall.
Under the pink quilted covers
his face bloated and pink
with his fifth pink hand sewn onto his mouth.
Even in the pink crib
inventing curses for your sister's pink, pink ear?
The walls are permanent and pink.
The magnolias had sat once, each in a pink dress,

curling like pink tea cups
but not meaning pink, but blood and
the pink tongues and the teeth, those nails.

3

SYLVIA PLATH PINK

A workman walks by carrying a pink torso.
It is pink, with speckles.

Tomorrow the patient will have a clean, pink plastic limb.
Pink and smooth as a baby.

A funny pink world he might eat
Flickers among the flat pink roses.

The gilt and pink domes of Russia melt and float off
But he is pink and perfect.

1995

FORTUNES

You are just beginning to live.
You are original and creative.

You have a yearning for perfection.
Your winsome smile will be your protection.

You are contemplative and analytical by nature.
You will take a chance in the near future.

You have an active mind and a keen imagination.
Listening is half of a conversation.

You love sports, horses and gambling but not to excess.
From now on your kindness will lead to success.

Your luck has been completely changed today.
Be direct, one can accomplish more that way.

You will get what you want through your charm and personality.
You will enjoy good health, you will be surrounded by luxury.

Someone is speaking well of you.
Now is the time to try something new.

1996

EVERY NIGHT, BYRON!

SATURDAY

Tonight Ira went
to a dinner party
at Jenifer Berman's.
She works at *BOMB*.
I met her once: lost
it when I smelled her
cat on her clothes.
David stayed home
and watched *The
Stepford Wives* on
TV. I jumped on-
to the couch, curled
up in my favorite
throw (the fuchsia
mohair) and watched
it with him. To my
surprise, there was
a dog in the movie,
a little Jack Russell
named Fred. He
moves from New
York City (where
I live) to the small
town of Stepford
and strange things
happen. At some

point, Fred disap-
pears (actually he's
kidnapped by an
evil sheriff). This
causes his owner
Katharine Ross a
certain amount of
distress. Now, I
have to admit that
this caused *me* a
certain amount of
distress also. I stuck
it out and was re-
lieved to see Fred
alive and well at
the end of the film,
but the fact that he
just sits there and
lets Katharine Ross
get strangled by her
robot clone . . . well,
this so upset me I
jumped down and
crept under the bed
(Ira and David call
under the bed my
"den") and didn't
come out until after
midnight, when Ira
came home with
the Sunday *Times*.

SUNDAY

David woke up at
6 a.m. (early for him)
to go to a doll show
in New Jersey with
his friend Jeannie
Beaumont. She's
visited our apart-
ment several times.
She and David have
two things in com-
mon: they're both
poets and they both
collect old (excuse me
—"vintage") Barbie
dolls. There's a whole
wall of them in our
living room, in two
tall white IKEA cab-
inets (another poet
friend of David's,
Robyn Selman, who's
handy with tools,
helped him put them
together) with glass
doors. I sometimes
sit and stare up: the
ones with the big
bubble hairdos look
just like balls. Once

during a fight Ira
threatened to pull
off their heads and
let me chew on them,
but I knew he wasn't
serious—they cost
hundreds of dollars
and besides, David
would have been
too upset. After he
left, Ira and I slept
in till ten, then slow-
ly started our day.
My morning walk
was later than usual,
as was my breakfast
(though Ira was es-
pecially generous
with the Raisin Bran
he always sprinkles on
my dry food). Sipping
his coffee, he perused
the Business, Travel
and Real Estate sec-
tions. Then he moved
from the kitchen table
to the couch, where he
spent the afternoon
reading manuscripts.
I kept trying to get him

to throw "fluffy bone"
(my blue bone-shaped
toss 'n fetch fuzz toy
with squeaker)—to
no avail. By the time
David came home, I'd
given up and taken a
two or three hour nap.
David's packages in-
terested me at first,
until I realized they
were full of the same
old (as Ira calls it)
"Barbie crap": a shiny
black wardrobe case,
a nude red haired doll,
and a colorful outfit
still in the cellophane.
Ira asked him how
much all of it cost.
David hemmed and
hawed: "When
words and people
fail me, I have no
choice but to take
refuge in things." Ira
didn't buy it; neither
did I. Just a high-
falutin excuse for
an expensive hobby.

MONDAY

I was born on December 26th (the day after Christmas), 1991, in Glastonbury, Connecticut (near Hartford). I barely remember my mother (an extremely high-strung show dog named Balbrae Katy Did) or my many siblings. I do remember the day Ira and David came. I was just two months old—a little ball of black fur. The breeder lady had already given me a name: Fluffy. Can you imagine me with such a common moniker? Whenever prospective owners arrived, she'd set us on her cold kitchen floor and let them

pick and choose.
Two of my brothers
had disappeared
that way, and I was
determined to be
next. So when
Ira crouched down
to get a close look,
I dashed across the
speckled pastel li-
noleum and leapt
right into his lap.
"That's the one,"
David said. "He
picked you." I
glanced up at him,
grateful for his in-
sight. And in case
there was any doubt
in Ira's mind, I
frantically started
licking his face with
my little pink tongue.

On the drive home,
I discovered they'd
chosen my name.
Byron. I later learned
it has great sentimen-
tal significance. They
had both lost close

friends (David, the
poet Rachel Sherwood;
Ira, the painter Carl
Apfelschnitt) who'd
loved the poems of
George Gordon (Lord
Byron), the famous
English Romantic.
Naturally when I
found this out I was
moved and flattered,
and made a vow
to live up to my
distinguished name.

I also learned that
I was the first pet
they, as a couple,
had ever owned.
I correctly sensed
this would give me
certain advantages.
Of course both of
them had grown up
with dogs. David
spent much of his
childhood in the
suburbs of Los An-
geles with a Samoyed
named Rashon. He
was apparently a very

sweet and sensitive
canine, and David
was devastated when
he died after suffer-
ing a heart attack
one Fourth of July.
His family then got
Skipper, a rat terrier
that turned out to
be quite a problem:
he'd bite the mail
as the postman put
it through the slot
in the front door,
leaving teeth marks
in each letter; he'd
snarl and snap at
anyone who tried
to reprimand him;
and he'd urinate
all over the house—
clearly a sign of
pent-up hostility.
But Skipper liked
David the best and
would follow him
everywhere. Ira
wasn't as lucky.
Lady, their shep-
herd mutt, didn't
care for him a bit.

It was a case of out-
right jealousy: she'd
been around for
years when Ira
came along, and
she felt the baby
stole the spot-
light from her.
Her bitterness may
have contributed to
her pitiful end: she
lost control of her
functions and ruined
the expensive wool
carpeting in their
house in the Bronx.

TUESDAY

I've lived in SoHo
my whole life. It's
an O.K. neighbor-
hood, though over-
run with tourists
on weekends (this
irks Ira and David,
and more and more
I hear them complain
that it's turning in-
to one big outdoor
shopping mall). I've

always been happy
here: so many sights
and smells and sounds.
However, there is
something that hap-
pens occasionally
that really pisses
me off. But first, a
little background:

I'm a Cairn Terrier.
Over 200 years ago,
on the ancient Isle
of Skye and in the
Scottish Highlands,
my ancestors earned
their keep routing
vermin from the
rock piles (called
cairns) commonly
found on Scottish
farmland. These
early terriers were
highly prized and
bred for their work-
ing ability, not
appearance. Such
characteristics as
courage, tenacity
and intelligence,
housed in a stur-

dy body clad in a
weather-proof
coat, armed with
big teeth in strong
jaws, were sought
generation after
generation. Today
the Cairn Terrier
in America is a
sensible, confident
little dog, independ-
ent but friendly
with everyone he
meets. True to our
heritage, the breed
still has very large
teeth, large feet with
thick pads and strong
nails (the better to
dig with!), muscular
shoulders and rears,
and a fearless tenacity.
The immediate im-
pression should be
that of a small, shaggy,
alert dog, head, tail
and ears up, eyes
shining with intel-
ligence, poised and
ready for anything.

Perhaps the most
famous Cairn is the
one that played Toto
in *The Wizard of Oz*.
Now, of this I am
certain: I don't look
anything like the
dog in that movie.
I'm big for my breed,
have huge ears (even
as a puppy they were
elephantine), and
since my owners
seldom send me
to the groomer, I
traipse around one
of the chicest neigh-
borhoods in Man-
hattan looking like
an unidentifiable
(albeit charming)
mess. So this is
what pisses me off.
Every now and then,
when I'm out on
a walk, people will
stop, point at me
and yell "Toto!" at
the top of their lungs.
Or they'll chant

"Follow the yel-
low brick road"
or "There's no
place like home."
Or cackle like the
Wicked Witch of
the West: "I'll get
you, and your little
dog, too!" It hap-
pened again last
Sunday afternoon.
Since West Broad-
way was mobbed
with tourists, Ira
took me over to
Thompson Street,
which was pleas-
ant to begin with.
Then, as I was
about to sniff
a promising green
garbage bag, some
queen comes run-
ning towards me
screaming "Auntie
Em! Auntie Em!"
His friends laughed.
I ignored them.

I'm reminded of
an incident that

upset David far
more than this
Toto stuff has ever
upset me. One day,
during a routine
walk around the
block, a woman
passed us and said,
"You're not going
to let him squirt on
the recyclables, are
you?" I was, at that
very moment, lift-
ing my leg on a
stack of wrapped
newspapers. David
looked at her and
said, "Mind your
own business." "It
is my business," the
woman quipped.
I won't repeat the
words they then
exchanged, but I
will tell you that
the entire affair
ended with David
and me standing
on a corner in the
middle of SoHo,
surrounded by

tourists, and him
shouting something
that only made him
look bad. I didn't
like this woman
either, but he let
her get under his
skin. Later, Ira
told him how he
would have re-
sponded to her
initial remark:
"No, I'm going
to let him squirt
on *you*." "Oh,
why couldn't I
think of a come-
back like that!"
David moaned.

WEDNESDAY

Last night I dreamt
about Fire Island
(where I've spent
several summers):
I was running
down the beach,
on a seemingly
endless flexi-leash,
barking at smelly

horseshoe crab
shells, at sand-
pipers and gulls,
at other dogs, and
at deer nibbling
sea grass in the
dunes. I was to-
tally at one with
nature, with my
own nature, when
suddenly the sun-
ny sky turned dark
and I was a puppy
again, playfully
biting into the
cord of a floor
lamp and getting
the electrical shock
of my life. I let
out a bloodcur-
dling yelp. David
held me and cried.
I could have died!
This is my scariest
recurring night-
mare. I must have
been whimpering
in my sleep be-
cause Ira woke me,
saying "It's all
right, little guy,"

and lifted me on-
to the bed, where
I slept between
the two of them
the rest of the night.

THURSDAY

This morning over
three-berry muffins
from New World
Coffee, David and
Ira discussed their
upcoming vacation.
(My begging paid off:
a flurry of sweet muf-
fin crumbs in my
"Good Dog" dish!)
They're flying to
Boston for four
days, to visit Damon
Krukowski and
Naomi Yang, who
are, among other
things, terrific mu-
sicians. I've heard
their CDs—*More
Sad Hits* and *The
Wondrous World
of Damon & Na-
omi*—many times.

You'd think I'd be
disturbed by the fact
that I'm being aban-
doned for four whole
days, but I'm not.
Whenever they go
away, Ira pays Jayne
Anne Harris to take
care of me. She runs
a pet-sitting business.
I get farmed out to
her parents, Mr. and
Mrs. Harris. They
make such a won-
derful fuss over yours
truly: biscuits, baby
talk, extra-long walks
in the West Village.
There's always a
tennis ball at their
house, and some-
body—usually one
of the grandkids—
who'll throw it for
me as much as I want.
Fritz, their cat, is a
pal of mine. He's
the only feline I've
gotten to know, and
it's been a complete
pleasure. We're

basically the same:
we eat, sleep, play,
and seek affection
from humans. Mr.
Harris' hobby is
building model air-
planes. Sometimes
when he's working
on them, both Fritz
and I lie at his feet and
keep him company.

Before the Harrises,
I used to stay with
Uncle Clutch. He's
the reason David
and Ira decided to
get a Cairn. They
looked after him
for a month when
his owners, Cookie
Landau and Gerhard
Reich, went to Mex-
ico, and thought all
Cairns would be
as mild-mannered
and quiet. Boy, were
they in for a surprise!
Clutch (so christened
because he was born
in the cab of a pickup

truck; his brothers
were Axle and Diesel)
originally belonged
to Carl Apfelschnitt.
The poor pup had
some pretty tough
breaks: first, his
mother (Scruffy
Louise) dropped
dead—right in front
of him!—while chas-
ing a car (I guess her
heart just gave out);
then Carl was diag-
nosed with AIDS
and, when he became
too sick, entrusted
Clutch to Cookie.
She'd smuggle him
into the hospital
in a wicker basket
(No *Wizard of Oz*
cracks, *please*). Clutch
was orphaned twice;
perhaps that's why
he's so detached. I
have to nip, gnarl
and nudge to get him
to wrestle with me.
We used to put him
up every Christmas.

In exchange, I'd stay
at his place (outside
Philadelphia) when
David and Ira left
town. I loved romping
through the woodsy
area in their back-
yard. Unfortunately,
the last time I was there
I came home covered
with ticks. David
really hit the roof.
Shortly thereafter,
Ira found Jayne Anne.

I have, of course,
been included in
a number of David
and Ira's excursions.
Like I said yesterday,
I've spent several
glorious summers
out on Fire Island,
in the tacky but re-
laxed community
of Cherry Grove.
I've also been to
Woodstock, Great
Neck and the Bronx,
and even went on
a three-week trip

to California: San
Francisco, Nipomo
(David's family lives
there) and Los Angeles.
On airplanes,* I flew
in the cargo compart-
ment, in my claustro-
phobic pink Kennel
Cab. Luckily they
shoved little white
pills down my throat
before each flight—
I slept like a puppy.
(David should've
been drugged as
well; his worrying
drove Ira insane.)

*Other forms of
transportation I've
taken are: taxis, rental
cars, buses, ferries
(to and from Fire
Island) and trains.
Oh, and a canoe.

I've been alone here
all day and am begin-
ning to get restless.
Earlier, I took a nap
on the couch. A loud

noise woke me: I ran
to the window and
barked. Then I dozed
on the lambswool
blanket on the bed,
in a blissful sunspot,
until David's phone
rang. After the beep,
Marcie Melillo (she
sells David Barbie
dolls) left a message
saying the brunette
ponytail he wants
is available. This
should make him
happy (for a few
minutes, anyway).

I just stuck my nose
in Ira's laundry bag
(nothing new) and
checked my food
dish (still empty).
Took a sip of water.

Two tulip petals
fell on the Saarin-
en coffee table in
the living room.

Though I prefer the
companionship of

humans, I manage
to maintain a modest
social life. I've al-
ready mentioned
Uncle Clutch. In
California, I met
Gina and Max (Amy
Gerstler and Ben-
jamin Weissman's
dogs) and Rita and
Spunky (the Trin-
idad's Doberman
and Pit Bull, respec-
tively). On Fire Island
there was Cagney
(an elderly Westie),
Helga, Zooey, and
another Max. Here
in Manhattan there's
Lizzy (Robyn Selman
and Stacey D'Erasmo's
Cocker Spaniel; she
was also named after
a great poet: Elizabeth
Bishop), Macho (a
Wirehair that lives
on Wooster; he barks
at me from his third-
story window and
I, needless to say,
bark back) and Mazie
(the old Golden Re-

triever at the florist).
My other canine
acquaintances in-
clude River, Aspen,
Zephyr, Jupiter. . . .

At last! Footsteps
on the stairs! I
thought this after-
noon would never
end! I wonder which
one it is. I hope it's
Ira—he takes me
for better walks.
I'm so excited I'm
shaking myself,
shaking myself. The
key's in the lock!

FRIDAY

Things got off to
a raucous start
today. When Ira
tried to pull me
out of my den, I
growled so fiercely
I even scared my-
self. Can't say
I didn't deserve
the smack I got.

I thought he was
going to give me
a bath, but it was
only a false alarm.
When it comes to
activities which
resemble medieval
torture, baths are
at the top of the
list. Right up there
with walks in the
pouring rain. Both
leave me wet and
shivering, not to
mention humil-
iated and dejected.
Anyway, my mood
improved when
David let me lick
his face after he
finished shaving
(I love the taste
of menthol Edge).
Then, as he was
getting dressed, he
said the magic words:
"Wanna go to the
office?" I practically
did somersaults. It's
the high point of
my week; David

goes into Ira's office
every Friday to do
the bookkeeping and
brings me with him.
A brisk five-minute
walk: down Spring
to 6th Avenue, right
to Charlton, left to
Varick, right, then
right again into the
lobby of 180, wait
for the elevator, up
ten floors, left, left,
through the door,
run to the corner
desk, and there she
is: Dianne Conley,
Ira's Marketing
Manager, one of my
favorite people in
the whole world.
I greeted her with
yips and kisses.
That's when I no-
ticed the bandage
on her hand. She
told David what
happened. Turns
out Dianne has been
feeding Jenifer Ber-
man's cat while

Jenifer is away at
a writers colony.
Well, last night
the cat went com-
pletely bonkers—
fur standing straight
up like its tail was
stuck in an electric
socket, hissing like
a little demon—and
viciously attacked
her—for no reason
at all. That darn cat!
I sensed something
was wrong with it
that time I smelled
Jenifer's jeans. Poor
Dianne ended up
in an emergency
room, had to have
a tetanus shot and
several stitches. I
felt so bad for her.
Plus she couldn't
play with me like
she usually does.
Thank God Katja
Kolinke, the sweet
intern from Ger-
many, was there. I
fished a paper cup

out of a wastebasket
and convinced her
to throw it again
and again and again.
Before I knew it, it
was time to go home.
It was already dark
outside. I proudly
led the three of us—
me, Ira and David—
one for-the-most-part-
happy little alternative
family, through the
streets of SoHo on
a Friday night. I was
still feeling pretty
frisky, but both of
them seemed tired.
They had their din-
ner delivered from
Il-Corallo (the usual:
Insalata Arcobaleno
and Pizza 4 Formaggi,
of which David fed
me a meager piece
of cheeseless crust)
and watched *The
X-Files* (too bizarre
for me) on TV. After-
wards, Ira came into
the bedroom to read.

I joined David in the
living room. He
stretched out on the
couch and watched
two episodes of *The
Mary Tyler Moore
Show* on "Nick at
Nite." Then he read
a few chapters of *The
Love Machine*. Then
wrote in his notebook
for a while. Then
turned the TV back
on and watched two
movies in a row: *Son
of Fury* (an engrossing
revenge epic from the
forties starring Tyrone
Power, Gene Tierney
and Frances Farmer)
and *The Hidden Room*
(a very effective Brit-
ish suspenser about
a possessive husband
who devises an ingen-
ious plan to kidnap
and murder his wife's
lover). In the latter, a
nimble white poodle
named Monty is also
held captive and, in the

film's thrilling climax, single-handedly saves the day. Satisfying to see a dog play such an important role. David reached for the remote control and clicked off the TV. "C'mon, B.," he said. "Let's go to bed." I followed him, slid into my den, and fell asleep thinking of all the silly nicknames I've had to endure: B., Ronie (rhymes with "phony"), Byronie, Ronus (rhymes with "bonus"), Little Goober (they got that from David's father) and the less formal Goob or Goobus, Grunty Kisser and Grunty Licker, Squeaky Yawner, Sock Thief, Tilty Head, Stinky Maroo, Licky Loo, Nipper, Nestler, Chien Lunatique (after one of their trips to Paris), and (Ira at his

wittiest) Cairn Terror-
ist. But mostly they
say Byron: "We love
you—every morning
... *every* night, Byron!"

1 9 9 7

EVENING TWILIGHT

Of sea and wind, and through the deepening gloom
These days are short, brittle; there is only one night.
Waxing and waning in the fog of the room,
You look like a lovely ship taking to flight

O'er the land. He considered his honeydew
As softly as falling-stars come to their ends
Against the church walls across the street. Two
Goes out drinking with four male college friends.

I remember "Howdy Doody" and "Queen for a Day."
Because it just happened a few minutes ago.
What I wanted to do was to find a way
Along the same lines as before. Old ice, new snow.

A handsome young man, dressed all in white, carries
Future findings, silver, in the cranial cockpit,
Screens blank as postcards from cemeteries,
In a language troublesome and private.

Driving home in my blue Mustang, I threw up
On less crudely painted pictures of familiar
Things we think of will be there. He, says, sand, she,
     a large cup
To razor-cross the cobra's kiss, to drink its venom.
     Her slender

Avocados, plums, the more delicate grapefruit.
One is the song which fiends and angels sing:
"Keep it up," he joked, "I'll ditch you for the cute
Pink flowers borne on the naked twigs in early spring,

And the sticky sweetness of provincial tears
Like untrained torch singers under a temporary moon."
The grave and that eternity to which the grave adheres—
Hands in your pockets, whistling the same old tune?

This poem is for Robert, remember Bob? He told me my
    lover's name
And he does not forget. Danny's voice on
The stitching-frame, weaving his fire and fame,
So when you wake up and find everything gone,

I'll have to wear dark glasses and carry the cane.
The skill comes in knowing when to close your eyes.
Heard far away in the distance: "Looks like rain."
He shudders his coat as if to throw off flies.

Inside, the rare bone of my hand and that harp
From some recess in the depths of my soul.
Waving a cup of grape, smart kid, his nose is sharp,
The objects of its scrutiny: trees, blue plums in a bowl,

Lincoln Continental, ocean waves, lunar eclipse
(Which caused disorder). Something on a pedestal
In the water of each other's mouths. Lips, those lips
Shake when a shovel strikes an amber bottle

At the sound of a man's command. These macho boys
On their bicycles, in the woods, are set upon by fur
Into such a sudden zest of summertime joys
I went back in the alley and I opened up my door. All her

Hushed oars dipping and squeaking. And the five sat
    all the time
So nicely, the cane too, on the red marble. No
I never smiled much here. Farewell, colleagues of the
    sublime!
Timmy's coming back to you from Orlando—

Florida, Vermont, Alabama, Mississippi! I guess
It is all my Midwestern parents talk about any more
In this sodden world. Nobody understood my distress:
I now commenced my search in earnest, but still, as before,

I would say the writing of poems is like dancing on ice
In the crisp dark night that has no stars. And
Women's voices, hurt, weeping. Intrusive electronic
    noises. Mice
Polish over old boards where he and she stand

During the commercials and plan their future—
Fearful and corpse-like fishes hooked and being played
To "Parables from Nature," 1894—a picture
Like your mind! I love you faded, old, exiled and afraid

Of my origin. I seemed to be reaching the heights of art
Whereof Life held content the useless key;

No one may see this put-away museum-piece, this
    country cart
Going "bye-bye" for a while. My friend and companion
    informs me

There's a moth flying in circles about an inch above
All that oriental splendor of bamboo and hotel palms
    and stale
Talk of a wife. Now that I know about the fear of love
You who live cannot know what else the seeds must be.
    Hail

Poets who mistake that gesture for a style.
Stay awake, keep the film going, ignore the body count,
    it's just
Family photographs, and this is a man, look at his smile,
A movement there! As if the towers had thrust

Through the window beams from a wandering car
And he grinds his teeth gently because the world pays for
A flag discolored by the rains. In my head drums are
Surface things. Intentions matter not at all. God does
    not read your

Penny horoscope, letters never mailed. The door may
Melt where the guideless cloud melts—Oh! favored by
Bodies shining in their feathers. A half moon at midday,
I have seen it come these eight years, and these ten years,
    and I

Grow indifferent to dog howls, to the nestling's last peep;
What would I give for words, if only words would
Emerge; but you sleep somewhere, who in my waking
   never sleep.
You like a golden laugh. Idol of tacky teenage-hood,

I tell you the past is a bucket of ashes, I tell you
We put the urn aboard ship with this inscription: This
Transparent body casting long dark shadows through
The sky, in blue for elms, planted its lightest kiss

In the middle of Florence. Florence in flames. Like
The hour glass marking the passing of more wasted
   time.
I knew: the last of the coke, the dope, me and Mike
On the land spit. The sea wears a bell in its navel.
   And I'm

Anxious, exhausted, holding a luger. Grey as
A rosary of rock crystal. Wisteria blossoms. Plum
Clouds float and sheep graze. A lot of dust has
A crack at love in the warm months to come.

The quick red fox jumped over the lazy brown dog.
But note this moon. Recall how the night nurse
Can sometimes see it still in the shimmering smog
Of knowing?—I stand and hold up this universe

In the hush of space, in rooms of leaves. A high
   round

Snowman holding up the North Pole. Incredible!
   we'd say
Conversations. In the morning, I hear the sound
In the warm wind, delta reeds vibrating, a-sway,

The last flick of the wolf's tail as it disappears in
Something you smoke, or a telephone number. Late:
29 minutes past 3 a.m. Without flipping into a spin,
Candles on the lawn go out. You make a path across
   the slate

To escape utterly from others' anchors and holds!
The gifts do not desert us, fountains do not dry
Before the spectacle of our lives with joined hands.
   The storm unfolds
Instead of eyes. A slow gray feather floated down
   the sky.

1997

IN MY ROOM

I listened to "Walk Right In." I listened to
"Walk Like A Man" and "The End Of The World." I
listened to "He's So Fine" and "I Will Follow
    Him." I listened to

"Surfin' U.S.A." I listened to "It's My
Party" and "One Fine Day." I listened to "Surf
City" and "Wipe Out" and "Judy's Turn To Cry."
    I listened to "My

Boyfriend's Back." I listened to "Sally, Go 'Round
The Roses" and "Sugar Shack." I listened to
"Surfer Girl" and "Little Deuce Coupe" and "Be True
    To Your School" and "In

My Room." I listened to "You Don't Own Me." I
listened to "I Want To Hold Your Hand" and "I
Saw Her Standing There." I listened to "She Loves
    You." I listened to

"Dawn (Go Away)" and "Navy Blue." I listened
to "I Only Want To Be With You" and "Please
Please Me" and "Fun, Fun, Fun" and "Glad All Over"
    and "Can't Buy Me Love."

In my room I listened to "Do You Want To
Know A Secret." I listened to "Love Me Do"
and "P.S. I Love You." I listened to "My
    Boy Lollipop" and

"Chapel Of Love." I listened to "Don't Let The
Sun Catch You Crying." I listened to "I Get
Around" and "Don't Worry Baby." I listened
    to "Rag Doll" and "The

Little Old Lady (From Pasadena)." I
listened to "Where Did Our Love Go." I listened
to "A Hard Day's Night" and "And I Love Her." I
    listened to "The House

Of The Rising Sun" and "Oh, Pretty Woman."
I listened to "Baby Love" and "Leader Of
The Pack." I listened to "You've Lost That Lovin'
    Feelin'." I listened

to "Downtown" and "This Diamond Ring" and "King Of
The Road." I listened to "The Birds And The Bees"
and "Ferry Cross The Mersey" and "Can't You Hear
    My Heartbeat" and "Eight

Days A Week" and "Stop! In The Name Of Love." I
listened to "I'm Telling You Now" and "I Know
A Place." I listened to "Mrs. Brown You've Got
    A Lovely Daughter."

In my room I listened to "Ticket To Ride"
and "Help Me, Rhonda." I listened to "It's Not
Unusual" and "Back In My Arms Again."
    I listened to "Do

The Freddie" and "Yes, I'm Ready" and "Cara,
Mia" and "What The World Needs Now Is Love." I
listened to "Mr. Tambourine Man" and "This
    Little Bird" and "What's

New Pussycat" and "I Like It Like That" and
"I'm Henry VIII, I Am." I listened
to "Satisfaction." I listened to "Don't Just
    Stand There" and "Baby,

I'm Yours" and "Sunshine, Lollipops And Rainbows"
and "Save Your Heart For Me." I listened to "Hold
Me, Thrill Me, Kiss Me" and "Unchained Melody."
    I listened to "I

Got You Babe" and "Down In The Boondocks" and "You
Were On My Mind" and "It's The Same Old Song." I
listened to "California Girls" and "Help!" and
    "Nothing But Heartaches."

In my room I listened to "All I Really
Want To Do" and "It Ain't Me Babe" and "Eve Of
Destruction." I listened to "Catch Us If You
    Can" and "Summer Nights."

In my room I listened to "Hang On Sloopy."
I listened to "You've Got Your Troubles" and "Do
You Believe In Magic" and "Home Of The Brave"
    and "Baby Don't Go."

In my room I listened to "Yesterday." I
listened to "A Lover's Concerto" and "Make
Me Your Baby" and "You're The One" and "Every-
   body Loves A Clown."

In my room I listened to "Get Off Of My
Cloud." I listened to "Roses And Rainbows" and
"1-2-3" and "Let's Hang On!" and "Rescue Me."
   I listened to "I

Hear A Symphony." I listened to "Turn! Turn!
Turn!" and "I Can Never Go Home Anymore"
and "Over And Over." I listened to "The
   Sounds Of Silence" and

"You Didn't Have To Be So Nice." I listened
to "We Can Work It Out" and "Day Tripper" and
"As Tears Go By" and "Lies." I listened to "My
   Love" and "Lightnin' Strikes."

In my room I listened to "California
Dreamin'" and "These Boots Are Made For Walkin'" and
"Elusive Butterfly" and "Working My Way
   Back To You" and "You

Baby" and "Kicks" and "Shake Me, Wake Me (When It's
Over)." I listened to "Time Won't Let Me" in
my room. I listened to "Monday, Monday" in
   my room, in my room.

1997

[371]

GARBO'S TROLLS

Often, the reclusive
actress, then in her late
sixties, fought intrusive

sleep-robbing thoughts (her great
silent romance with John
Gilbert, for instance—fate

played a dirty trick on
him during the furor
about sound: couldn't con

"customers," her word for
fans, with a voice that high,
Adonis or not; or

her unlikely start, shy
and overweight, her rise
to fame, her quest for pri-

vacy; or her disguise—
dark glasses and scarf—and
how she'd come to despise

the press, her upraised hand,
spotted with age, blocking
her face in the newsstand

photos she passed walking
aimlessly around mid-
town Manhattan, shocking

even the most jaded
celebrity spotters)
and fought all her wretched

3 a.m. pains (doctors
were out: she was afraid
of air conditioners

so she stubbornly stayed
home and suffered) by crouch-
ing before the brocade

Louis XV couch
in her living room. "Damn
sandman," she'd mutter, grouch-

y from lack of sleep. Sam
Green sat rapt on his end:
"She'd say 'Let's go' and slam

down the phone. She could send
for me any time." Green,
an art dealer, befriend-

ed the eccentric screen
legend in seventy-
one; they were often seen

wandering the city
together. The invite
came years later. "Thirsty,

Mr. Green?" she asked right
after a brisk walk. Few
had been inside. Delight-

ed, Green followed her to
the elevator. He
took in the fifth-floor view

of the river while she
mixed drinks in another
room. Munching cocktail pea-

nuts, one fell, rolled under
the couch. He knelt to pick
it up and discovered

something odd: "A Nordic
creature . . . you know, a troll,
a plastic gnome with thick

orange Dynel hair and coal-
black eyes, peeking out at
me." Behind it: a whole

row of trolls. Stunned, Green sat
on the floor. His next vis-
it, he ascertained that

they'd been rearranged; his
theory is that "Miss G."
was on some nights so mis-

erably sleepless she
would act out little fan-
tasies with trolls. "Maybe,

when her precious sandman
refused to show, she'd stage
famous folk tales from Scan-

dinavia or age-
less scenes from her films: Queen
Christina with her page-

boy and butch velveteen
attire; pale Camille swoon-
ing in tulle; or the lean

Anna K., misfortune
prodding her off the train
platform. Maybe, by moon-

light, she would entertain
herself this way." Green could-
n't ask her to explain

her trolls, of course, but would
look underneath the so-
fa whenever he could.

He'd wait till her death, though
she dropped him, to betray
the troll secret. Garbo

walked alone, and would stay
sphinx-like and elusive
until her final day.

1 9 9 7

THE LATE SHOW

(CIRCA 1970)

Natalie Wood, in the middle
of reciting a Wordsworth poem,
bursts into tears and runs out
of the classroom. Carroll Baker
gasps in an oxygen tent, her
platinum Harlow hair damp
and flat. Kim Stanley throws
a champagne glass at her mother's
taxi, screaming "There is no god!
There is no god!" In a chiffon
cocktail dress and ankle-straps,
Joan Crawford staggers down
the beach, convinced her lover,
Jeff Chandler, is out to murder
her. Lana Turner learns that
she and her daughter, Sandra
Dee, are in love with the same
man. Jilted and demented, Suzy
Parker crouches in an alleyway
in a soiled trench coat, sifting
through Louis Jourdan's trash.
To avoid forging the signature
of her twin sister, whom she's killed,
Bette Davis grabs the red-hot end
of a fire iron with her writing hand.
Doris Day, in a black lace peignoir,

sobs into the telephone: "Who are
you? Why are you doing this to me?"
Julie Harris hears Hill House
beckoning, beckoning. Geraldine
Page begs Paul Newman for a fix.
Simone Signoret wipes her finger-
prints off the glass as James Caan
collapses, dead at her feet. Lee
Remick pours herself another
drink. Trembling, Ingrid Berg-
man watches the gaslights dim.
Shirley MacLaine breaks down,
admits her attraction to Audrey
Hepburn. Barbara Stanwyck tries
to keep Capucine. Elizabeth Taylor
scrawls, with lipstick, "No Sale"
across a mirror. Deborah Kerr
smolders. Shelley Winters shrieks.
Kim Novak screams and backs out
of the bell tower, into thin air.

1998

WATCHING THE LATE MOVIE WITH MY MOTHER

It was our special time:
just the two of us
alone in the family room
on a Saturday night,
everybody else—my father, brother
and two younger sisters—
asleep in the back of the house.
She reclined on the brown couch;
I was sprawled on the carpet
in front of the TV, totally
absorbed in the drama
on the small screen:

Elizabeth Taylor in a white slip,
Paul Newman on crutches,
arguing in an upstairs bedroom;
Natalie Wood and Carolyn Jones sneaking
off from their summer camp
and canoeing, by moonlight,
to the adult resort across the lake;
or Tippi Hedren tiptoeing away
from her boss's safe, her
beige pump slowly slipping
out of her coat pocket.

My mother lay there
in her lavender bathrobe,
head propped on a couple of throw
pillows, with her double chin
and her salt-and-pepper hair,
bags under her eyes,
easily moved to tears
by love or death scenes.

During a used car
commercial, I fixed popcorn
in the kitchen, poured it
into the large green Tupperware
bowl, quickly added
melted butter and salt
as not to miss a minute
of the movie. I scooped
a small bowl for my mother,
grabbed napkins, set a glass
of ice water on a cork coaster
on the table next to the couch.

Often, she fell asleep
before the end and I'd have
to nudge her: "The movie's
over, Mom, go to bed."
Once alone, I quietly unlocked
the kitchen door and snuck
outside, my cigarettes tucked
in the pocket of my plaid robe.
In the driveway, I smoked

several in a row, ducking behind
a hedge whenever a car
came by, its headlights sweeping
the dark street.

Occasionally, a dog barked
on another block. Dew
shimmered on the dichondra
in our front yard. I looked up
at the moon, the trees, what
stars I could see through
the glow of the city in the
distance. I inhaled the last drags
deeply, doused the butt in curb water.
Then, as frightened and excited
as Marjorie Morningstar
or Marnie, I tiptoed back
into the house.

1998

SLICKER

came in a pink,
orange and white
striped metal tube,
with a black curlicue
border and a splayed
gold base. It came
in any number of
mod shades: Nippy
Beige, Chelsea Pink,
Poppycock, Hot Nec-
taringo, Pinkadilly,
Dicey Peach. There
were several tubes in
my mother's makeup
drawer in the bath-
room five out of six
of us used (my father
had his own bathroom,
as forbidden as the
walk-in closet where
his *Playboys* were
hidden under a stack
of sweaters on the top
shelf). All the girls
at school had Slicker
in their purses; I
watched them apply
The London Look

at the beginning and
end of each class. I
marveled at what else
spilled out: compact,
mascara brush, eye
shadow, wallet, troll
doll, dyed rabbit's
foot, chewing gum,
tampon, pink plastic
comb. At home I
stared at myself in
the medicine cabinet
mirror and, as my
brother pounded
on the locked bath-
room door, twisted
a tube and rubbed,
ever so slightly,
Slicker on my lips.

1 9 9 8

KID STUFF BY OSCAR WILDE

The Etch A Sketch is laced with fitful red,
The circling Spirographs and Hula Hoops flee,
The Water Wiggle is rising from the sea,
Like a white Barbie Doll from her bed.

And jagged brazen Balsa Planes fall
Athwart the Magic Slate of the night,
And a long Slinky of yellow light
Breaks silently on Thingmaker and hall,

And spreading Silly Putty across the wold,
Wakes into View-Master some fluttering bird,
And all the Mexican Jumping Beans are stirred,
And all the Coloring Books streaked with gold.

1998

FROM THE LIFE OF
JOE BRAINARD

(1 9 6 5)

Moves
to new
apart-
ment.

Inspired
by the
color
scheme

of *The
Umbrellas
of Cherbourg,*
paints

the walls
in vari-
ous pastel
shades,

but
when
result
disap-

points
him,
moves
again.

1998

A POET'S DEATH

RACHEL SHERWOOD, 1954–1979

What can you say about a twenty-five-year-old girl
who died? —ERICH SEGAL, *Love Story*

The first time we talked was in the rooftop
cafeteria at Cal State Northridge.
Misplaced poets, we sat amidst a crop
of clean-cut freshmen while, round the college,
smog-smudged San Fernando Valley beckoned,
panoramic and bland. I'd just returned
from my debauched year up north—sad, drunken
sex at the baths, in dark parks. You still yearned
for St. David's, your stint as a foreign
exchange student. In Wales, something fearless
woke you up: you drank, wrote, fucked. Now, stuck in
the suburbs, we talked poets, punk rock. This
was the late seventies, disco's zenith.
We both wanted to look like Patti Smith.

We both wanted to look like Patti Smith
on her *Horses* album: disheveled, pale,
thin, intense. You were scanning Meredith's
"Modern Love" for British Lit. I thought stale
anyone before Sexton. You laughed, threw
back your head. I puffed a Marlboro Light.
In truth, you were too hearty, and I too

uptight, to do punk. I praised, as twilight
dimmed the gray valley, a poem you'd read
at the student reading: a pitcher cracks,
foreshadows a car crash. The skyline bled
behind you. I'd also read that night—racked
with stage fright, trembling uncontrollably.
You seemed at ease, more confident than me.

You seemed at ease, more confident than me,
more independent. Lived on Amigo
Avenue with a roommate, a moody
science major; and your alter ego,
a tomcat named Baby Tubbs. Still at home,
I had no wheels. You drove a battered white
hatchback full of newspapers, beer cans, comb,
brush, books—half wastebasket, half purse. One night
early on, we split a fifth of scotch, spread
your tarot cards on the living room floor.
You predicted long life for me, then said
of yourself: "I *might* make twenty-five." Your
roommate walked by, shot a look. Later, I
passed out beneath Lord Byron's watchful eye.

Passed out beneath Lord Byron's watchful eye—
the poster tacked above your secondhand
couch—I dreamt I was falling down the side
of a mountain, a scarecrow, twisted and
limp, limbs ripped, bouncing from rock to rock. On
every wall an idol: Toulouse-Lautrec

cancan in kitchen, young Chatterton's wan
figure over your desk. Shuffling the deck,
you asked the same question, drew the same black
card: Death. Together we consulted all
your oracles: Ouija board, zodiac,
I Ching, palm, a fickle Magic 8 Ball.
Hoping for more time, you inquired, believed
like a convict praying for a reprieve.

Like a convict praying for a reprieve,
you were more alive than the complacent
suburbanites I despised. Drunk and peeved
at the world, I started an argument
that ended with you hurling a full Coors
at me as I fumed down your stairs. Four weeks
passed before we spoke, a rift I endured
by writing a poem about the freak-
ish night a black cloud followed us—we lit
candles, toasted oblivion. Battle
scarred, we entered the undergraduate
poetry contest at Northridge. Daniel
Halpern guest judged . . . or was it May Swenson?
After your death, I'd be happy you won.

What can you say about a twenty-five-
year-old girl who died? That as a child she
loved horses. And dogs. And cats. That Monty
Python made her laugh. That she was alive
to the disruptions of her time. That she

liked Byron, Rod Stewart, Mozart, Waugh, Poe,
Keats, the Cars. That she lived on Amigo
and was my friend. That she once threw her keys
in anger; once threw a *New Yorker*, shout-
ing "I hate John Ashbery!" And that she
once, after a speed- and scotch-fueled orgy—
Some Girls blasting, her last boyfriend passed out
beside us—straddled, rode me like a horse.
Rachel, can I say this: your cunt felt coarse.

After your death, I'd be happy you won
the contest—at least you had that. "Don't turn
on me," you pleaded. Losing wasn't fun,
but I couldn't begrudge you your prize. Burned
out from an abortion, a vicious bite—
a German shepherd lunged at your nose, slit
its tip—and a violent unrequit-
ed affair with your "Don J," a closet
case obsessed with Kerouac, you spoke of
making a change. By then it was summer:
Blondie on the car radio, Fourth of
July, craving fireworks. I remember
headlights; reaching for the steering wheel, you.
Next thing I knew, I woke in ICU.

Next thing I knew, I woke in ICU:
machines beeping around me, doctors and
nurses hovering in an eerie blue
light. Tube down my throat, I scrawled, with bruised hand,

your name, question mark. My sister was steered
in, wept to tell you were dead. The night they
moved me to a private room, you appeared,
pulsating white presence, in the hallway
outside my door. "I'm all right," you said, "You
don't have to worry about me." I'd lie
there in traction for six weeks, almost two
decades ago, a ghost that fell from my
own scarecrow dream, numb to that deadly drop.
The first time we talked was on a rooftop.

JANUARY 27–MARCH 10, 1999

NATURE POEM

Till the Clouds Roll By
A Patch of Blue

How Green Was My Valley
Splendor in the Grass

The Petrified Forest
The River of No Return

Lilies of the Field
The Bad Seed

A Tree Grows in Brooklyn
Autumn Leaves

Lost Horizon
Gone With the Wind

2001

GLOSS OF THE PAST

Pink Dawn, Aurora Pink, Misty Pink, Fresh Pink, Natural Pink, Country Pink, Dusty Pink, Pussywillow Pink, Pink Heather, Pink Peony, Sunflower Pink, Plum Pink, Peach of a Pink, Raspberry Pink, Watermelon Pink, Pink Lemonade, Bikini Pink, Buoy Buoy Pink, Sea Shell Pink, Pebble Pink, Pink Piper, Acapulco Pink, Tahiti Beach Pink, Sunny Pink, Hot Pink, Sizzling Pink, Skinnydip Pink, Flesh Pink, Transparent Pink, Breezy Pink, Sheer Shiver Pink, Polar Bare Pink, Pink Frost, Frosty Pink, Frost Me Pink, Frosted Pink, Sugarpuff Pink, Ice Cream Pink, Lickety Pink, Pink Melba, Pink Whip, Pinkermint, Sweet Young Pink, Little Girl Pink, Fragile Pink, Fainting Pink, Helpless Pink, Tiny Timid Pink, Wink of Pink, Shadow of Pink, Tint of Pink, Shimmer of Pink, Flicker of Pink, Pink Flash, E.S. Pink, Person-to-Person Pink, City Pink, Penny Lane Pink, Pink Paisley, London Luv Pink, Pretty Pink, Pastel Pink, Pinking Sheer, Pink Piqué, Pink Silk, Plush Pink, Lush Iced Pink, Brandied Pink, Sheer Pink Champagne, Candlelight Pink, Fluffy Moth Pink, Softsilver Pink, Pinkyring, Turn Pale Pink, A Little Pink, Pinker, Pinkety Pink, Heart of Pink, Hug that Pink, Passionate Pink, Snuggle Pink, Pink-Glo!, Happy-Go-Pink, Daredevil Pink, By Jupiter Pink, Stark Raving Pink, Viva La Pink.

2003

A REGRET

Kurt, early
twenties. Met
him after
an AA
meeting in
Silverlake
(November,
eighty-five).
I remem-
ber standing
with him up-
stairs, in the
clubhouse, how
I checked his
body out.
But not who
approached whom.
Or what we
talked about
before we
leaned against
my car and
kissed, under
that tarnished
L.A. moon.
Drove to my
place and un-
dressed him in

the dark. He
was smaller
than me. I
couldn't keep
my hands off
his ass. Next
morning, smoked
till he woke,
took him back.
He thanked me
sweetly. I
couldn't have
said what I
wanted, though
must have known.
Drove home and
put him in
a poem
("November")
I was at
the end of.

Later that
day it rained
(I know from
the poem).

2 0 0 3

WHO'S THERE?

Iris or Olaf?
Captain Howdy?
Ephraim? Sybil's Pan?
The planchette rose off
the Ouija board and
floated midair.
Medea (the daughter)
screamed. Or did I
scream in my
seat, ten years old,
at that Saturday
matinee in Reseda?
Surely I did.
I *was* Medea.

2003

HACK, HACK, SWEET HAS-BEEN

What Ever Happened to Baby Jane? is an excellent movie and well
  worth owning on DVD.
Bette Davis goes over the top as Jane Hudson, a former child star
  gone to seed.
She slouches around in a fright wig, bedroom slippers, and makeup
  that looks put on with a putty knife.
In a decaying Hollywood mansion, she tortures her crippled sister
  Blanche (Joan Crawford), once a screen idol.

Bette Davis goes over the top as Jane Hudson, a former child star
  gone to seed.
It's impossible to look away from her clownish chalk-white face.
In a decaying Hollywood mansion, she tortures her crippled sister
  Blanche (Joan Crawford), once a screen idol,
And deludes herself into believing she can make a theatrical
  comeback by reviving her old vaudeville act.

It's impossible to look away from Jane's clownish chalk-white face.
She sings her signature song from when she was a little girl, "I've
  Written a Letter to Daddy,"
And deludes herself into believing she can make a theatrical
  comeback by reviving her old vaudeville act.
But when she gets a look at herself in the mirror and sees what time
  and age have done to her, she screams.

She sings her signature song from when she was a little girl, "I've
    Written a Letter to Daddy."
Meanwhile, her wheelchair-bound sister is trapped upstairs.
When Jane gets a look at herself in the mirror and sees what time
    and age have done to her, she screams.
Hearing this, Blanche presses a buzzer in her room to see what has
    happened.

Her wheelchair-bound sister is trapped upstairs.
Blanche desperately tries to get away, but all avenues of escape are
    cut off by the deranged Jane.
Blanche presses a buzzer in her room.
Jane brings Blanche her lunch on a silver tray.

Blanche desperately tries to get away, but all avenues of escape are
    cut off by the deranged Jane.
Crawford wisely underacts; if her performance isn't as showy as
    Davis's, it's not any less accomplished.
Jane brings Blanche her lunch on a silver tray.
In one of the cinema's most macabre moments, Blanche lifts the
    cover off the dish to find a dead parakeet.

Crawford wisely underacts; if her performance isn't as showy as
    Davis's, it's not any less accomplished.
During production, the feud between these two divas was highly
    publicized.
In one of the cinema's most macabre moments, Blanche lifts the
    cover off the dish to find a dead rat.
The real-life animosity makes for some compelling on-screen sibling
    rivalry.

During production, the feud between these two divas was highly
    publicized.
Davis had a Coke machine installed on the set to anger Crawford,
    whose late husband was an executive at Pepsi.
The real-life animosity makes for some compelling on-screen sibling
    rivalry.
Davis's foot allegedly made contact with Crawford's head during a scene
    where Baby Jane punts Blanche around the living room.

Davis had a Coke machine installed on the set to anger Crawford,
    whose late husband was an executive at Pepsi.
Crawford insulted Davis's daughter, who appeared in a small role as the
    teenager who lives next door to the Hudson sisters.
Davis's foot allegedly made contact with Crawford's head during a scene
    where Baby Jane punts Blanche around the living room.
In retaliation, Crawford put weights in her pockets so that when Davis
    had to drag Crawford's near-lifeless body she strained her back.

Crawford insulted Davis's daughter, who appeared in a small role as the
    teenager who lives next door to the Hudson sisters.
Davis bitched to director Robert Aldrich about Crawford's drinking
    (both women were alcoholics) and padded brassieres.
In retaliation, Crawford put weights in her pockets so that when Davis
    had to drag Crawford's near-lifeless body she strained her back.
Despite their utter dislike for each other, the film was a critical and
    commercial success and it revitalized their sagging careers.

Davis bitched to director Robert Aldrich about Crawford's drinking
    (both women were alcoholics) and padded brassieres.
Davis commanded a larger salary, Crawford a higher percentage of the
    gross.

Despite their utter dislike for each other, the film was a critical and
commercial success and it revitalized their sagging careers.
Davis received her tenth and final Oscar nomination for her portrayal
of Baby Jane.

Davis commanded a larger salary, Crawford a higher percentage of
the gross.
They hoped to duplicate their success in a follow-up, again directed by
Aldrich, called *Hush, Hush . . . Sweet Charlotte.*
Davis received her tenth and final Oscar nomination for her portrayal
of Baby Jane.
Davis's torment of Crawford (who had campaigned against Davis's
nomination) became so oppressive that Crawford feigned illness
in order to get out of the production.

They hoped to duplicate their success in a follow-up, again directed by
Aldrich, called *Hush, Hush . . . Sweet Charlotte,*
With Davis as the title character, a reclusive Southern belle accused of
an axe murder.
On location in Louisiana, Davis's torment of Crawford became so
oppressive that Crawford feigned illness and held up filming for
weeks.
Eventually she was replaced by Olivia de Havilland.

With Davis as the shrieking Charlotte, a reclusive Southern belle
accused of an axe murder,
Rafter-rattling overacting is the call of the day.
Crawford was replaced by Davis's friend Olivia de Havilland,
Who plays Charlotte's seemingly sweet-tempered cousin Miriam to
the hilt.

Rafter-rattling overacting is the call of the day.
In a decaying plantation mansion, strange things start happening.
De Havilland plays the seemingly sweet-tempered Miriam to the hilt,
Intent upon driving Charlotte out of her mind and getting her mitts
    on the family fortune.

In a decaying plantation mansion, strange things start happening.
Awakened late at night by a haunting harpsichord, Charlotte finds
    her dead lover's disembodied hand.
Intent upon driving Charlotte out of her mind and getting her mitts
    on the family fortune,
Olivia de Havilland sends a severed head rolling down the staircase
    at Bette Davis.

Awakened late at night by a haunting harpsichord, Charlotte finds
    her dead lover's disembodied hand.
While not as tight as *Baby Jane*, *Charlotte* features some unforget-
    table moments, including a scene where de Havilland slaps
    Davis senseless
Then sends a severed head rolling down the staircase.
Many fans would rather have seen Crawford smack Davis across the
    face.

While not as tight as *Baby Jane*, *Charlotte* features some unforget-
    table moments, including a scene where de Havilland slaps
    Davis senseless
And viciously snarls, "Now will you shut your mouth!"
Many fans would rather have seen Crawford smack Davis across the
    face.
The film was another big hit, although Davis was miffed that one
    critic labeled her "Hollywood's *grande-dame* ghoul."

"Now will you shut your mouth!"

Reviewers with a yen for violence applauded the picture.

Davis was miffed that one critic labeled her "Hollywood's *grande-dame* ghoul."

Throughout the sixties, the names of Bette Davis and Joan Crawford were synonymous with horror movies.

Reviewers with a yen for violence applauded the picture.

This sparked a trend towards casting over-the-hill leading ladies in gothic horror flicks.

Throughout the sixties, the names of Bette Davis and Joan Crawford were synonymous with such movies.

Davis starred in *Dead Ringer* and *The Nanny* among others, and Crawford in gorier fare like *Strait-Jacket* and *Berserk!*

This sparked a trend towards casting over-the-hill leading ladies in gothic horror flicks.

Barbara Stanwyck, Tallulah Bankhead, and Joan Fontaine made forays in the genre.

Davis starred in *Dead Ringer* and *The Nanny* among others, and Crawford in gorier fare like *Strait-Jacket* and *Berserk!*

In *Strait-Jacket*, Crawford portrays a deranged woman who discovers her husband in bed with his lover and hacks their heads off.

Shelley Winters, Debbie Reynolds, and Geraldine Page made forays in the genre.

Crawford caused the most damage to her reputation by accepting ludicrous scripts.

In *Strait-Jacket*, she portrays a deranged woman who discovers her husband in bed with his lover and hacks their heads off.

After her release from a mental institution, she's suspected of a fresh series of beheadings.

Crawford caused the most damage to her reputation by accepting ludicrous scripts,

Tawdry grade-B entries churned out for quick profit.

After her release from a mental institution, she's suspected of a fresh series of beheadings.

The killer is revealed as Crawford's daughter.

In *Berserk!*, another bloodbath churned out for quick profit,

Crawford plays a ringmistress whose circus is plagued by a rash of gruesome murders.

The killer is revealed as Crawford's daughter.

Sadly, her last Hollywood film was the dismal *Trog*.

Crawford plays a ringmistress whose circus is plagued by a rash of gruesome murders.

She admitted these movies were terrible: "I made them because I needed the money or because I was bored or both."

Sadly, her last Hollywood film was the dismal *Trog*,

The most embarrassing enterprise to which she had ever subjected herself.

"I made them because I needed the money or because I was bored or both."

Unlike Crawford, Davis made repeated attempts to escape the low-budget horror mold,

Embarrassing enterprises to which she kept subjecting herself.

None were as stylish or suspenseful as *What Ever Happened to Baby Jane?*

Davis made repeated attempts to escape the low-budget horror mold.

As the sixties wore on, the films she was offered became more and more exploitive.

None were as stylish or suspenseful as *What Ever Happened to Baby Jane?*

She campaigned vigorously for the role of Martha in the movie version of *Who's Afraid of Virginia Woolf?*

As the sixties wore on, the films she was offered became more and more exploitive.

One of the biggest disappointments of her career was not getting the role

She'd campaigned vigorously for, Martha in the movie version of *Who's Afraid of Virginia Woolf?*

Instead, she ended up in *The Anniversary*, as the fiendish eye-patched mother of three sons, one of whom "likes to wear ladies' underthings."

It was one of the biggest disappointments of her career.

She cried when she saw herself in rushes.

She'd ended up in *The Anniversary*, as the fiendish eye-patched mother of three sons, one of whom "likes to wear ladies' underthings."

She's loud, over-the-top, unhinged, dangerous, and luminous.

Davis cried when she saw herself in rushes.

She slouches around in a fright wig, bedroom slippers, and makeup that looks put on with a putty knife.

She's loud, over-the-top, unhinged, dangerous, and luminous.

What Ever Happened to Baby Jane? is an excellent movie and well worth owning on DVD.

2 0 0 4

SONNET

The day she died, my mother divided
up her jewelry, placed each piece in Dixie
cups (on which my father had written, with
magic marker, the names of her children
and grandchildren): her aunt's pearls, her mother-
in-law's topaz and amethysts, her own
mother's plain gold cross. Earlier, I'd held
a mirror while she put on her lipstick
(Summer Punch) and ran a comb through what was
left of her hair. She stared at the gray strands
in her hand—not with sadness, but as fact.
When she placed the last ring in the last cup,
she looked up at me and said, "We never
have enough time to enjoy our treasures."

2 0 0 4

WRITTEN WITH A PENCIL FOUND IN LORINE NIEDECKER'S FRONT YARD

Bewitched
    the boys were out
        in force

Drunken-
    ness and lust

—and full moon
bouncing back
        and forth that
black

above the bars

            *

Last night
    it burned
        cigarette

tip
    thru old
        blanket

hole-punched
    gray paper
        sky

Tonight it
    outright
        blinded

One headlight
    or drive-in sci-fi
        eye

        *

I've been
        alone
long enough

Even the moon
wears a ring

and is full

2005

ODE TO THELMA RITTER

There's no one like you in the movies
anymore, Thelma, no lovable, middle-aged
character actress, gravelly voiced and
hard-boiled, with a sharp-tongued flair
for the cynical as well as the comical. You
could work miracles with a little screen time,
turning out indelible performances in a matter
of minutes: Bette Davis's acerbic sidekick
in *All About Eve*, Jimmy Stewart's down-to-
earth nurse in *Rear Window*, Doris Day's
perpetually hung-over maid in *Pillow Talk*.
You played women with names like Clancy,
Aggie, Bertha, Birdie, Lottie, Leena, Della,
Stella, Sophie, Sadie, Maude, Mae, and Moe.
But what of you, Thelma? Online I find only
this mini-biography. Born in Brooklyn on
Valentine's Day in 1905. Trained at American
Academy of Dramatic Arts. Stage career
mostly unsuccessful. Married Joseph Moran
in 1927; briefly gave up acting to raise two
children. Started working again in radio in
1940. Bit part in *Miracle on 34th Street* launched
noteworthy screen career. Appeared in thirty
films between 1947 and 1968. Died of a heart
attack in 1969 in New York. Thelma, six times
you were nominated for Best Supporting
Actress, and six times you lost. You, who
could save any movie with your wisecracks!

A Google search uncovers this little-known fact:
"Shirley Booth was not the first choice to play
Hazel. Thelma Ritter was. Miss Ritter wanted
the role badly, but due to illness had to bow out."
Booth would win two Emmys in the early '60s
for playing television's sassiest maid—your
rightful part. O elusive trophies! O tired heart!
You, who survived the Titanic in one picture,
would say sadly, world-wearily, in the next:
"I have to go on making a living so I can die."

2 0 0 5

QUEEN BEE

FOR ROBYN SCHIFF

"It's really not like me,"
says the timid cousin.

"Then you
be like the dress."

See how slyly
she removes her

sleep mask.
How maliciously

she swats the dolls
with her riding crop.

How she
gleefully destroys

the lives of those
around her.

O evil matriarch!
O wicked frock!

2005

A POEM UNDER
THE INFLUENCE

FOR JEFFERY CONWAY

Last night I dreamt of Barbie, or to be precise, a Barbie outfit: a big
    pink gown

that came with unusual shoes: clear plastic half shells, about the size
    of her "Plantation Belle"

hat, sprinkled with silver glitter. Her feet fit into high-heel-shaped
    indentations

in the base of each shell. That's all I recall. I rarely remember my
    dreams.

It's July 22, two days after my birthday. Three months ago I wrote in
    my red journal:

From a dream: The ending of a short, uncollected poem by Anne Sexton:

> *"I drank my coffee*
> *and contemplated the white candle."*

The next day I wrote: *Dream: Feet half over the curb, Barry holds me by*
    the back

of my neck w/one hand, leans me forward. "What do you know about the
    Goddess?" he asks.

"That she's powerful," I say, "And that I'm afraid of her." Between these
    two entries:

Why do I find rape scenes exciting? Further back, in January, I dreamt
    I was pissing blood

that looked like ketchup. This is more dream remembering than
    usual. Years pass,

it seems, and . . . nada. (A psychic once told me that means I do a lot of work

in the sleep state.) Though I tend to remember dreams during times of crisis or change.

In the summer of 1988, for instance, when I drove from Los Angeles to New York,

I remembered them like mad. That was a trip! Janet Gray and I tooling across

this great land of ours, chain smoking and reading out loud from the baroque second novel

of a "flamboyant" L.A. poet (a narcissist of pathological proportions), laughing

ourselves to tears. We stopped at McDonald's on a daily basis and ordered as healthily as possible

(in my case, a Quarter-Pounder with Cheese and carton of milk). Toward the beginning

of our journey (New Mexico, I think) one of Janet's dogs, a sweet Irish setter named Britt,

freaked out and had (we later figured) a stroke. She lay panting in the back

seat. Unrelenting August heat, no A/C. At one point I turned around and realized

Britt had died. Telling Janet, who was at the wheel, her cigarette smoke streaming

out the open window, was no easy thing. We must have been in Texas by then.

I am typing this on pink paper in tribute to Sylvia Plath, who wrote her great poems

on "pink, stiff, lovely-textured" Smith College stationery, her vision "special, rose-cast."

She even bought a pink light bulb for the room in which she worked.
    ("Life is all about

lighting," says Stevie Nicks—and she should know!) Also in tribute to
    Jacqueline Susann,

who pecked away on a hot pink Royal manual, and wrote (she said)
    subsequent drafts

of her novels on different-colored paper: pink, green, yellow, blue,
    white.

("She doesn't write," Gore Vidal said famously, "she types." Another
    critic jealous

of her huge success said she typed on a cash register.) Susann used
    (she said)

a blackboard and color-coordinated chalks (pink, green, yellow, blue,
    white) to chart

the progress of her characters and her plots. As a teenager I loved the
    idea of writing

being color-coordinated, like women's fashion accessories. Pink,
    green, yellow, blue, white—

the bright colors of Jackie's Pucci outfits, her kaleidoscopic "banana-
    split nightmares,"

which she liked because they were light and easy to wash on the road.

(New York, 1997: Ira and I shop for Pucci ties to wear to "The Other
    Jackie,"

a panel discussion "of the enduring influence of Jacqueline Susann,"
    at The New School,

where I teach. Ira, who as editor-in-chief of Grove Press has brought
    Valley of the Dolls

back into print, moderates. I sit on stage with Jackie's friends, editors,
    and biographer,

Rex Reed among them. My tie—a cascade of gold, salmon, magenta,
    lime green, red-orange,

and pale pink tendrils and swirls—is my badge of honor. A slide of
    Jackie is projected
on a screen behind me as I stand at the podium and deliver my talk.
    I feel her
smiling down on me—Our Lady of "Literary Trash," who called
    inspiration "juice.")

Confession: I have in my possession two check stubs, one yellow and
    one pink,
of royalty payments for *Valley of the Dolls*, which I stole when, for ten
    days in the summer of 1998,
I cataloged Jackie's papers, photographs, and memorabilia. I'd been
    hired by the Susann estate and brought
out to Los Angeles—the only time I've flown first class. Kim
    Rosenfield and Rob
Fitterman were on that flight; we chatted in a waiting area at JFK.
    I was both elated and embarrassed
when first-class passengers were invited to board before the others,
    the pitiful commoners
who would have to crouch together in coach. "All poets should fly first
    class!"
I pronounced with mock egalitarianism. And in that vain rush forgot
    my laptop.
I was buckled in, blithely testing the legroom, before it dawned on me
    I'd left it behind.
Felt a fool as I dashed off the plane, past Kim and Rob, boarding by
    then, to retrieve it.
One of the first things the Susann executrix asked me to do was
    destroy all of Jackie's financial records.
"No one needs to see this," she insisted. I tried to convince her that
    the income

of "one of the best-selling novelists of all time" might be of interest
   to *someone* . . .
to no avail. I complied, but secretly plucked, at the last minute, five
   check stubs
from the trash. A forgivable theft, n'est-ce pas? I presented one to Ira
   (for luck),
one to Lynn Crosbie (for her unmatched—except maybe by me—
   devotion to J.S.),
one to Wayne Koestenbaum (for teaching *Valley* in his Pornographic
   Imagination class at The Graduate Center),
and kept two for myself. The pink stub is from Bernard Geis
   Associates for
"royalties on net sales of VALLEY OF THE DOLLS for the month of
   April 1966."
Seated at a dining table piled with Jackie's scrapbooks, letters, and
   manuscripts,
it was impossible not to feel like a beggar at a banquet. Naively, I asked
   the executrix if there
were any extra *Love Machine* ankhs. She scoffed, said she'd just given
   one to Michele Lee, who would wear
it when she played Jackie in *Scandalous Me*, a terrible (is there any
   other kind?) made-for-TV movie.
Her response effectively put me in my place, and let me know that
   ankhs don't grow on trees,
at least not in the San Fernando Valley, where at fourteen I discovered
   V.O.D. in a paperback rack
in a Thrifty Drug Store, and where at forty-five I sifted through the
   remnants of Jackie's career.
Remnants haphazardly stuffed in a dozen or so boxes, collecting dust
   in an Encino garage.

How many popular authors have met such a fate? It was an honor, really, to get that close

to what was left of her life. The executrix did allow me to take a few keepsakes:

a poster, some duplicate photos, a manuscript page with Jackie's scribblings, an author copy of the French

edition of *La Vallée des Poupées*: *Vive comme l'éclair, Neely plongea dans un des W.C. dont elle verrouilla la porte.*

On entendit un bruit de chasse d'eau. Translated: Quick as lightning, Neely plunged into one

of the water closets whereupon she bolted the door. They heard the sound of a flush.

A couple nights ago I noticed, at the corner of Belmont and Clark, a clothing store called Pink Frog.

A few doors down, in the window of Hollywood Mirror: a vintage metal wastebasket, pale pink,

with painted seahorse, seaweed and starfish, and glued-on plastic pearls; and a pink feather boa.

On Clark: pink neon. On Buckingham: pink flowerbeds. On the train going down to Boy's Town:

a golden pinkishness, as of a rose's brief peak: sunset through a slit in distant storm clouds.

A steady stream of airplanes, in flight pattern over Andersonville, descending toward O'Hare.

Once, traveling from Los Angeles to New York, Ira upgraded us to business class

and we sat across the aisle from Eileen Heckart. I was certain the plane wouldn't crash

(my fear of flying was at fever pitch) because an Oscar winner was on board.

Once, Sharon Mesmer and I flew from New York to Baton Rouge;
　　Andrei Codrescu

had invited us to read at LSU. We were assigned different rows. I had
　　an aisle seat.

The man to my right, who worked on the crew of *Roseanne*, didn't
　　believe me

when I said I'd never seen the show. (I had no TV till 1990, when Ira
　　and I

moved in together.) I tried to read but couldn't concentrate: an
　　overweight

woman had left first class and stood yakking with passengers in coach.
　　She kept

bumping me. It was, of course, Ms. Roseanne Barr. I refused to look
　　up from my book.

Once, Ricki Lake graciously let me go ahead of her while boarding a
　　flight.

Once, Jack Skelley and I drank scotch flying cross-country; I'd brought
　　a fifth of J & B in my bag.

October, 1982: I was finally going to New York City. How excited and
　　frightened I was.

Tim Dlugos and Dennis Cooper (he'd flown out earlier than me and
　　Jack) met us at JFK.

My first glimpse of Manhattan, through the window of our cab: the
　　skyline—

so majestic and arresting—rising silently, at twilight, above the traffic
　　and noise.

That sparkling panorama would always, during the years I'd later live
　　there, returning tired

or weary from some journey, bring the magic back. Except at the end,
　　naturally, after 9/11.

I stayed with Tim—host extraordinaire—in Brooklyn: Cobble Hill:
    his apartment on Strong Place
and for fourteen days ran around the Big Apple as if it were Disneyland.
    At an opening
I met Joe Brainard. I remember standing with him, both of us awkward
    and shy,
and glimpsing, through the crowd, Martha Diamond's blazing
    skyscrapers. Late
one night Eileen Myles and I rode the Staten Island Ferry—just like in
    her poem
"Romantic Pain" (we both caught colds). I visited Ted Berrigan and
    Alice Notley
on St. Mark's Place. Ted, "huge of frame," bedridden in the middle of
    their railroad flat,
cigarette ash dusting his beard and clothes, asked me to go buy him
    some Pepsi;
I was happy to comply. "For David, Civilized Poet and graceful guest,
    all the best,"
he wrote in one of the books I had him sign. He knew I was there for
    Alice: "See,"
he called out to her, "I told you someday they'd come to see *you*." (In
    time I'd fall
in love with his work as well.) Alice and I sat in the front room and
    shared a six-pack
of Budweiser (the tall cans). "Delirious afternoon," she wrote in one of
    her books.
And in another: "Oh God he wrote all over his—Am I this failure a
    Woman? Save me".
Tom Carey had arranged for me to meet James Schuyler at the Chelsea
    Hotel.

Running behind (drinks with Cheri Fein), I called to say I'd be late. Tom consulted

Schuyler and came back to the phone: "Jimmy says not to bother to come." Stunned,

I stammered, "Well, tell him I think he's the best living American poet." The next morning,

Tim shook me awake. Tom had called. When he told Schuyler what I'd said, Schuyler snapped,

"You can tell the little idiot he just missed meeting the best living American poet."

I moaned, prone on the fold-out couch. (Later, thankfully, Jimmy and I became

friends.) Tim loomed: "You drink too much." If you spot it you got it, as they say.

Soon both of us would pass through the Looking-Glass, into our sober lives.

Once, Ira and I had breakfast in Paris, lunch in London, and dinner in New York—in one day.

I didn't know such a thing was possible. Once, Dennis, Ira, and I went on every

ride in Fantasyland (something I'd always wanted to do as a child): Alice's

descent, Mr. Toad's Wild Ride, Peter Pan's flight over London at night—all those

tiny lights! The Magic Kingdom was ours: no lines. *Of such moments is happiness made.*

The next pink thing I see I'm going to put in this poem. "That guy needs more air in his tires."

"I don't think I know how to have fun." "We should have taken Lake Shore Drive."

Seven days before Christmas, Bob and I are stuck in traffic on 90/94,
    Dan Ryan Expressway,
downtown Chicago. We're driving to Cleveland, in Bob's black
    TrailBlazer, to see
the exhibition of Supremes gowns at the Rock and Roll Hall of Fame.
    "My camera
sounds sick." "We've been on the road an hour and we're not out of
    Chicago yet."
Fred (our nickname for Bob's Magellan GPS [Global Positioning
    System]) is our guide.
He continually interrupted me ("slight right turn in .5 miles"; "remain
    on the current road")
when I read Bob the beginning of the poem. This is a straight stretch,
    so Fred's finally quiet.
"I think we're in Indiana." Krazy Kaplans Costume Castle. "I hate
    having dandruff."
"I hadn't noticed." Rest area: we both pee. Bob's first glimpse of
    Manhattan was from New Jersey,
driving in from Philadelphia. He fell for the city right out of the
    Holland Tunnel—
the starkness of Canal Street at night; businesses with rolled-down
    gates, all locked up and
guarded; the aggressiveness of the driving a great rush. Eventually
    he'd convince
his boss to transfer him East. "I love all these lines and then all these
    cylinders out here."
"Let's talk about Scott again." "No, let's talk about Rafael." Amish Acres.
    "Oh,
there's snow." "According to Fred we have four hours and four minutes
    to go."

God bless America: an endlessly repeating background—like on
    The Flintstones—of the same
fast-food restaurants and large chains: McDonald's, Wal-Mart, Dairy
    Queen, Dunkin'
Donuts, Wendy's, Linens 'n Things, Home Depot, Burger King,
    Super Target, Taco
Bell, KFC. After a nap, I slip in a Supremes CD. *Though the love I give*
    is not returned
for that boy my heart still yearns. "I suppose The Supremes' lyrics
    were not the best guide to life."
"I mean occasionally I'd have sloppy, desperate, drunken sex." "Look
    at that windmill."
Crooked Creek. The Candy Cane Christmas Shoppe (open year
    round). "A little man-made lake
with some houses around it." "I wouldn't want to live there—this or
    any other life." Breast
cancer ribbon bumper sticker (the next pink thing). Welcome to
    Ohio. Pretty cemetery.

> *Over the years,*
> *many of the gowns*
> *worn by The Supremes*
> *were given descriptive*
> *names by the group*
> *and their fans. For*
> *ease of identification,*
> *all the gowns in this*
> *exhibit are titled.*

> Black Swirls
> White De Mink

Purple Fantasy
Turquoise Freeze
Pink Feathers
Crème de Menthe
Carousel
Yellow Wool
Tropical Lilac
Black Diamonds
Pink Lollipops
Feathered Bronze
Goldie
Black Butterfly
Green Valley Fringe
Cotton Candy
Blue Icicles
Orange Freeze
Green Petals
Red Hot
Sunburst

There was even a dress called Sophisticated Lady, like Barbie's biggest
    and pinkest
outfit from the mid-sixties: *Romantic old rose taffeta ball gown with silver
    filigree lace*
*trim on bodice and drape of skirt. Silver tiara, long white gloves, pink pearls
    and evening slippers.*
*Fitted American Beauty Rose velveteen evening coat, lined to match gown,
    has dainty silver buttons.*
This was Barbie's most expensive ensemble at the time: $5.00. Her
    wedding set, Bride's Dream,

cost $3.50; the doll itself (with red jersey swimsuit, pearl earrings,
     shoes, and

"special wire stand to keep Barbie on her feet for all Fashion Shows")
     cost $3.00.

Confession: I recently purchased Sophisticated Lady from a Barbie
     dealer for $150.00—

"NM/C" (near mint/complete); "Crisp gown with glitter version tiara"
     (Mattel

produced the outfit with two kinds of headbands: clear plastic with
     molded-in silver glitter

and solid gray plastic with no glitter; I'm sure most Barbie collectors
     prefer the former)

—one of several Christmas presents to myself. Confession: this is not
     the first time

I've purchased Sophisticated Lady. My collecting: a saga I doubt I'll
     ever fully understand.

Let's just say that—like many collectors—I've bought and purged,
     only to buy again.

Confession: last Monday (February 21) at Columbia College, I gave my
     poetry workshop

a writing assignment (Joe's I Remember) and went to my office to bid
     on Bride's Dream

on eBay. A gorgeous example, NRFB (never removed from box). I got
     it for $430.00

(a decent price), placing my bid nine seconds before the end of the
     auction.

How the heart races, bid sniping on eBay, waiting until seconds
     before the auction closes

to click "Confirm Bid." Confession: this is not the first time I've
     purchased Bride's Dream—

loose or NRFB. It's ironic, I said to my therapist, that at this particular
    moment
(over Ira/ready and willing to date/feeling like there's room for a
    relationship in my life)
I should find myself buying (again) Barbie's wedding dress. I did, after
    all, sell
the previous NRFB Bride's Dream I owned on eBay right after Ira and
    I broke up.
"I wouldn't mind having a wedding ring," I said to Bob not too long ago,
    idly twisting
a flattened straw wrapper around my ring finger. "You might want to
    find a boyfriend
first," he said drolly. Ira always wanted rings; I resisted. Instead, we
    bought
St. Christopher medals at Tiffany's. Had them engraved with each
    other's name
and wrapped, with white ribbon, in little boxes—my first taste of
    Tiffany blue.
December, 1992. One of the most romantic gifts: it's what the narrator
    of *Breakfast at Tiffany's*
gives Holly Golightly as a Christmas present. For years I wouldn't get
    on an airplane without
that St. Christopher around my neck. *Holly was not a girl who could keep
    anything, and surely by now*
she has lost that medal, left it in a suitcase or some hotel drawer. Unlike
    Holly, I've held onto mine.

What a stroke of pink luck that *What a Way to Go!* should come out on
    DVD while I am writing
this. A movie I first saw the year it was released (1964) and which had a
    monumental effect

on my young mind. How to capture that sense of rapture? I'm eleven.
    I'm sitting with
a group of neighborhood boys at the Northridge Theater, down in
    front, beneath that massive
Cinemascope screen. A couple of our mothers sit a few rows back.
    Shirley MacLaine
(wearing a black bikini) walks into a completely pink universe: pink
    swimming pool, pink
patio furniture, pink Grecian statues, pink plants and trees. In the
    next scene, MacLaine emerges
from a pink limousine wearing nothing but pink: pink slinky gown,
    pink floor-length mink,
pink earrings, purse, shoes, gloves. Most astonishing of all: her
    towering pink wig. I've written
about this elsewhere: upswept "swirls of cotton-candy-like pink hair."
    Pity, if you will, this
budding homosexual, this strange child ensconced in the dark in the
    suburbs of Los Angeles
the year after JFK was assassinated, transfixed by such pinkness. Did
    he share his pink epiphany
with the other boys? with his mother? Or did he secret it away, let it
    dominate his overactive
imagination like so many of his interests—Barbie paramount among
    them—unacceptable in
a boy. I remember that *What a Way to Go!* was on a double bill with
    That Man From Rio,
but don't remember how (or if) I responded to Jean-Paul Belmondo's
    homely good looks.
The Beatles (already a sensation: "I Want to Hold Your Hand" topped
    the *Billboard* charts in

February '64) would soon clue me in: contrary to popular sentiment,
     I thought Ringo was
the sexy one. Later: Sonny Bono and Bekim Fehmiu (of *The
     Adventurers*) turned me on.
I believe I saw a photograph of the latter wearing a skimpy black
     bathing suit, in a magazine.
What would I have done without *Playboy*'s "History of Sex in the
     Cinema" pictorials?
And one in particular: July, 1968. I turned fifteen that summer, was
     masturbating
furtively, whenever I could. There was a photo in the spread that I
     couldn't get enough of:
two guys, one blond and one dark, naked except for fig leafs covering
     their genitals,
talking to a naked woman (who resembled Natalie Wood). The way
     the darkly handsome
man looks down at the woman—intently, licentiously—drove me
     wild. As did the fact that
his fig leaf fails to cover, completely, the pouch that holds his crotch.
     As did the idea
that whatever he wanted to do to the woman would involve the more
     feminine blond man.
A few pages later: a rape scene from a sword and sandal epic: two
     soldiers pinning
a maiden down—its attraction always confusing. Next to it: Keir
     Dullea and Rossana Podestà
embracing, wet and naked. Dullea's expression undid me: half-
     closed eyes and parted lips:
ecstatically surrendered to desire, as if stoned. I've been haunted by
     his beauty ever since.

Did I mention the pink plastic DVD case? An all-pink Shirley
    MacLaine adorns
both the cover and the DVD. The whole pink package designed by
    some queen, no doubt.
Was it obvious I was looking at, rather than recalling from memory,
    that *Playboy* pictorial?
In our travels, Ira and I scoured flea markets and antique malls: he
    for modern furniture
and retro household items, I for bits and pieces of the past. I picked
    up a few copies
of the slick men's magazine along the way. (Its centerfolds—what
    most boys couldn't wait
to open wide—still terrify to some extent.) And picked up all manner
    of movie memorabilia,
including stills, lobby cards, and posters from *What a Way to Go!*
    Why shouldn't I try
to possess that pink world? Or each miniature piece of Barbie's vast,
    highly accessorized
universe? Or every Yardley Slicker I can win on eBay? *Pocketa-pocketa.*
    (Attachment, as I
once discussed with Ann Lauterbach, is a powerful thing. We were
    walking across
Rutgers campus at sunset, on the way to her reading. The sky was
    shot with streaks
of hot, almost phosphorescent pink. When we stopped to admire it,
    I said: "Nature's
really putting on a show for us.") And why shouldn't I also extol the
    dark side of attachment,
to all that horrified or traumatized? Like movies that scared the hell
    out of me

when I was a child. The first—I don't know the title—involved an
    underwater death.
A fifties black-and-white sci-fi flick? Futuristic submarines? A man
    tries to swim
through a circular passageway, but it contracts, closes and traps him,
    and he drowns.
I remember the horror of it, how I gasped in identification, couldn't
    breathe. My parents
were out for the evening. Mrs. Snyder, from around the block, was
    babysitting.
She used to let us stay up later than usual and watch movies on TV;
    we'd make
root beer floats and Jiffy Pop. In fact, the contracting circular
    passageway in the movie
resembled a flat silver Jiffy Pop pan, how it pinwheels toward the
    center. Are
my memories commingling? Then came *Invaders from Mars*, with its
    eerie music
and the sandpit behind the little boy's house that kept swallowing
    the townspeople:
they returned zombie-like, a strange implant in the base of their
    necks. I saw it at a revival house
in San Francisco in the mid-seventies and was surprised by how silly
    it was; it had
haunted me so. The murder raid in *The Searchers* also stayed with
    me: a pioneer family
massacred by marauding Comanches. I watched it two or three
    times in a row one Saturday
at my friend Mark's house, on his portable black-and-white TV.
    "Million Dollar Movie": Channel 9

would run the same film all weekend—an obsessive's dream in those
   pre-VHS days. Was amazed
years later to discover that Lucy, one of the daughters captured by the
   Indians, is murdered
offscreen. I could have sworn there was such a scene, so vividly had I
   imagined it. Was also
amazed to learn that *The Searchers* is in color: it had for so long been
   black-and-white in my mind.

Then came *Queen of Outer Space*: beneath her elaborate mask (gold,
   glittery, with swirly antennae) hideous pink,
red, and black radiation burns. Then *The Hypnotic Eye*: beautiful
   women, in a trance,
disfigure themselves: one, shampooing her hair at her kitchen stove,
   sets herself on fire;
another washes her face with acid. Then *Bluebeard's Ten Honeymoons*:
   George
Sanders disposing of a woman's body on a dark train track, burning
   other victims
in his fireplace—the telltale smoke billowing from his chimney late
   at night.
Then *Blackbeard, the Pirate*: buried up to his neck on a beach, he
   drowns as the tide comes in.
Other indelible scenes from a childhood spent watching, on TV and
   at matinees, as many movies as possible:
Tom and Becky Thatcher lost in the caves in *The Adventures of Tom
   Sawyer*; a woman stoned to death
in *Barabbas*, Anthony Quinn condemned to the sulfur mines in the
   same movie; Ben-Hur's mother and sister
cowering in the shadows of a leaf-littered courtyard, lepers in rags;
   Brandon De Wilde rescuing

Carol Lynley from the abortionist at the end of *Blue Denim*; Inger
    Stevens and Don Murray shot
(not really, it turns out) at the end of *The Borgia Stick*; the woman's
    disembodied talking head
in *The Brain That Wouldn't Die*; the pilot bisected by an airplane
    propeller in *Catch-22*;
Lee Remick harassed by a psychopath in *Experiment in Terror*; a blood-
    splattered kitchen in
The House on Greenapple Road; a skeleton prodding Vincent Price's
    wife into a vat of acid
in *House on Haunted Hill*; the river raft caught in the rapids in *How the
    West Was Won* (it breaks
apart, Agnes Moorehead drowns); a dead body in a car trunk in *The
    Lady in the Car with*
Glasses and a Gun; a mother and child engulfed in molten lava in
    The Last Days of Pompeii;
the rape in *Last Summer*; Dorothy Malone trapped on a sinking ship
    in *The Last Voyage*,
Robert Stack frantically trying to free her; the cruelty (to Shirley
    Temple) of Miss Minchin
in *The Little Princess*; Jill St. John attacked by man-eating vines, a
    native girl chased
through a giant spider web tunnel in *The Lost World*; the rape in *Rider
    on the Rain*;
Rock Hudson gagged and screaming, being wheeled to extinction at
    the end of *Seconds*;
the dismemberment of Sebastian Venable in *Suddenly, Last Summer*;
    the haunted house
in *13 Ghosts*; Rod Taylor saving Yvette Mimieux from drowning and
    from the hairy,

blue-skinned, subterranean mutants in *The Time Machine*; Diana
    Barrymore (Dorothy
Malone) self-destructing in *Too Much, Too Soon*; the deaths—by
    runaway wagon,
by Indians, by flash flood—in *Westward the Women*; Irene Papas
    murdered by angry villagers
in *Zorba the Greek*. In one movie, or maybe it was a TV show, a
    stewardess sucked out
of an airplane. How ill the thought of such a fate made me feel. It felt
    real. Still,
I had a desperate desire to see, to know about murder and death and
    destruction.
I begged my mother to let me watch *Children of the Damned* (kids with
    telepathic powers
and glowing eyes!), but she refused. Why she let me see *The Nanny*,
    with demented,
murderous Bette Davis, is a mystery; she must have thought it was a
    sweet little story about
a children's nurse. The few times my father took me to the movies,
    it was to epics like
Lawrence of Arabia and *Cleopatra*. Both bored me to tears. Too young
    to appreciate
Liz's bad acting and heavy makeup, I sat waiting, waiting for her to be
    bitten by the asp.

Another day (July 9), another piece of pink paper. I'd wanted, when
    I started this poem,
to write it rapidly: twenty stanzas in as many days. Here it is a year
    later, and
I'm not even halfway done. So my early fifties whiz by. A few years
    are all we have—

yet there is a sense of timelessness in the temporal. One gets lost in
    dailiness, in one's own
compulsions, in the never-ending to-do list. In my case: the Post-its
    (pink, green, yellow, blue)
that for over twenty years (since I got sober) have reminded me to pay
    my rent,
to take out the trash, to call or write someone back. And have caught
    the fleeting image
or thought, things (especially this past year) to include in poems.
    "Pink Poets," for instance.
A preliminary list: Sexton and Plath, James Schuyler, William Carlos
    Williams, Elaine Equi.
Or "Scorpio Poets" (here we have some overlap): Sexton and Plath,
    Schuyler,
Alice Notley, Amy Gerstler—poets whose work has meant the world
    to me.
Maybe it's my Scorpio moon: all I have to do is touch one of their
    poems and I get ideas.
So many poets, so few kind ones (the aforementioned excluded).
    Lawsamercy, honeychil'!
What you spect? 'Taint like you was entering a nunnery or nutin', when
    you took up da pen.
Why, today, do I think of unkindness? She of the horse manure,
    murderer of woodchucks,
who after I wined and dined her the day of her reading, treated her
    like royalty really,
trashed my work in a condescending email. How that hurt—an
    abrupt, inexplicable attack.
Threw me for a loop early last summer; not till I started this poem did
    I begin to shake

her meanness off. Or he of the Paleolithic vulva, who so childishly
    lashed out when
I had the audacity to reject (rather tactfully, I thought) his "first-rate"
    (his words) poems.
To live to seventy or eighty, enjoying long and successful careers as
    professional poets,
and not to develop a sense of grace, let alone the simplest manners.
    What's wrong with
this picture? In the seventies, when I was studying with Ann
    Stanford at Cal State Northridge,
she returned from a trip to New York, where she'd given a poetry
    reading. When
I asked her how it went, she said, "I hate John Ashbery." It was the
    only unkind thing
I ever heard her say. I wish I'd asked her to explain. Mean poets? A
    concept, at that point,
I don't think I'd have wanted to accept. Poetry was akin to a religious
    calling. So naive.

Why dwell on the negative. Better to look pinkly through a glass at
    the tarnished past,
count my blessings (on both hands), and call it a day. But I have to
    ask: why, early on,
did Ann Stanford (my mentor) and Rachel Sherwood (my first poet
    friend) both say,
independent of each other, that they hated John Ashbery? A
    warning? Of course Rachel
was talking about his work. Well, many years later I would feel, at a
    party at Darragh Park's,
little J.A.'s sting. And having been stung, feel vindicated when I
    came across the following

in Ted Berrigan's *Train Ride*: "The grotesque John Ashbery of / the
    bad character".
Of course Ted is being tongue in cheek. In all fairness, Ashbery was
    pleasant enough
on other occasions: Jimmy's birthday dinners at Chelsea Central, the
    day Jimmy's ashes
were buried at Little Portion Friary. Douglas Crase once told me that,
    walking with Ashbery
in SoHo, he pointed out where Ira and I lived, said he'd recently been
    to one of our parties.
Ashbery looked up toward our apartment and snipped, "*I've* never
    been invited
to one of their parties." An anecdote as gratuitous as it is telling? I
    often felt,
at those glittering New York literary cocktail parties, like a Christian
    in the lions' den.
Once, when Ira and I arrived at an Upper West Side party for Wayne
    Koestenbaum,
the hostess (a Knopf poet with whom I'd been anthologized) barreled
    past us to greet an
obviously more important guest. She slammed into my shoulder,
    then gave me an angry look,
as if her foyer were a rush-hour subway. I still cringe whenever I
    happen upon her name.
Oh that was a black decade, the nineteen-nineties. First Tim died,
    then Jimmy,
then Joe; everyone scrambling, all the while, dog-eat-dog style, for the
    success, for the fabulous,
supercalifragilistic fame they felt entitled to. New York doesn't stop to
    grieve

the loss of poets, or of youthful idealism. One is left to tend one's
    own wounds in

one's SoHo loft, corner of West Broadway and Spring, as high rents
    force out the mom-and-pops

and the art galleries flee to Chelsea and one winds up living—a true
    prisoner of New York—

in the center of an outdoor upscale mall teeming with shop-till-you-
    drop tourists and daytrippers.

Ira tried, in his way, to protect me. But how many times, upon
    entering the lions' den,

did he leave me to fend for myself? He knew how to work a room;
    it was one of his gifts.

I both admired and resented him for it. "And you are?" Such vile
    condescension from an

acquaintance, a real "vomit number" (to quote Truman Capote),
    at an Alice Notley reading at St. Mark's.

If I had it to do over again, I'd say "You know perfectly well who I
    am" and turn

my back. Regrettably I just stood there and listened to her boast her
    accomplishments.

In January 1990, I read at Intuflo in SoHo—Broadway and
    Thompson. Little did I know

that, within a few months, I'd be living with Ira a block away. I read
    "Eighteen to

Twenty-One" that night, and couldn't understand why the audience
    thought my sex life

was so funny. Jill Hoffman came up to read after me and made a
    flippant remark

about my work. "Don't call David's poems dirty!" Eileen Myles yelled
    from the back

of the room. Eileen had balls—I loved her for that. Ironically, our seven-
    year friendship
would soon come to an end. Susan Wheeler was also at that reading. I
    nervously asked her,
as I was being introduced, to hold my cigarettes. That was the
    beginning of a beautiful friendship.

Once, in a workshop, Ann Stanford told us never to use "pink" or
    "gossamer" in a poem.
She had a personal prejudice against these words. I agreed with her
    about "gossamer,"
but "pink"? I proceeded (youthful rebellion?) to pinken all of my
    poems.
To this day, if I can fit "pink" in a poem, I do. Just now, on Byron's
    morning walk,
we passed the woman who lives four doors down Hollywood Ave.,
    Mrs. Broyle
(according to the plaque on her house). She was sitting in the swing
    on her front porch,
wearing a pink T-shirt. "How is your dog?" I asked. (A few weeks ago
    she'd told me
her fourteen-year-old Schnauzer, Micky, was having heart problems.)
    "I had to
put him down." "I'm sorry to hear that." "I miss him. We get attached
    to them, you know.
They're like children." She gave Byron three of Micky's treats: one
    bacon and two
green biscuits. Home, he still expected the usual post-walk treat, so I
    gave him half
a beef biscuit. Then he scarfed down his breakfast. Hard to believe
    Byron himself

is almost fourteen. Just now, while I was making toast, Peni called to
    tell me that she

and Jen (Maureen Seaton's daughter) were in an accident on the way
    to the airport

and are in transit to the hospital with arm injuries, that they might
    need me to

walk their dog Jane later this afternoon. Last night after a meeting,
    Peni and Jen

took me out to dinner for my birthday. I spilled Diet Coke on Jen's new
    white skirt.

"I'm so sorry, Jen." She almost burst into tears. Felt awful, blamed it
    on full moon,

Mercury retrograde madness. The past few days have been wild:
    no Internet

connection, Byron and I caught in downpour, cab driver from hell,
    therapy felt

like five minutes, restaurant full, slow service, no cake on birthday,
    mistakes,

delays, *Night of the Living Dead* shoppers coming at me with carts in
    the supermarket.

Thought yesterday (Friday) was Saturday. Today (Saturday) is July 23,
    three days

after my birthday. I'd intended to write yesterday, July 22 (the day I
    started this poem

a year ago—full circle, perfect), but Priscilla called: Patrick was at
    St. Joseph's

with a burst appendix: she and Megan were going to see him, I should
    come with them.

Megan brought Patrick a stuffed dog; I bought him a pink feather boa
    in the hospital

gift shop. Patrick just out of surgery: his usual humorous self. His
    immediate impulse,
upon seeing us, was to crack a joke, but it hurt too much to laugh.
    Priscilla and I sat with him
as he faded in and out. He said he thought, when he first came to,
    that he was playing
"Frère Jacques" on his recorder. *Are you sleeping?* The association (he
    said) was obvious.

Last Wednesday (July 27) on Wabash Ave. I passed a guy in a pink
    shirt. "David?"
It was poet Larry Janowski. "Oh, hi." I was lost in post-therapy
    reverie (I'd cried, envisioning
wholeness) and fumbled the moment, kept walking, the opportunity
    for human contact
taking a back seat to interiority, and that flash of passing pink. The
    things I've missed
in life, lost in my own head. I don't know how many times I've
    learned (after the fact)
that people have felt I slighted them, when in actuality I simply
    wasn't present, fully,
but absorbed in my own (usually grim) imaginings. "I thought you
    were conceited."
"No, just cripplingly shy." Once, when a certain individual (a
    publisher of gay and
lesbian poetry) treated me rudely, I asked a mutual friend why he
    disliked me.
Friend later reported: "He says you snubbed him at an AA meeting
    five years ago."
Once, walking home from high school, Susan Dick (redheaded,
    freckled, bespectacled)

said, "David Trinidad, you have a black cloud over you." All too true.
    But Sue, how to

disperse it? I remember seeing, in a john at school, a sticker above a
    urinal: RAP LINE

and the number: the prefix plus R-A-P-P. I must have been sixteen or
    seventeen, had

already tried confession, but bolted (never to return to the Catholic
    church) when

the priest admonished, in an emphatic whisper: *You must put these
    evil thoughts out of your mind.*

I dialed (one night from a gas station phone booth) and a man
    named David answered.

Agonized, I somehow managed to give voice to my problem. Thank
    God David was on

the other end of the line. We became friends (I called him frequently
    from that phone booth);

in an attempt to help me, he took me to talk to a counselor at a free
    clinic. Scared

and confused, I sat across from this middle-aged woman and once
    again blurted

my secret: *I think I'm a homosexual. What should I do? How can I meet
    others like myself?*

Somewhere in the black depths of my memory is the image of her
    expression—

indignant? outraged? cruel?—as she uttered: "What do you think I
    am, a pimp?"

Thirty years later, I asked David (he himself had come out by then;
    we'd stayed in

touch) what he remembered of this event. Nothing, to my great
    disappointment.

I was in therapy with Laura in New York, casting back to the angry
    blanks of adolescence.
I hoped that David had complained about this woman to the clinic.
    I wanted to believe
she'd been chastised in some way. I remember, at eighteen, fingering
    my shoelace as I sat
across from Dr. Phelan. My parents sent me to him (to "change" me)
    after the rape.
"I can't change you," he said during our first session, "but I can help
    you become
a better-adjusted homosexual." The path had twisted, turned; I'd been
    dealt some pretty
rough blows, but somehow had ended up in his office. Under his
    guidance, I sat my parents
down and told them I was gay, that I intended to pursue the lifestyle
    of my choice.
My mother cried. "I take no responsibility for this," insisted my father.
    Since he
was paying for it, and since it had in his eyes failed, he cancelled my
    therapy.
"I'm going to miss you, David," Dr. Phelan said, at the end of our final
    session.
How sad and special his words made me feel, lost as I was, leaving his
    office for the last time.

Pink Moonbeams: my most recent eBay acquisition: late sixties two-
    piece negligee set,
in soft or hot pink: gown topped by white lace bodice with pale pink
    ribbon straps
and flower detailing; peignoir lace-lined, with pink marabou sleeve
    trim. I got the hot

pink version. Bought it from dolldogfan, a seller I purchase from
    regularly. Her
real identity is Karen Caviale, one of the editors of *Barbie Bazaar*,
    "the official Barbie
doll collector's magazine." I remember reading, many years ago, an
    article in *Barbie Bazaar*
about a woman who collected "pink box"—not vintage, but the garish
    blonde dolls
Mattel produces to cash in on the collectors' market. She filled an
    entire room
with "pink box." Then one night lightning struck this room and her
    collection
went up in smoke. Poof—just like that. The great collector in the sky
    punishing
her for her gullibility, her poor taste? I love the idea of lightning hitting
    its pink mark.
But all of this is gratuitous, given where I am in my therapy and my
    poem.
"Do you want to talk about the rape?" Prem asked last Wednesday. "No,
I'd rather wait and see what comes out in the poem." But I did tell him
    my dream:
I was trying to escape from a large house (a mansion?), had just made
    it out the
front door when Nick (the man who raped me) popped out of a closet
    and tried
to drag me back in. Something was printed on his gray T-shirt—
    a word? He seemed
more powerful: had he developed super powers? Byron was somewhere
    in the
house, in danger. I was worried that Nick would hurt him. Dreamt this
    three and

a half weeks ago, on July 12, my first remembered dream in over eight
  months.
Dr. Phelan once said there were warning signs that I could have read,
  had I been more
aware, about Nick's character. Did I see and not see? I honestly didn't
  know. I was so
inexperienced. Eighteen, on my own for the first time (I'd gotten a job
  as a stock boy
at K-Mart, rented a guest house in Reseda), first year of college, living
  out a fantasy
of myself as a free spirit, like Holly Golightly ("*Traveling*") or Patty
  Duke in *Me, Natalie.*
Did the rape ever take the wind out of those pink sails. Nick: "Do you
  have any lubricant?"
What did I know about anal intercourse. So he fucked me dry, a steak
  knife (my
mother had given me a set when I moved out) in his right hand. I
  remember that
he whacked my thigh with it, drawing blood, when I resisted, to let me
  know he
meant business. I remember that, before he turned on me, I played
  him the soundtrack
to *Valley of the Dolls* and he said the theme song was about suicide,
  an interpretation
I didn't understand. I remember that I said to him: "I hope you find
  what you're looking for."
Something I'd heard in a movie? And that that was what made him
  turn. "What
do you mean by that?" Thank God my neighbor (a blonde woman who
  raised chinchillas)

saw us scuffle: Nick pulled me back into the guest house when I tried
    to leave. And that

she knew my last name: she looked up my parents in the white pages.
    Nick answered

the phone when it rang, held the receiver to my ear (he had tied my
    hands behind

my back). "Are you in trouble?" said my mother, "Do you need help?
    Just say yes or no."

"Yes." "*Put him on.*" "She wants to speak to you." Nick listened, hung
    up, untied me,

and left in a hurry. I later learned what she'd said to him: "David's
    father and I

will be there in a few minutes. We have a gun. If you're smart, you'll
    leave right now."

My parents did arrive within minutes, and my mother did have a
    loaded pistol

in her purse—like a woman in an Almodóvar film. My three-month
    stint as a

free spirit ended then and there. I went home, never to return to that
    guest house,

except to collect my things: a beaded curtain, some sheets I'd tie-dyed
    in high school,

posters of Janis Joplin and Jane Fonda, a framed photograph of Bette
    Davis that I'd bought

at an antique store on Ventura Blvd. I'd have been too afraid to
    continue living there anyway.

On my mantelpiece: a pink vinyl Barbie and Ken case, a pink painting
    by Denise Duhamel,

and a 24-inch-long pink plastic Remco Showboat. The case shows Ken
    in Tuxedo

and Barbie in Enchanted Evening, her famous pale pink satin gown,
with its slim

skirt and long, draping train. I bought it last summer, when Joris
and I braved the sales room

at the Barbie National Convention. I paid him to drive me to the
Hyatt Regency O'Hare,

where I spent (quite quickly) the better part of a sizable tax return.
Joris (who,

being an *X-Files* addict, was fascinated by the climate of frenzied
collecting)

snapped a number of photographs: row upon row of dolls,
impervious in their clear-lidded

coffins; bubblecuts with price tags tied like nooses around their
necks; a bin filled

with doll heads ("$7 each")—a tangled, post-guillotine mass. When I
was in Miami

last February, I admired Denise's paintings of Olive Oyl's boot-clad
feet (which

hang in Maureen Seaton's guest apartment, where I was staying).
"Would you paint

something pink for me?" I asked the night Denise, Maureen, Nick,
and I ordered in

Chinese food and played Celebrity. In June Denise sent me
"Milkshake," a pink drink

with glued-on doodads: green and pink straws, plastic musclemen
figures, and felt flowers.

The Remco Showboat is one of three toy theaters I was obsessed
with as a child.

It came with punch-out characters and scenery, and scripts for four
plays: Pinocchio,

Cinderella, Wizard of Oz, and Heidi. Pull tab to lift curtain: Dorothy
   (holding Toto)
and the Witch of the West stand center stage. Behind them we see
   Dorothy's house.
Under it: a pair of feet wearing red-and-white-striped stockings.
   The shoes are gone.
Twisting into the distance: the tornado that transported her to this
   strange land.
Shirley Temple's Magnetic TV Theater (by Amsco) came with actors,
   props, and backdrops
for Goldilocks and the Three Bears, Red Riding Hood, and Sleeping
   Beauty. By grasping
a Figure Guide and placing your hand beneath the stage, directly
   below an actor
set in a Figure Base, you could make magnetic contact and move
   that actor forward,
backward, sideways, around in circles, and in and out the exits—
   like magic!
Somewhere there's a Kodak slide of me, age five, kneeling beside
   my Shirley
Temple theater. 1958, the year before Barbie was born: I wear a
   crewcut and a wistful smile.
The Barbie and Ken Little Theatre, which my sisters got for
   Christmas in 1964, haunted
my waking hours and rendered me sleepless at night. Tortured gay
   boy on the verge
of puberty. How could he be anything but gaga over the
   magnificently detailed costumes
Mattel designed for this sturdy, easy-to-assemble structure. Red
   Riding Hood

had a basket with checked napkin and wax rolls (to take to Grandma)
    and a gray plush
wolf head for Ken. Cinderella had a patched "poor" dress and broom,
    and—
after her transformation—a yellow satin ball gown with silver appliqué,
    lamé bodice,
and white tulle overskirt. The Prince had a green and gold brocade
    jacket with rhinestone
buttons, white lace collar and cuffs, green velvet cape, gold cap with
    white plume
and jewel, and a magenta velvet pillow for Barbie's glass (clear plastic)
    closed-toe pump.
At the National Barbie Convention in San Diego in 1997, I purchased
    Red Riding Hood
and the Wolf, NRFB, for $795.00. The following year, Ira and I flew to
    Las Vegas
to witness Damon and Naomi's marriage. Somewhere there's a
    photograph of us eating
at an In-N-Out Burger. I look fat. Another night we ate at Spago in the
    Forum.
Throughout the meal, I kept excusing myself and walking the streets
    of ancient Rome,
sky changing from day to night above me, to a phone booth in Caesar's
    Palace,
where I called to increase my bid on a NRFB Cinderella being auctioned
    in New Jersey.
I won it for $1,200.00. My need to possess what I wished I could have
    possessed that
Christmas morning in 1964, justifiable at the time, seems desperately
    sad to me now.

Also on my mantel, in a Plexiglas display case: my collection of vintage
    Yardley makeup: pink-
white-and-orange-striped Slicker tubes (fifteen of them), Glimmerick
    (*shimmers eyes*
like a thousand candles), frosted Sigh Shadow ("whisper-soft" brush-on
    eye powder
in such shades as Sealace and Rainbow Pink), Slicker nail polish, face
    Slicker, Oh! de London
cologne, London Lashes, Pot O' Gloss. I've even obtained, thanks to
    eBay, a Slicker whistle
and a Slicker key ring. Did you know that in 1968 Yardley of London
    "published"
their Poetry Collection, "six lyric, lacy lipsticks," "six love poems for
    lips": Couplet Coral,
Ballad Beige, Mauve Ode, Poetic Pink, Roundelay Rose, Sonnet Peach?
    Or that in 1971
they put out Slicker Lip Licks, so teenage girls could kiss "him" in his
    favorite flavor:
Raspberry, Strawberry, Rock Candy, Root Beer, Maple Sugar, Bubble
    Gum, Mint, Banana
Split? How many times must I return to the Thrifty Drug Store of my
    youth and
relive that initial, painful attachment? Just inside the automatic door,
    left through the
turnstile: the makeup counter. I can still see the woman behind it: her
    powder blue
Thrifty's smock, her glasses hanging by a chain around her neck, her
    perfect hair-sprayed
helmet of gray hair. The trick was to walk as slowly and nonchalantly
    as possible, taking in as

much of the Yardley display as I could in just a few seconds. I've
    written about this elsewhere:
"the rows of striped lipstick tubes pure eye candy." What must she
    have thought of this
obsessed trespasser in Cosmetics. He'd turn right, then two aisles
    over, left, to Toys.
More torture: the Barbie outfits in their pink-and-white-striped
    cardboard frames.
He'd pretend to be interested in the little bottles of model airplane
    paint. But he'd
be eyeing those chiffon and taffeta gowns, those high heels and
    necklaces and gloves
stitched into Mattel's colorful display packages. If he could pick up
    one of those
packages and press the dress, the accessories—the cellophane would
    make a crinkly sound.
He didn't know that housewives all over Japan, commissioned to
    work at home,
had strained their eyesight, pricked their fingers with needles, and
    hunched over
and wrecked their backs affixing Barbie's clothing to those
    captivating displays. Nor did he know
that three decades later he'd begin to collect the lipsticks and doll
    outfits he coveted from a distance.
NRFB: never removed, never handled by anyone since that Japanese
    housewife gently pulled
the white thread through the hem of the dress and, on the back of
    the card, tied a tight knot.

Also on my mantel, in a stack of books: Dodie Bellamy's latest, *Pink
    Steam*. Last year,

after a visit to Chicago, she wrote: "I keep thinking about your Yardley
   vitrine."
In the eighties, in San Francisco to do a reading, Kevin and Dodie
   drove me to
the Barbie Hall of Fame in Palo Alto. Somewhere there's a photo
   (Kevin took it)
of me standing in front of a case of Barbies. My destiny—though I
   couldn't have foreseen
it then. It wasn't until 1993 or 4, rummaging through a cardboard box
   at the 23rd St.
flea market, that I would discover Francie's phonograph and garter belt.
   Francie,
Barbie's teenaged "MOD"ern cousin, was created in 1966, Mattel's
   attempt to reflect
the swinging youth culture. Shorter and less busty than Barbie, Francie
   came with "real"
eyelashes and an infinitesimal mascara brush. The phonograph was
   part of Dance Party,
an outfit that included pink crepe dress, white hose, pink heels, two
   records (one
with a blue label, one a red; both said "Barbie"), chocolate sundae,
   spoon, and napkin.
The garter belt (which had four pink plastic garters) came with First
   Things First,
a lingerie set—white nylon sprinkled with brightly colored flowers—
   "to go with
all of Francie's fab outfits!" Which I watched my sisters unwrap,
   uninterested in my Christmas
presents. That morning, Ira had dragged me to the flea market. And
   there I stood, in the

middle of Chelsea, holding Francie's diminutive garter belt in the palm
of my hand. So
my collecting began, and I went far on my own pink steam. Somewhere
there are photos
of the display cases in Ira's and my loft. Lynn Crosbie wrote about them
in *Phoebe 2002*:

"Don't touch anything in the display cases!" David said,
and I stared at them for hours.

The tableaus of Barbies, Midges, and Skippers,
reclining, posing, babysitting, and so on,

each dressed to the nines.

The kitchen was fully detailed, and included
plates, silverware, a turkey roasting in an oven.

The best moment was when M.G. Lord, author of *Forever Barbie*, came
to dinner.
She studied the dolls (over a hundred at that point) then said, "It takes
a collector
to do it right." The worst was when Jeffery walked in and said, "Oh, how
girlish."
Another low was when the lips on a blonde bubblecut disappeared
before my eyes (exposure
to sunlight). I contacted a restorer well known in the Barbie collecting
world.
We became friendly over the phone. I told her I wrote poetry; she
expressed interest

in reading my work. I included a copy of *Answer Song* when I mailed
  her the doll—
$8.00 for a repaint. When next we spoke, she was considerably less
  friendly. She'd
opened the book to "My Lover," an explicit litany of my sexual
  experiences;
was certain I'd intended to shock her. "You should be more careful
  who you show
this to. I loved Sylvester when I was into disco, but this was too much
  for me."

Just three more pink threads and this poem will be finished. Poem
  I'm going to miss.
Poem which promised so much: *We know how to give our whole life
  every day.* Poem
which became, some time ago, as much about what I can't fit in as
  can. All those memories
crowding around the edges. How I once came out of a blackout on
  the San Diego Freeway,
doing 70. I'd been to a party at Dennis Cooper's. Was that the party
  he poured a drink on my head?
How that infuriated me. The same party I kissed Amy in the
  kitchen; she looked so sexy
in her red dress. Years later, when we talked about it, she said kissing
  me was like kissing
Virginia Woolf. Or how, in elementary school, I did a diorama of the
  Green Room
based on a photograph (in a spread on the White House) in *National
  Geographic.* What magic
I worked with a little cardboard, construction paper, and glue. I
  guess that's as close

as I could come to having my own dollhouse. I seem to recall that my
 teacher thought I
had cheated (help from parents), my diorama was that good. Or how
 Jeannie and I first met:
in either 1992 or 1993, on either the 13th or the 30th floor of the
 Empire State Building,
at a meeting of the NYBC (New York Barbie Club). *How does
 anything know its kind?*
Fate sat us next to each other; we discovered we knew each other's
 poems. What a gift
her friendship has been: to be able to share the ups and downs of
 two worlds: poetry
and collecting. How to make this all fit? Simply bounce here and
 there, like a time machine
gone haywire? Here I am in San Francisco, 1976, wearing my Emily
 Dickinson T-shirt.
Taped to the wall behind me: pictures of E.D. and Rimbaud (torn
 from library books)
and Anne Sexton's poem "Her Kind," which I'd written with magic
 marker on a sheet
of butcher paper. Here I am in London, sometime in the nineties,
 standing in front of
23 Fitzroy Road, the address where Sylvia Plath died. I wear an
 orange shirt and black blazer,
and dark sunglasses, so no one can see the eyes of this death
 monger, this gauche American.
Here I am back in Los Angeles, circa 1983: Elaine Equi and I wander
 through Hollywood
Memorial Cemetery in search of Rudolph Valentino's grave. The
 ghost of Clifton Webb

keeps us company. And here I am in Chicago, month before last,
	crying my eyes out over an

aborted affair. Don't worry, I won't put your name in my poem, pal,
	but you know who

you are: you of the mixed messages, you of the chickenshit emails,
	you of the disappear.

And the fear, the fear, the fear (as Anne, badly imitating Sylvia,
	would say). "Remember

that not getting what you want is sometimes a wonderful stroke of
	luck." Thank you,

Dalai Lama, for your quotable wisdom. And remember that
	unfortunate moment in bed:

"You make me want to fuck you." "I don't get fucked." Did that ever
	stop me in

my tracks. "Really?" Headshake: No. "Even over time, with intimacy
	and trust?"

Same headshake. If I had it to do over again, I'd say "Then why did
	you sit on me

and press my cock against your crack?" Ironic: I was always the one
	who didn't want

to get fucked: "I had a bad experience when I was young." Strange to
	be on the other

side of that Looking-Glass. What's the point of all that intense
	foreplay if it doesn't lead

to *acute core-reaching fucking?* Deep breath. Let him go. Bless you and
	fuck you.

Is that the best you can do? So much for acceptance. *I want a
	complete and equal love.*

A few loose ends (of the pink variety). This week Jeannie sends me a
	color xerox of an ad

from the June 1954 issue of *McCall's* magazine: "The Pink Shoe." Four
   scintillating styles.
In fine print beneath number two (*Wonderful with summer's whirling
   skirts is this delicate
kid-stripping sandal*): "Drawings by Andy Warhol." Chuck Stebelton
   sends me an email
announcing his new book, *Circulation Flowers*: "it's alarmingly pink!"
   "I'm enjoying
your pink correspondence with Elaine," Connie Deanovich wrote me
   in the mid-nineties,
after she read, in separate magazines, pink poems we'd dedicated to
   each other.
At the end of my drinking (early eighties), I often spoke on the phone
   with Michael Silverblatt.
In those small hours, Michael would recount his conversations with
   Pauline Kael.
One night he told me Kael was working on a review of *Sophie's Choice*,
   which I hadn't seen,
and described a scene in the movie where everything was pink. I said
   that reminded me
of the pink sequence in *What a Way to Go!* Then related the entire plot
   of that childhood favorite.
Sure enough, my association made its way into Kael's *New Yorker*
   review: "Was it
inspired by the 1963 movie *What a Way to Go!*, with Shirley MacLaine
   trying to
cheer up her husband, Pinky, by having the rooms in their mansion
   all painted pink?"
Kael gets several things wrong: the film came out in 1964, and it's
   Pinky (Gene
Kelly), not MacLaine, who out of sheer egotism douses their world with
   pink paint.

Obviously some fact checker couldn't have cared less about such
    pink minutiae. Michael
arranged for me to meet Pauline when I went to New York in
    October of '82. I visited her
in her *New Yorker* office. She was kind, given I was barely able to
    speak (awestruck),
and signed a copy of *Reeling* for me. I later gave that book away. And
    dropped Michael.
He'd have to wait ten years to get his revenge. When *Answer Song*
    came out, he
interviewed me for his radio show. He asked me to read a piece, then
    hit me with:
"What makes you think that is a poem?" It threw me; I shut tight as
    a clam. Thank God
that interview was unairable. If I had it to do over . . . Well, he was a
    low bottom friend.
At least Sheree, when she forbade me to participate in any of Bob's
    memorials, was aboveboard
about her anger. And Bob's: he never stopped railing at me,
    according to his *Pain Journal*,
even though I'd tried, a year before his death, to make things right.
    I'm grateful that
Henry and I were able to patch things up. Jeffery and I visited him
    when I was in New York
last April, two months before he died. It was hard to believe that
    nearly a decade and a half
had passed since the three of us last sat in Henry's kitchen and
    laughed. I thought it
serendipitous, since I was writing this when he died, that a
    memorial for Henry
should be held at a cafe called Pink Pony. Kept that pink coincidence
    in the back of my

mind. God bless Henry Flesh, who died ten pages shy of finishing
  his third novel.
And God bless Ed Smith, another old friend who died during the
  writing of this poem.
Ed who initially rubbed me the wrong way (I took his irreverence
  personally), but who,
once I got sober, I grew to appreciate. At news of his suicide, I
  reached for his books, and out fell,
from one of them, a slip of paper: this collaboration, signed by both
  of us, written on 10/30/88:

                    half
                    beautiful

                    don't
                    sway

                    point
                    north

You drive in a circle. A pink one. The first time I saw Barbie: Linda
  Moran invited me into
her backyard (I was seven or eight): there on a picnic table was a
  black patent leather
wardrobe case. She pulled back the clasp: inside, the blonde ponytail
  with big breasts,
but what really interested me were all the clothes hanging on little
  plastic hangers—
a white nurse's uniform, a tight-fitting black nightclub dress, a see-
  through pink negligee.
And the miniatures Linda poured out of the accessory drawers—a
  wooden bowl with three

balls of yarn and knitting needles, gloves and purses, tiny plastic
     high heels, a wax apple,
a pink stuffed dog—were bliss to behold. I remember that Linda's
     mother, Priscilla,
stood watching us from their living room window. (Fast forward to
     the nineties:
in a bus on the way to a doll show in Hackensack, New Jersey, I meet
     Cyndi, also on her way
to the show, who tells me that her mother was so into Barbie she
     used to wake her in the
middle of the night and ask, "What happened to Barbie's sunglasses?
     Where's Barbie's comb?")
My first memory: January 31, 1957 (I was three and a half), 11:18
     a.m., Pacoima, California:
two airplanes collide in the clear skies over the San Fernando Valley:
     one of them,
its left wing sheared off, begins a steepening, high velocity dive
     earthward and slams
into a Pacoima churchyard, killing all four crew members on board.
     Upon impact,
hundreds of pieces of flaming metal and debris slash across the
     playground of Pacoima
Junior High School, where some 220 boys are just ending their
     outdoor athletic activities.
Several boys are killed. I remember that our house shook, that I was
     watching cartoons
on TV. My mother was vacuuming in another room. I also
     remember my mother,
hysterical, dragging me across a vacant lot; my brother was in the
     elementary school
across the street from the junior high. *Your destination waits where
     you left it*: Thrifty Drug

in Chatsworth, week of July 5, 1967 (I was almost fourteen): I spin
    the paperback rack
like the wheel of fortune: it stops at a novel with "dolls" in the title,
    its white cover
spattered with red, blue, and green-and-yellow pills. My life will
    never be the same.
"Pink will always be there for you," Elaine said the other day, when I
    said I was sad the poem
was coming to an end. "I've never forgotten how deep and important
    our friendship was,"
Eileen said in an email a year ago. Did she know how meaningful
    that would be for me?
When I was dealing with a disgruntled colleague, Laura Mullen said,
    "Yes, but you're a
whole person, David." One of the nicest things anyone's ever said to
    me. I'm grateful
that on her deathbed my mother said: "You've been a good son." And
    that when Allen Ginsberg
died, tulips Ira and I had sent were in the room. Were they red?
    Pink? *You drive in a circle.*
I can still hear Allen say, after reading one of my poems in a
    workshop at Brooklyn College,
"Where's the epiphany, Trinidad?" Somewhere there's a photograph
    of us standing
in front of St. Mark's Church. I wear a red shirt. Recently, I came
    across some
notes I'd taken, many years ago, during a session with a psychic. I'd
    asked her about rape:

> *vital attention from*
> *powerful person—*
> *that's why it's exciting*

Still, in my red journal, a few months before starting this poem, I
    asked the question again.
You drive in a circle. (Both Maureen and Susan called in the last few
    minutes. "I can't talk,
I'm at the end of my long poem." Thank God for my friends.) In
    1993, I asked Amy
to sign *Nerve Storm*. She wrote: "For David, A Doll who needs no
    valley". In 1982,
I asked Lewis MacAdams to sign *Africa and the Marriage of Walt
    Whitman and Marilyn Monroe.*
He said: "What should I write?" "Bliss in this life," I said, quoting
    one of his poems.
He smiled and jotted it down. At the end of fourth grade, I asked a
    substitute teacher
to sign my blue autograph book. I regret that in the late eighties, in a
    fit of purge,
I threw that book away; I wish I could include her name. But I've
    never forgotten
what she wrote: "David, you are an unusual boy. May it continue into
    adult life."

JULY 22, 2004–DECEMBER 16, 2005

TO TIM DLUGOS

That time you said Tom (regarding his stealing and selling
Ginsberg and Schuyler manuscripts to buy drugs)
had more reparations to make than Germany
after the war, you laughed your inimitable laugh:
self-satisfied, infectious. I sat rapt on my end of the line.
Now you're dead fifteen years, who once broke down
and confessed to Raymond, after a night at the baths,
your helpless addiction to unprotected sex. Update:
Eileen got a teaching job in San Diego. Dennis is
in Paris with a Russian boyfriend, Brad still looks thirty,
Tom is priest of a parish on Long Island. Ira and I split
up, and I left New York: teach poetry at an arts college
in the South Loop in Chicago. Turn my students
onto your work. Live north of downtown, on West
Hollywood Ave. (you'll never escape it, I can hear you
say, Hollywood is your state of mind) in Andersonville,
an old Swedish neighborhood full of gay men my age.

I'm at my computer thinking of your last days, how one
afternoon on G-9, sitting with you in awkward silence,
you asked point-blank: "Why did Dennis drop me?"
I stammered something about rivalry over a boy, afraid
to tell you, for some reason (you'd been sober many years),
that how you'd drunkenly lashed out during that rivalry
was the most accurate explanation. Then: "You've gained weight."
An uncharacteristically cranky moment, my friend, in an
otherwise grace-filled death. "I'll lose it," I said. And have.
Yesterday, walking home from the gym at dusk, I was struck

by the sky: a color you, who celebrated such nuances,
would have appreciated: Popsicle blue. Tim, I can still hear
your laugh, the closeness of your voice when you'd call,
late at night, to read a new poem or to relish the indiscretions
of others: "He's been crossed off guest lists I didn't know existed."
Nursing a ten-year crush, I was always reticent, let you—so smart
and so sharp—take the lead. I think I could keep up with you now.

2 0 0 6

JAMES SCHUYLER

I went to his sixty-sixth birthday
dinner: sixteen years ago this past
November. I remember that it was at
Chelsea Central (his favorite restaurant:
great steaks) on 10th Avenue, and
that Ashbery was there, and a few
others, including Joe, impeccably
dressed and gracious, who picked up
what must have been (I thought
at the time) an exorbitant bill.

I remember him saying more than
once, "Joe always picks up the bill,"
then smiling a slightly wicked smile.

Sitting with him (those excruciating
silences!) in his room at the Chelsea,
my eyes would wander from his book-
shelves (*The Portrait of a Lady* stood out)
to the pan of water on the radiator
to the records strewn on the floor
to some scraggly plants (ivy? herbs?)
in ceramic pots at the base of the French
doors that opened to the balcony and
balustrade and sound of traffic on 23rd
Street six floors below. He read me
"White Boat, Blue Boat" shortly after he
wrote it, and a poem about Brook Benton

singing "Rainy Night in Georgia" that
didn't make it into his *Last Poems*, though
I remember thinking it beautiful. He
complained, in a letter to Tom, about
how much I smoked, and how emotional
I'd get during movies: he must have been
referring to *Field of Dreams* (he had a yen
for Kevin Costner). When he took me
to see *L'Atalante*, a film he loved, I was
bored. Once, we took the subway (he
hadn't ridden it in years) to the Frick;
I remember admiring Romney's Lady
Hamilton. It hurt that he didn't invite
me to the dinner after his Dia reading
or to the reception after his reading at the
92nd Street Y, though he did, at the latter,
read "Mood Indigo," dedicated to me.
When he said my name from the stage,
Joan and Eileen, sitting to my left, turned
and stared at me; frozen by the enormity
of the moment, I couldn't look back.
When he came to a reading I gave at
St. Mark's, Raymond impressed upon
me what an honor it was: Jimmy didn't
go to many poetry readings. What else
is there to say? That when I visited him
at St. Vincent's the day before he died
Darragh said, "He likes to hear gossip."
So I said, "Eileen and I are talking again."
That at his funeral I sat alone (Ira couldn't
come); that that was the loneliest feeling

in the world. That afterwards Doug said
"You look so sad." How should I have
looked, Doug! And that a year after he
died, I dreamt I saw him in the lobby of
the Chelsea Hotel. He was wearing a
hospital shift and seemed to have no
muscle control over his face—like in inten-
sive care after his stroke. He saw me
and said, "It's nice to see some familiar
faces." I approached him, but he
disappeared.

2 0 0 6

CLASSIC LAYER CAKES

Mother is gone, / only Things remain. —DENISE LEVERTOV

9773 Comanche Ave. A pale yellow, ranch-style tract house in the suburbs of Los Angeles. White shutters. Decorative cast iron trellis (leaves and acorns), painted white, around the front porch. Dichondra. Gardenias. Ivy in the parkway, beginning to climb a Modesto Ash. Snapdragons in the flowerbeds. Bottlebrush in the backyard.

The phone number, when we moved there in the late fifties, was Dickens (DI) 9-1647. The prefix was later changed to 349.

Osso, Lassen, Winnetka, Plummer: the streets that boxed in our world.

My mother in her frilled apron, dusting and vacuuming; sweeping and mopping; rinsing, scouring, scrubbing. Driving her station wagon to the supermarket. Pushing the cart. Crossing each item off her shopping list. Her large, slightly loopy handwriting slanting towards the right. Perusing *The Brand-Name Calorie Counter* at the check-out stand. Folding her receipt and Green Stamps into her purse. Pulling into the driveway. Unloading the brown grocery bags, setting them on the speckled linoleum in her pink kitchen. Emptying them, folding them, flattening them, stacking them.

What treats she'd take out of those bags: Wheat Thins, Triscuits, Oreos, Nilla Wafers, Bugles, Sno Balls, Twinkies, Cheez-Its, Ritz. Laura Scudder's potato chips came in twin-paks, in big red, yellow, and brown striped bags. After my mother died, at a store near her home, those colors caught my eye. I bought a package, folded and saved it (threw away the chips). The expiration date, stamped on the bag, is June 23, 1996.

the fork marks in her peanut butter cookies

her pink and light green Depression glass
her collection of souvenir spoons
The Ray Conniff Singers
Sing Along with Mitch
the milk glass (hobnail, ruffled) in the Early American hutch
her German cuckoo clock

She sent away to Northern Paper Mills, makers of fine toilet tissue, for a set of American Beauty Portraits: 11 x 14 prints of sweet little girls: one holding daisies, one cuddling a kitten, one bundled up against the snow. Which she framed and hung in the hall. There was also one of an infant peeking out of a pink blanket.

My brother and I are outside, in the front yard, when it begins to rain. Soon it is pouring. I find this exciting, dance around in my soaked clothes and then lose myself in play: floating my Mickey Mouse pirate ship in the rushing river the gutter has become. Pleased with ourselves, we knock on the door—to surprise my mother. But she is furious. She grabs and undresses us, wraps us in towels, and makes us dry off in front of the fireplace.

So much to be afraid of: earthquake, mudslide, wildfire, plane crash, train wreck, car accident, Communism, nuclear war, riots, gas shortage, Skylab, burglar, rapist, kidnapper, mass murderer, botulism, polio, rabies, tetanus, lockjaw, gangrene, infection, germs, sirens, black widow, rattlesnake, calories, high cholesterol, heart attack, cancer.

PTA meetings. Tupperware parties. Den Mother. "Avon calling."

One year, she threw a surprise birthday party for my father. Invited neighbors and some of his Lockheed colleagues. It never happened again; my father didn't like being surprised. I remember shish kabob skewers on the barbeque on the back patio and a huge brandy snifter filled with cantaloupe, honeydew, and watermelon balls.

I also remember a shower she gave for one of her friends. There were dishes full of mixed nuts and pastel pillow mints, and candied almonds wrapped in tulle and tied with curling ribbon. They played a game where each woman, blindfolded and using a spoon, had to lift as many cotton balls as she could from that same brandy snifter.

My mother lying on the couch in front of the TV, watching the late show, crying. *Since You Went Away*: Claudette Colbert and her daughters (Jennifer Jones and Shirley Temple) holding down the home front. *The Fighting Sullivans*: five brothers, stationed on the same battleship during World War II, perish together. Family tragedy: my mother's nineteen-year-old cousin George also died at Guadalcanal.

Years later she tells me her deepest secret: when they were children, George molested her.

her suffering, her experience, her emotion

After the war ended, her mother, Marguerite, died of leukemia. My mother was fourteen. A family photo taken during Marguerite's illness: my mother's angry expression. "I didn't want that picture taken."

Moments before she died, Marguerite cried out: "George is calling me."

Imitation of Life: the scene where Sarah Jane (Susan Kohner), full of remorse and grief, throws herself on her mother's coffin.

Her migraine headaches. Her weight problem. The mornings she slept late, unable to get out of bed.

In the mid-eighties, my parents were traveling in their motor home. Parked at a campground one night, they became friendly with a couple their age, sat talking over drinks. The woman, when the subject of Rock Hudson, gay men and AIDS came up, said: "What do they expect us to do?" "They expect us to help them," my mother replied.

In the previous passage I initially wrote "mother home" instead of "motor home."

My father once said she loved children and the elderly, but wasn't fond of many people in between.

Her first breakdown: she woke up in the middle of the night, looked out her bedroom window, and saw—hanging in the backyard—a pair of golden drapes.

My mother's burden, all her adult life: my father's anger. His daily outbursts, his constant belittling. It eventually wore her down, defeated her. How many times did I hear her say, in the middle of one of his fits: "Shhh! What will the neighbors think." She once told me he never showed his temper until they were married. After she died, my father said that when they were newlyweds, my mother got so angry she threw a cast iron ashtray at him. It really hurt—he walked around the block in pain. His anecdote made me laugh. *Good for her.*

A phone call from my father. "Your mother has cancer." "Where?" "Down there." Ira and I spend Christmas in Paris as planned, but it is cold and rainy, and I am depressed. I lie awake in our hotel room late one night watching a film in which Santa Claus battles the Devil—in Spanish, with French subtitles. Unable to enjoy the surreal juxtapositions, I long to understand what is being said.

How in the midst of her illness, returning from the hospital, she bribed an ambulance driver to stop at McDonald's. How when I was in high school and she'd pick me up at the library on weeknights, we often drove through McDonald's on the way home. "Don't tell your father." How it used to tick me off that she'd pick at my French fries. "Why didn't you get your own?"

When we were sick she'd bring us Campbell's chicken noodle soup, saltines, and ginger ale on a TV tray. A rerun of *I Love Lucy* was also medicinal.

Thinking it the first of many such trips I'd have to take, I flew from New York to Los Angeles. Rented a car and drove to central California, where my parents had retired. She was in an extended care facility in Santa Maria. The first thing she said to me was: "Did you bring me a poem?" Later, waking and finding me sitting there, she said: "This can't be fun for you." "It's why I came, to see you." At one point, when I was telling her about my teaching, my writing, she pronounced: "It's taken you a long time, but you've come up in the world."

How, before she died, decades seemed to drop away. She looked younger, prettier, than she had in years.

her Kleenex tissues
her Aqua Net hairspray
her Jergens Lotion
her Camay soap
her Calgon bath oil beads
her Clairol shampoo
her Avon lipstick samples: tiny white plastic tubes
her jar of Topaze cream (a yellow jewel embedded in its lid)

The morning she died, she called my father from the hospice. Said she'd thought she was going to die the night before. Thought that she was hemorrhaging. And that her mother, Marguerite, was coming for her.

I was eight months sober when she had her first breakdown. My mother was convinced that their house had been bugged, that their neighbor, a redheaded woman, was the leader of a suburban drug ring. There may have been some truth to this. One night when I visited my parents (they were still on Comanche Ave.), the tires on my car were slashed. I went to see my mother when she was in the psych ward at Northridge Hospital. I remember almost nothing—only that we sat together and talked. That Christmas, in the middle of preparing the holiday meal, my mother, fed up with my father's nagging, asked me to take her "anywhere." We drove up to Chatsworth Park, sat looking at the lights of the San Fernando Valley. "Do you think someone's looking out for you?" she asked. "You mean like God or a Higher Power or something?" "Yes." "Yes," I said, "I do believe that."

I spent the morning with her, helping her divide up her jewelry. I took a break for lunch, drove up the coast to a doll store I'd found in the Yellow Pages. I remember having a funny feeling as I drove back.

When I walked in the house, the phone was ringing. It was my father: "Get here quick!" The wildest ride of my life: doing 90 on 101, in my mother's Taurus, thinking "Wait!" The dreamlike sensation of watching myself from outside myself: This wasn't really happening. I pulled into the parking lot. As I walked towards the hospice, I saw a woman (a nurse?) out of the corner of my eye, pointing and gesturing that I should run. So I ran. My sister pulled me into the room.

What I said to my mother as she was dying:
"Thank you for being my mother. I love you."
"You're onto the next step of the journey. God be with you."
"You've done a good job, Mom. You can let go now."

I saw the nurse look at her watch, heard her say "time of death." Then I crumpled beside the bed, sobbing.

My father said he cried once, while she was dying. "That's the only time I'm going to cry." I remembered my mother telling me that she'd tried to get him, after he'd retired, to go with her to a therapist. He'd refused, saying he was too set in his ways, wasn't about to change now.

I remember thinking: Now I know what a dead person looks like.

Later I'm told that after she hemorrhaged she yelled: "Oh God, take me now!"

The house my parents retired to was also pale yellow. When my father and I went to Costco to buy food for the reception after the funeral, he insisted that the cake be pale yellow, like her houses.

My father says it was all the sodas, all the Cokes, that killed her.

I remember the two framed ballerinas in her lavender bedroom. I re-member the soft light and silence when, alone in the house, I'd intrude on my parents' privacy: explore their walk-in closet, riffle through drawers. Her dresses and ruffled slips, her clip-on costume earrings. On the dresser: ceramic figurines: Pinky and Blue Boy, the Virgin Mary. In a bedside drawer: her rosary and prayer book, and a bundle of her and my father's love letters (tied with a white ribbon).

A day or two after the funeral, before I went back to New York, my sis-ter pulled me aside and handed me my parents' love letters. "You should keep these," she whispered, "Dad will just throw them out." I did keep them for a while, but couldn't bring myself to read them. When I sold my papers to Fales Library at NYU, I included the letters, still tied in ribbon. I remember the air of mystery, of secrecy these let-ters had when I was a child; that they still have.

My mother in the rear view mirror, waving and undoubtedly crying, at visit's end, as I drive away.

A month after my mother's death, I have a phone session with Helen. She tells me my mother was ready to go, that her mother, Marguerite, and a friend were there to greet her. She says that my mother isn't com-ing back right away, that she is undergoing a process of "soul healing." She can do this in the Ethers; she doesn't have to be here on Earth. Helen hears healing sounds. Musical healing. Healing at the deepest level of being. My mother will begin, when she's ready, a whole new cycle, one of pleasure, peacefulness, and beauty. She also says that my mother and Marguerite are together, and that they're aware of the con-versation Helen and I are having.

Most reincarnational philosophies teach that a long period of celestial rest usually intervenes between incarnations—a time for assimilating the har-

vest of life's experiences. Then, refreshed and invigorated, the individual re-
turns, not in sadness and despair but, as childhood attests, in eager joyous-
ness to undertake a new adventure in learning and growing.

What I had them put in her coffin: a lucky penny and two fortunes: "You will be singled out for promotion" and "There is a prospect of a thrilling time ahead for you."

Helen said the woman I saw out of the corner of my eye, who encouraged me to run, was my mother. She wanted to make sure I'd be there at the end.

Time of death: 6:05 p.m., Wednesday, May 8, 1996. Insult to injury: that she should die right before Mother's Day. My father, as we made the funeral arrangements, said: "I guess it won't be much of a Christ mas this year."

One of the ironies of her death: that I should develop a closer relationship with my father. How he asked me to be his executor: of the four children, he said, I am the one who can communicate. He's been supportive of my poetry, and I see that he is proud of what I've accomplished, though when I was younger it seemed he did all he could to thwart my efforts to be a writer.

In the weeks before Christmas, my mother hides presents around the house: under beds, in cupboards and closets. I am given to snooping; she tells me not to poke around. I find a gift for my brother—the *Combat!* board game—in the hamper in my father's bathroom. Unable to contain myself, I let her know I'm in on the secret. Instead of welcoming me as her conspirator, she slaps me across the face.

Things she put in our Christmas stockings: candy canes, oranges, batteries, maple leaf candies, yo-yos, pennies, socks.

How she always wanted Christmas to be perfect; how it was always spoiled by my father's tirades. Decorating the tree: boxes of ornaments, strands of colored lights, on the living room floor. Christmas morning: ribbon and wrapping paper everywhere. He resented the mess.

her special holiday china: Franciscan Desert Rose

One year, instead of tinsel, she covered the tree with angel hair. I remember her saying to be careful, when I tried to help, because it could cut your fingers, get in your eyes. The fact that something so pretty could also be dangerous could not have been lost on me.

I wish I could do this memory better.

Using sponges, dipped in colored Glass Wax, to stencil the windows with snowflakes, reindeer, candles, wreaths. Watching her arrange her cookies—drizzled, sprinkled, powdered, frosted—on the three-tiered serving tray. Gazing at the Sears Christmas catalog, pretending *not* to look at the pages of girls' toys: Barbie and her friends; metal two-story dollhouses; child-size cardboard kitchens and supermarkets; play food; Suzy Homemaker vacuum cleaner and ironing board; cake mix sets with electric ovens.

Come into Miss Cookie's Kitchen. I purchased, on eBay, this 1962 Colorforms set. My sisters must have had it, because I distinctly remember how you could open Miss Cookie's refrigerator, oven, and cupboards and press her yellow teapot, her green cake, and her pink milk bottle inside. Taped to the upper right-hand corner of the box is the original gift tag—a smiling Santa face. Printed across his white beard is the name Patti.

Christmas, 1963: my sisters receive Deluxe Reading's Barbie-scale Dream Kitchen. Even while opening my own presents, I can't keep my eyes off of it. "Santa" had opened the box and set up those colorful plastic appliances: pink sink and brown dishwasher (both with running water), yellow oven (with rotating turkey and glowing red burners), turquoise refrigerator (with swing-out shelves). Countless accessories: dishes, silverware, utensils, food. Three decades later, it will take me a number of pre-eBay years to piece together a complete set, mostly by scouring doll shows. Precious: the plastic cakes (with hairline cracks), the ice cube and egg trays, the tiny boxes of sugar, crackers, and lemon cookies.

August, 2005: I visit my friend Bec in Largo, Florida. My first night there we sit up late, talking, admiring her Barbie collection. From a closet she produces a Deluxe Reading Kitchen, never played with, in its original box. It's a hard feeling to describe: confronting what I desired and couldn't have, in such pristine condition—brand new, as if it had been transported via a time machine. Thrilling, and yet sad. After looking at it, I say: "My mother couldn't have known how important this stuff was to me." Bec agrees. I feel my mother's presence in the room. The next morning, Bec says: "I felt that your mother was with us last night." "I did too," I tell her.

A turning point in my collecting: when I realized I had bought myself every Barbie item my mother had bought my sisters.

Ira, Dianne, and I wander around the Chelsea flea market. I spot an old Sears catalog and start flipping through it. Ira comes over to look at it with me. The dealer, a woman in her thirties, says we can buy, but not look at it. "How can I tell if I want to buy it unless I look at it?" The woman reaches for the catalog and slides it away from us. "Cunt," I say. I look back as we make our way through the market, can see how agitated she is. We have to pass her table on the way out. She charges up to me and says: "What would your mother say?" Ira and Dianne are afraid I'll lose it, since my mother has just died. But I don't respond. "She's right," I say to them. And feel the reprimand has come straight from my mother.

After she died, I bought, at an antique mall, a stack of magazines from the early sixties. *Better Homes and Gardens. Family Circle. McCall's.* Late at night I'd look through them—at pictures of housewives in kitchens and dining rooms; at ads for laundry detergent and floor wax; at recipes for Rice Krispie treats and pumpkin pie—and cry.

My mother in her apron, baking. My mother combining, mixing, blending, and stirring. My mother flattening the dough on the breadboard with her rolling pin. My mother squeezing the handle of her flour sifter. My mother kneading, blanching, creaming, and whipping. My mother pouring tomato aspic into a Jell-O mold. My mother measuring, folding, removing, and filling. My mother greasing the cookie sheet. My mother placing paper cupcake liners in her muffin pan. My mother beating, sprinkling, crimping, and tinting. My mother cutting the dough into strips for a lattice crust. My mother consulting her *Betty Crocker Cookbook.* My mother using a spatula to evenly spread frosting to the edge of the first layer. My mother frosting the sides. My mother applying more frosting with free, easy strokes. My mother spreading frosting on top, making swirls with the back of a spoon.

Angel Food. Pineapple Upside-Down. Lemon Chiffon. German Chocolate. Red Velvet. Classic White.

Licking the last streaks of batter from the bowl, or one of the beaters when she finished whipping the cream. After making a pie, she'd transform remnants of dough into "Rolly Pollys": strips sprinkled with cinnamon and sugar, then rolled and baked. Through the glass oven door, I'd watch them puff up and turn brown.

gardenias from the front yard floating in a shallow bowl on the kitchen table

A photograph taken the day I graduated from Nobel Junior High. Northridge, California. June, 1968. I stand, stiffly, in front of the entrance on Tampa Ave., in suit and tie, squinting at the camera (my father), trying to smile. My mother stands a few feet to the right, facing me. She wears a sleeveless floral print dress. Her hair has been done. In her left hand she holds the commencement program and her purse. Her right hand is raised to her throat, in proud excitement. She is smiling broadly.

Last time I visited my father, there wasn't a trace of my mother in the house. He'd gotten rid of everything. Given most of her belongings to my sisters. Saved a few things for me, in a small box on the top shelf of a closet in a guest room. The Tiffany china (tulips) I'd sent her from New York several Christmases, a couple pieces of her cut glass.

I miss my mother.

Searching eBay for *The Sound of Hollywood*: The Medallion Strings performing themes from *The Apartment*, *The Sundowners*, *A Summer*

Place, Spellbound, The Alamo, Never on Sunday, Midnight Lace. Staring at the photo of the blue-on-blue album cover and deciding not to bid. Enough to simply remember lying in front of the hi-fi in the living room, while she cleans or cooks in the kitchen, listening to those dramatic tunes.

2 0 0 6

TINY MOON
NOTEBOOK

FOR TONY TRIGILIO

A perfect half
moon. Walking
Byron. Hot
breezy night.

*

Above the roof of
the building across
the street: a bright
gibbous moon in a
nest of silvery clouds.

*

Corner of Hollywood
and Glenwood.
Above trees: moon,
just about full, obscured
by small puffy clouds.
First hint of fall.

*

Full moon, moonlit-
clouds—through
trees.

*

Clouds moving
across the round
moon. The night
Jim died.

*

Walking down Clark
St. with Doug. The
moon, waning, against
a black backdrop,
above Alamo Shoes.

*

Leaving Jim's place
with Priscilla: a
gibbous moon, lightly
smeared, between
telephone wires.

*

Doug and I walking
out of Whole Foods in

Evanston: gibbous moon
on a clean blackboard.
Doug eating a cookie;
me, a Rice Krispie treat.

*

The moon, almost full,
glowing a little, but alone
in the sky. A yellow
leaf fell in front of me.

*

Radiant and
full, the moon,
alone in the
sky.

*

Walking Byron
(with Doug) on
Hollywood Ave.—
whiteness through
the trees.

*

Hollywood and Ridge:
waning gibbous,

out of focus.
Beneath it: a
bluish wisp.

*

Outside Ebenezer Church:
the moon, shy of
half, and fast-moving
gray streaks.

*

Glenwood and Hollywood.
Everything pointing up:
steeple of Edgewater Baptist
Church, trees—one stripped
clean, one hanging on to half
its yellow leaves. The tip
of the latter touching the sharp
point of the half moon.
It looked like a blade.

*

Half moon on its
back, quickly enveloped
by orangish-gray gauze,
through wind-tossed
trees.

*

Gibbous moon in
the thicket of an
almost bare tree.
Halloween.

*

Day moon over
the Art Institute.
How did it get
so big?

*

Moon—removing
her gray veil.

*

Not yet dark, the moon,
nearly full, with nimbus,
in a net of bare branches.

*

Gibbous moon
in black branches,
burning through
swiftly moving mist.

*

Hopping out of a
cab at Hollywood
and Clark: gibbous
moon in a cloudless
sky.

*

First Christmas
lights. No moon
for the longest time.

*

Crescent moon.
Then: a low plane.

*

Half moon, hazy,
directly over
the clock tower
at Dearborn Station.

*

Half moon, white
as a tooth, through
a mass of bare

swaying branches.
Shroud-like clouds
moving across.

*

Clear, icy
night. Gibbous
moon—white
and gleaming.

*

Byron sniffing
shoveled snow.
The moon, not
quite full, free
of branches by
the end of the block.

*

Same moon,
high in the sky,
lighting the ice-
tipped branches.

*

The moon—as full
as it can be and not
be full. Do the craters
make any shapes?

*

Full, horror film
moon, complete
with clinging branches,
shredded clouds.

*

A small faint dot,
barely burning through.

*

Waning, bright
and white.
Wintery.

*

Morning moon
in a slate blue sky.
Some of it was
eaten away
in the night.

*

Moon over
Manhattan.
It too is
far from home.

*

Quarter after midnight,
with Jeffery and Soraya,
corner of 9th St. and 6th Ave.,
the moon, its top
sheared off, above the building
where Balducci's used to be.

*

2:30 a.m., in Marcie's
kitchen window:
a crescent Cheshire
cat grin, rising
fast, above Denver's
twinkling lights.

*

I thought it was
the moon, but it
was a clock at the top
of a cell phone
tower.

*

The day after
Christmas. Home
from O'Hare.
Hello Byron!
Hello (half) moon!

*

Through the overcast:
a wedge of light
glowing, then dimming,
almost disappearing, then
glowing again.

*

A waxing, afternoon
moon.

8/1 – 12/28/06

DEAR PRUDENCE

Does anyone remember Mia Farrow's haircut?
She paid Vidal Sassoon $5,000.00 to give her
a gamine or "elegant pixie," as it was officially
called, look. That was in 1968. Does anyone
remember that she was married to Frank Sinatra
at the time? He was thirty years her senior. For
him, the haircut—"If I'd wanted to marry a boy,
I woulda married a boy"—was the final straw.
Mia was served with divorce papers on the set of
Rosemary's Baby. Does anyone remember *MAD*
magazine's spoof of the movie: "Rosemia's Boo-
Boo"? Perhaps they were referring to her haircut.
Did you know that Frank Sinatra was the first
singing teen idol? He was as big in the forties as
The Beatles were in the sixties. In fact, the term
"bobby soxer" was coined to describe the overly
zealous, usually teenage fans who swooned when
they heard Ol' Blue Eyes croon. They wore poodle
skirts and rolled their socks down to their ankles.
Now single, Mia was free to travel to India to med-
itate with The Beatles. Or was that before the haircut?
I can't find a timeline anywhere online. Does anyone
remember? I always thought "Dear Prudence" was
written for Mia: she was inside meditating too much
and The Beatles wanted her to come out and play
with them. But it turns out—I just learned this from
Wikipedia—that John Lennon wrote the song for
Prudence Farrow, who'd accompanied her sister

Mia on her pilgrimage to study with the Maharishi. Apparently Prudence was having anxiety attacks and was afraid to leave her cabin. A few years later, Mia *did* become the subject of a song, one not nearly as nice as "Dear Prudence." Does anyone remember Dory Previn? American singer-songwriter and poet. After her first husband, composer André Previn, left her for Mia Farrow, Dory wrote "Beware of Young Girls," a savage attack on Mia and her motives for befriending the Previns—her sweetness all an act to steal André away from her. Dory had a break-down (she started screaming on a plane), but then bounced back by releasing, between 1970 and 1976, album after album of original songs. Popular among feminists, Dory sported big round sunglasses and a huge afro of red hair. Fros were in style at the time. Does anyone remember? A song on one of Dory's albums—"Mary C. Brown and the Hollywood Sign" —was about a hopeful who hanged herself from the letter "H" because she failed to achieve stardom. The song was turned into a rock opera—which bombed. Does anyone remember? I always thought it was ironic that when Woody Allen left Mia for Soon-Yi, whom Mia had adopted when she was married to André Previn, no one commented on the fact that, twenty years earlier, Mia had been the source of a similar drama; that it was, in a sense, Mia's karmic comeuppance. Dory, by then a recluse, must have had a good laugh. Whatever happened to Prudence Farrow? Does anyone know? There's very little about her on the Internet, and no photographs. Only that

she now teaches elementary school, and that she still
practices transcendental meditation. TM is a technique,
based on Hindu writings, by which one seeks to achieve
a relaxed state through regular periods of meditation
during which a mantra is repeated. Having escaped
the limelight from which you so famously shied away,
has it helped, dear Prudence, keep the demons at bay?

2 0 0 7

NOTES AND ACKNOWLEDGMENTS

"Hand Over Heart": The italicized lines in the last stanza are paraphrased lyrics from The Shangri-Las' spoken-word song "Past, Present and Future" (1966).

"Poem" ("Friday evening: "): This poem commemorates one of two private rehearsal readings that James Schuyler gave in preparation for his first public poetry reading at the Dia Foundation in New York on November 15, 1988.

"Plasticville": Plasticville is the name of a model train village manufactured in the '50s and '60s by Bachmann Brothers, Inc. Such miniature structures as gas stations, cathedrals, schoolhouses, supermarkets, and barns enhanced the realism of electric toy-train layouts. Tiny plastic people, animals, picket fences, street lamps, trees, and other accessories were also available.

"Evening Twilight": A cento made up of lines from 116 different poems. The order is alphabetical by poet; thus the poem begins with Matthew Arnold and ends with James Wright. "Evening Twilight" is the title of a poem by Baudelaire.

"Kid Stuff by Oscar Wilde": "Wham-O created the Water Wiggle, a wacky-looking plastic head that attached to the end of any hose and turned it into a wild, water-spraying snake that propelled itself willy-nilly as kids ran screaming for cover." From *The Toy Book* by Gil Asakawa and Leland Rucker.

"A Poem Under the Influence": *Of such moments is happiness made.* Anne Sexton; *Holly was not a girl who could keep anything . . .* Truman Capote; *Pocketa-pocketa.* Anne Sexton; *Lawsamercy, honeychil'! What you spect? 'Taint like you was . . .* See Truman Capote's "Nocturnal Turnings" in *Music for Chameleons; We know how to give our whole life every day.* Arthur Rimbaud, translated by Louise Varèse; *How does anything know its kind?* Jeanne Marie Beaumont; *acute core-reaching fucking.* Anaïs Nin; *I want a complete and equal love.* Anaïs Nin; *You drive in a circle.* Ted Hughes; *Your destination waits where you left it.* Ted Hughes.

"Classic Layer Cakes": *Most reincarnational philosophies teach . . .* From *Reincarnation: A New Horizon in Science, Religion, and Society* by Sylvia Cranston and Carey Williams; *I wish I could do this memory better.* Patricia Spears Jones. This piece was inspired by Kimiko Hahn's "Sewing without Mother."

Some of the poems in part one first appeared in: *The American Poetry Review, Another Chicago Magazine, Bloom, Clementine, Columbia Poetry Review, Hanging Loose, The International Literary Quarterly, The Iowa Review, La Petite Zine, Lo-Ball, Plath Profiles, Puerto del Sol, The Q Review, Shampoo, Tammy,* and *Tin House.* "Black Telephone" was included in *The Best American Poetry 2010,* edited by Amy Gerstler (Scribner, 2010). "9773 Comanche Ave." was featured in the Academy of American Poets' Poem-A-Day series (Poets.org) on September 28, 2010. "Anne Sexton Visits Court Green," "Chasing the Moon (with Anne Waldman)," and "Jacqueline Susann and her husband Irving Mansfield, Los Angeles, Cal., 1969" were first published in *TriQuarterly Online,* a publication of Northwestern University.

The poems in part two were selected from: *Pavane* (Sherwood Press, 1981), *Hand Over Heart: Poems 1981–1988* (Amethyst Press, 1991), *Answer Song* (High Risk Books/Serpent's Tail, 1994), *Plasticville* (Turtle Point Press, 2000), *The Late Show* (Turtle Point Press, 2007), and *Tiny Moon Notebook* (Big Game Books, 2007). "Poem" ("Friday evening:") originally appeared in *Santa Monica Review;* "The Portrait of a Lady" in *New American Writing;* and "Dear Prudence" in *Vanitas.*

Thanks to the editors of all of these publications.

DAVID TRINIDAD

lives in Chicago, where he teaches
poetry at Columbia College and
co-edits the journal *Court Green*.